# Greek Mythology

# Greek Mythology

## An Encyclopedia of Myth and Legend

### Richard Stoneman

The Aquarian Press
*An Imprint of* HarperCollins*Publishers*

The Aquarian Press
An Imprint of HarperCollins*Publishers*
77-85 Fulham Palace Road,
Hammersmith, London W6 8JB

Published by The Aquarian Press 1991
1  3  5  7  9  10  8  6  4  2

A CIP catalogue record for this book
is available from the British Library

ISBN 0-85030-934-4

Printed in Great Britain by
Mackays of Chatham, Kent
Typesetting by MJL Limited,
Hitchin, Hertfordshire.

# Contents

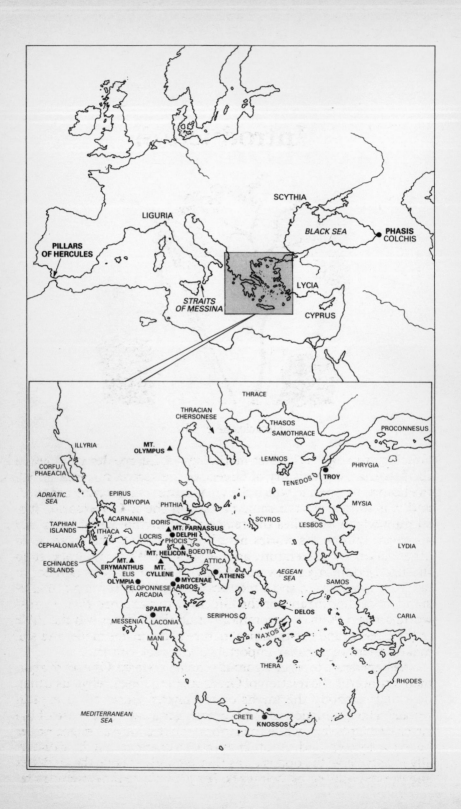

# Introduction

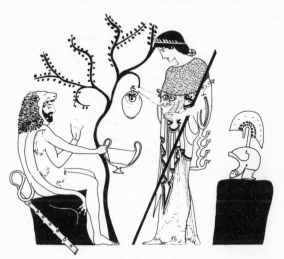

Heracles and Athena

Greek mythology is the first mythology of Europe. Its roots are in the Mycenaean prehistory of Greece of the second millennium BC, the historical period to which the great heroes of legend are assigned, and it is formed on the same pattern as the Indo-European substratum which underlies the religion and mythology of India and all pagan Europe. Its stories have become central like those of no other nation to the literature, art and music of Western Europe, from the late Middle Ages onwards. Many of them seem as familiar to us as our own history, and it requires an effort of distancing to understand what they meant for the Greeks who patterned their mental world around them. It is commonly said that Homer was the Bible of the Greeks, and the canonical nature of the myths made, and still makes, them of peculiar importance in Greek culture.

Greek myth is a topic of vigorous scholarly debate. One set of arguments concerns the relation of Greek myth to Greek religious ritual: do rituals embody the myths or are myths conceived to explain rituals? The foundation of the Nemean games is a clear case of the latter (see *Opheltes*) while the stories about Dionysus might rather be of the former kind. Another approach examines myths structurally to show how the oppositions they embody encode the anxieties and presuppositions of their users. For example, in the extreme statement of the anthropologist Edmund Leach, incest is wrong because it is an error in the grammatical structure of mythology. Less popular now are the Frazerian view that all heroes are faded gods and all myths and rituals reflect in some form the dying god on the model of Adonis and Attis (and Osiris and Christ), and the view (which was often that of the Greeks themselves) that the legends of the past are essentially historical and can be accepted as such if minor allowances are made. A variant of this latter view concentrates on those aspects of myth which express a 'pre-logical' way of codifying information of an ethnographic, historical, genealogical or geographical kind (for example M. L. West's work on *The Hesiodic Catalogue of Women*).

Our knowledge of Greek myths is conditioned by our sources. Though some few survive as living traditions (see below), in the main we are dependent on Greek literary texts, enlivened by a good deal of representational art and deepened by some archaeological finds. First and foremost we have the works of the classical period of Greek literature from the eighth to the fourth centuries BC — the epics of Homer, the Homeric hymns, the tragedies of Aeschylus, Sophocles and Euripides, as well as fragments of lost epics of the Homeric Cycle, and the odes of Pindar and other lyric poets which are rich in mythological detail, though few of them tell a story in simple linear sequence.

As early as the sixth century BC the myths were being criticized (for example by Xenophanes of Colophon) for presenting gods in an undignified way, and most reflective people found they had to find some way of dealing with the tremendous baggage of lore inherited from the 'primitive' Greece which had so quickly become a byword for a rational approach to the world.

In the fourth century a rationalizing approach to the myths became common and is especially associated with the name of Euhemerus, who interpreted the gods of myth as merely great men of the past. Similarly, Palaephatus' work *On Wonders* found a commonplace explanation for everything: the Sphinx for example became a lady bandit of Boeotia, a Bonnie without a Clyde. This process was assisted by the discomfiture which the Greeks felt with some of the mixed creatures (griffins, sphinxes) they took over from Near Eastern art: instead of heraldic emblems of dignity these became identified with Greece's fabulous monsters, and even more grotesque combinations as bogeys for children (*Lamia* for example).

Another kind of problem faced Apollodorus in the second century BC, in writing what remains our most indispensable encyclopaedia of Greek mythology: he had to try to construct a coherent narrative out of fragmentary and often conflicting traditions. A notable example of impossible chronology concerns the kings of Crete: see *Sarpedon*. But Apollodorus is in general a faithful witness who does not try to impose heavy interpretations of his own.

In Alexandrian poetry of this period arose a scholarly movement which was especially interested in tracing *aetia*, causes: poets like Callimachus and Theocritus narrated myths which could easily be allied to quaint practices or beliefs of their own day; while Lycophron borrowed something from contemporary Jewish prophetic literature in composing a riddling and obscure account of Greek mythology in the form of a prophecy by the Trojan prophetess Cassandra (whom he calls Alexandra).

As the Greek world became more sophisticated it was harder to see how the old forms of Greek religion fitted with the contemporary world, and the problem of justifying their study became more acute. (It is not an unfamiliar problem to present-day devotees of the classics.)

Strabo (64 BC-AD 21 or later), in the introduction to his *Geography* (I. 19-21) justified the study of Greek myths essentially as a propaedeutic to history and ultimately philosophy — a palatable way for children, and all uneducated persons, to absorb much miscellaneous information lightened with elements of wonder. Essentially for him the myths are like historical novels. There is an important moral component in the pleasures and terrors of myth (always good for children). It is an argument we might more readily apply to literature itself.

A new approach is that of Plutarch, writing in the second century AD when paganism was beginning to take on a more mystical and gnostic form. For him myth (he is writing about the Egyptian myth of Osiris) is a kind of refraction of religious truth: just as a rainbow in all its beauty is a refraction of the light of the sun, so the myths 'are but reflections of some true tale which turns back our thoughts to other matters' (*De Iside et Osiride* 358 F). Increasingly godhead was coming to be seen as something higher than the old gods, who now began to be thought of as *daemones*, as in Neoplatonic thought. With the triumph of Christianity the daemones became demons, evil spirits that haunt and tempt a man and bar his way to religious truth.

By this time Roman retelling of the myths had given them a purely literary dimension also. While mythographers like Hyginus regarded them as pieces of quaint lore, or useful explanations for the names of constellations, the genius of Vergil and Ovid gave them new meaning irrespective of their religious basis. Ovid's *Metamorphoses*, one of the greatest works of antiquity, is essentially a vision of the mutability of human affairs as evinced in the trials and transformations of nymphs, gods and heroes. His limpid style made the myths approachable again from a non-pagan standpoint and led directly to the enormous flowering of mythological themes in Renaissance art and literature. Ovid, almost alone of classical authors, was not forgotten in the Middle Ages.

Meanwhile the medieval world of the Eastern Mediterranean, the inheritor of Greek culture, could not shake off its gods, however much authors like John of Damascus (eighth century) or Michael Psellus (or whoever wrote the tenth/eleventh-century treatise *On the Operation of Demons* which goes by his name), inveighed against their lures. The bogeys and spirits of ancient Greece — Lamiae, Satyrs, Nereids — are as alive in modern Greek lore as they ever were, though Christianity has made their menace more pronounced. Alexander the Great has become a legend where before was history. The gods and heroes by contrast have receded into a semi-legendary historical past: their shrines have been superseded by Christian ones (Prophet Elias replacing Zeus on mountaintops, SS Cosmas and Damian acquiring the functions of the *Dioscuri*, and so on).

A recent book by Paul Veyne asks *Did the Greeks Believe in their Myths?* The author describes his work as an essay on the constitutive imagination. The Greeks created their myths in order to say important things about their experience of the world. The longevity of the ancient gods, in Greek folk tradition and in Western high culture, testifies that they still have things to say to us about our world. They are part of us and we cannot escape them: their terror and beauty are embedded in the Greek landscape and in our European experience.

### User's Key

Italicized names have their own entries. The Olympian gods are excluded from this system as they appear so frequently throughout.

# A

Achilles and Ajax playing draughts

**Acamas** The son of *Theseus* and *Phaedra* and eponym of the Athenian tribe Acamantides. He accompanied *Diomedes* to Troy to demand the return of Helen, and there fell in love with *Priam*'s daughter Laodice. They married and had a son Munitus, who died while hunting at Olynthus. Some say that Acamas took part in the capture of Troy by the *Wooden Horse*.

**Acarnan** The son of *Alcmaeon* who, with his brother Amphoterus, dedicated at Delphi the necklace of *Harmonia*. He became founder of the colony (later region) of Acarnania.

**Achelous** A river of Boeotia (modern Aspropotamo). The god of the river was the eldest son of *Oceanus* and *Tethys*, and like many river and sea gods could change his form at will. He fought with *Heracles* for the right to marry *Deianeira*. Heracles won.

**Acheron** One of the four rivers of the *Underworld*, across which dead souls were ferried by *Charon*. It was also the name of a real river in Acarnania, near the mouth of which there was a famous *Oracle* of the Dead (at Ephyra), where men could obtain advice from the gods of the underworld. Some of the machinery used by the priests to present 'visions' of the gods can still be seen today.

**Achilles** The son of *Peleus* and the sea-nymph *Thetis*, who grew up
to become one of the leading heroes of the *Trojan War*, and the central figure of Homer's *Iliad*. When the child was born Thetis prepared to make him immortal by placing him on the fire (as Demeter
did *Demophoon*) or, according to a later version, by dipping him
in the River Styx. Peleus found her at her task and cried out, break-
ing the taboo which in many cultures forbids mortals to speak to
their mermaid wives. Thetis fled, the magic unfulfilled, so that
Achilles remained a vulnerable mortal. (In the Styx-dipping version,
it was his heel alone, by which she held him, which remained vulnerable: hence, 'Achilles' heel'.)

Peleus gave him to the *Centaur Chiron* to bring up, on the slopes
of Mt Pelion. Chiron taught him to catch wild animals without nets,
by his native cunning, and — it seems — to eat their entrails raw,
a combination of Greek ephebic rites and the savagery of the young
Siegfried which sets the tone for the later life of this violent and impa-
tient hero. Achilles returned to his father and was educated by a tutor,
Phoenix. At this time *Patroclus*, the son of Menoetius, came to Peleus'
court and became Achilles' 'squire,' or inseparable companion (later
accounts commonly hinted at a homosexual relationship).

In another version, equally well known, Thetis knew that Achilles
was fated to die at Troy and sent him into hiding at the court of Lycomedes on Scyros: the latter dressed him as a girl and hid him among
his own daughters. (One of the daughters, Deidameia, later bore
Achilles a son, *Neoptolemus* or Pyrrhus. Obviously Lycomedes was
not the only one in on the secret!)

But when *Odysseus* came to Scyros recruiting for the Trojan War,
he uncovered Achilles' disguise by setting out a collection of presents
for the girls: ornaments and pretty clothes, but also a spear and
shield. Naturally the boy chose the latter and was hauled off to Troy.
He was 15 years old.

The first landing of the Greek fleet was in Mysia, where in battle
Achilles wounded the Mysian king *Telephus*. The wound would not
heal, and an oracle informed Telephus that only the inflictor of the
wound could cure it (sympathetic magic). Telephus went, dressed
in rags, as a suppliant to Achilles, who was at a loss until he at last
understood that the true inflictor of the wound was the spear. He
scraped some rust from the spear into the wound, and Telephus
recovered.

For the first nine years of the war at Troy, the city proved impregnable and the Greeks contented themselves with sacking cities and
islands round about. From Lyrnessus, Achilles carried off the beautiful *Briseis* as his concubine. This event is the root of the plot of
the *Iliad*, in which Agamemnon as commander-in-chief claims all
booty, including Briseis, as his own. Achilles in a rage storms off to

his tent and refuses to take part in the fighting. Eventually Patroclus goes into battle wearing Achilles' armour, to try to turn the tide of Greek misfortune, and is killed by *Hector*, the Trojan prince, with the help of Apollo. Achilles now goes into battle, killing many men and even fighting the River Scamander. He then kills Hector in single combat, ties his body to the back of his chariot and drags it three times around the city walls before concealing it in his tent. He builds a great pyre for Patroclus on which he slaughters 12 Trojan youths. Eventually Priam, led by Hermes, makes his way by night to Achilles' tent and pleads for the return of Hector's body. Achilles relents and the *Iliad* ends with Hector's funeral.

Achilles' further battles were described in other epics of the Cycle: they include his fight with the Amazon queen *Penthesilea* — they fell in love at the moment of her death — and with the Ethiopian prince *Memnon*, son of the Dawn. Achilles was himself killed by Priam's son *Paris*, who shot him with an arrow in his vulnerable heel. His ashes were buried in a barrow by the sea along with those of Patroclus: the tombs were pointed out by later travellers and were the object of special visits by *Alexander the Great* and the Emperor Caracalla, among others.

After his death, Achilles, in some versions, was transported to the White Island in the Black Sea, where he lived with the other heroes, married *Helen*, and spent his time brooding on revenge on the Trojans. Local legend had it that he once assailed a passing merchant and asked him to bring a certain girl, the last descendant of the Trojans. The merchant did so, thinking he was in love with her. As he sailed away from the island, he looked back and saw the ghost of Achilles tearing the maiden limb from limb. [Homer, *Iliad*; Pindar, *Nem*. 3; Philostratus, *Heroicus*]

**Acis** The god of the River Acis (Aci) in Eastern Sicily. His rival for the love of the nymph Galatea was the *Cyclops Polyphemus*. The latter hurled rocks at him, but they landed in the sea (Isole Ciclopi near Acitrezza) and Acis turned himself into a river.

**Acontius** A young man of Chios who fell in love with the Athenian maiden Cydippe at a festival in Delos. He threw her a quince on which he had scratched 'I swear by the temple of Artemis that I will marry Acontius.' Picking it up, she read it aloud (as the ancients always did) and thus was bound to marry him. [Callimachus, *Iambi*]

**Acrisius** King of Argos, who divided the Argolid with his brother *Proetus*, King of Tiryns. Acrisius had a daughter *Danae*, whom he imprisoned in a bronze chamber to prevent her being seduced. (The bronze chamber probably recalls the bronze lining of Mycenaean tholos tombs.) For the rest of his story see *Danae*, *Perseus*.

**Actaeon** Son of *Aristaeus* and Autonoe. He learnt the art of hunting from the *Centaur Chiron*. One day he was unfortunate enough to see the goddess Artemis bathing naked in a spring. In her anger she caused him to be turned into a stag and torn to pieces by his own hounds. The story is a popular theme in renaissance painting. [Ovid, *Metamorphoses*]

**Admetus** King of Pherae, in Thessaly, who married *Alcestis*, the daughter of Pelias, King of Iolcus. *Apollo* who was working as Admetus' cattle-drover, helped him to win her by providing him with a lion and a boar to which to yoke his chariot, as Pelias had made this a condition of giving his daughter away. Apollo further promised Admetus that he need not die on the day allotted by Fate, if he could find a willing substitute. His wife Alcestis agreed; but on the day of her death *Heracles* arrived in Pherae and went down to the *Underworld* to fetch her back (Euripides, *Alcestis*). Alternatively, Heracles was not involved and Persephone spontaneously sent her back in admiration for her self-sacrifice.

**Adonis** The son of an incestuous union between *Myrrha* or Smyrna and her father Theias, King of Syria or Cinyras, King of Cyprus — the girl's punishment for her refusal to honour Aphrodite. Her nurse helped her to satisfy her desire under cover of darkness, but when her father discovered the trick he tried to kill her. The gods rescued her by changing her into a myrrh-tree. In due course the tree gave birth to Adonis, whose name derives from the Semitic Adonai, Lord.

Aphrodite gave him to Persephone to bring up; the latter found him so beautiful that she refused to return him, and so henceforth he spent two-thirds of the year above the earth with Aphrodite and one-third in the underworld. In this he clearly resembles Persephone herself in the Demeter story: he is a vegetation deity and identical in essentials to the Semitic (Babylonian) Tammuz. In Athens and elsewhere a spring festival was celebrated in which small seed-trays (Gardens of Adonis) were planted with lettuce, watered until they sprouted, and then left to wither. The rite symbolises the transience of the life of vegetation and perhaps also — as it was a women's festival — the limitations of male potency.

Not easily harmonized with the underlying myth is the legend of Aphrodite's falling in love with the youth Adonis as he hunted (in this case he had been brought up by nymphs). He was gored by a boar — sent, in some versions, by Artemis, for unexplained reasons — on Mt Idalion or Mt Lebanon. Aphrodite's (Venus') mourning over the beautiful dying youth is a popular theme of Renaissance painting. From the drops of blood which fell on the ground the anemone originated (a type of anemone typical of the Syrian mountains is known as Blood-of-Adonis). The River Adonis which flowed through Byblos ran red with blood each year on the festival of his death. [Ovid, *Met.*; Détienne, *Gardens of Adonis*]

**Adrastus** King of Argos and son of Talaus. The latter was murdered in a riot by Adrastus' cousin *Amphiaraus*. Adrastus fled to Sicyon, whose king bequeathed him the kingdom. Adrastus made peace with Amphiaraus by giving him the hand of his sister *Eriphyle*, and returned to be King of Argos. *Polynices* of Thebes and *Tydeus* of Calydon both sought asylum at his court, and these four, with Capaneus, Hippomedon and Parthenopaeus, mounted the expedition of the *Seven against Thebes*, of which Adrastus was the leader.

Adrastus alone escaped from the unsuccessful siege of Thebes and took refuge in Athens. Ten years later he accompanied a second expedition of the sons of the previous champions (the *Epigoni*) against Thebes. This time they won, and Polynices' son Thersander became King of Thebes. But Adrastus' own son Aegialeus was killed and Adrastus died of grief at Megara.

Adrastus was venerated as a hero at Sicyon, where he received cult including tragic choruses, until the tyrant Cleisthenes of Sicyon, at war with Athens, transferred the cult to Dionysos. [Davies, *Epic Cycle*; Pindar, *Ol.* 6]

**Aeacus** Son of Zeus and the nymph *Aegina*. To populate the island of Oenone (later Aegina) on which he was born, he asked Zeus to turn its numerous ants into people, and called them Myrmidons (from *myrmex*, ant). By Endeis he was father of *Peleus* (and thus grandfather of *Achilles*, who led the Myrmidons to Troy) and Telamon, and by the sea-nymph Psamathe of *Phocus* (Seal). The two brothers killed their half-brother with a discus, and Aeacus exiled them from Aegina, thus acquiring a reputation for justice which led Plato to make him one of the three judges of the dead in the *Underworld*.

At another time, when all of Greece was stricken by a terrible drought, and the Delphic oracle pronounced that only the prayers of Aeacus could relieve it, he ascended Mt Panhellenion on Aegina and prayed to Zeus, and was rewarded with success.

According to another legend he also helped Apollo and Poseidon to build the walls of Troy. [Pindar, *Nem.* 4,5; Ovid, *Met.*; Pausanias, *Guide to Greece*]

**Aegeus** One of the four sons of Pandion, who became King of Athens. He was childless; on being consulted, the Delphic oracle told him that he should not loosen the spout of the wineskin until he returned to Athens. He consulted Pittheus, King of Troizen, about the meaning of the oracle; in response, Pittheus made him drunk and gave him his daughter Aethra to lie with. Some said that she was visited by Poseidon in the same night, and so *Theseus* was conceived. (Very probably Aegeus is in some sense a by-form of Poseidon, being likewise associated with the sea: see below.) Before leaving, Aegeus told Aethra to bring up her son without telling him the name of his father; when he was big enough to move a certain rock he would find underneath it Aegeus' sandals and sword as token of his paternity.

*Medea* then married Aegeus and they had a son, Medus. Medea and Medus fled Athens when Theseus returned.

*Minos* invaded Attica because Aegeus had murdered Minos' son Androgeos, thus originating the annual tribute of 50 youths and 50 maidens to the *Minotaur*.

When Theseus sailed on his expedition to Crete to destroy the Minotaur, he failed on his return voyage to change the black sails to the white ones that would announce his success. Aegeus in grief, thinking his son dead, hurled himself off the south-west corner of the Acropolis to his death. He is supposed to have landed in the sea, which thenceforth bore the name Aegean.

**Aegina** Daughter of the river-god Asopus. On the island of Oenone she bore Zeus a son, *Aeacus*. Oenone was thereafter called Aegina. Asopus was a common river-name in Greece; the best-known is that in Boeotia, but there was also one on Aegina.

**Aegisthus** The son of *Thyestes* and his daughter Pelopia, who abandoned him at birth. Pelopia stole her father's sword during the rape. She then married her father's brother *Atreus* who brought the boy up. When Aegisthus grew up, Atreus sent him to capture Thyestes. When the latter saw Aegisthus' sword, the secret was discovered. Pelopia killed herself and Aegisthus killed Atreus. Aegisthus and Thyestes then ruled Mycenae.

Later Aegisthus became the lover of *Clytemnestra* while her husband *Agamemnon* was away at war with Troy. The two of them killed Agamemnon on his return and ruled Mycenae for seven years until both were killed by *Orestes*, Agamemnon's son. Aegisthus is characterised in the tragic playwrights as a lustful, cruel but weak man dominated by his wife.

**Aegyptus** The hero who gave his name to Egypt, which he ruled, along with Arabia, while Libya was the kingdom of his brother *Danaus*. The brothers quarrelled and Danaus fled to the Argolid. The 50 sons of Aegyptus came to Argos to marry the 50 daughters of Danaus; but instead the daughters killed all the sons. See *Danaids*.

**Aeneas** The son of *Anchises* and the goddess Aphrodite, he was reared by nymphs until he was 5. He led the Dardanian troops on the Trojan side in the Trojan War. When he was wounded, the gods healed him; Apollo urged him to challenge Achilles but Poseidon restrained him, saying that he was destined to rule Troy.

So far Greek legend. In the tradition familiar to us, Aeneas became the founder of Rome, but that is an entirely Roman legend, told matchlessly in Vergil's *Aeneid*, and need not be elaborated on here.

**Aeolus** Son of Poseidon and ruler of the winds, which he kept pent in a cave on the island of Aeolia. He could release them at will, and at Hera's request gave the *Argonauts* a fair wind home. He also gave *Odysseus* a goatskin bag containing all the winds except that which would take him home to Ithaca. But Odysseus' companions thought the goatskin was full of wine and opened it, causing a terrible storm which drove Odysseus back to Aeolia again.

The character should be distinguished from the hero Aeolus, son of Hellen and Orseis, and eponym of the Aeolians, one of the three branches of the Greeks or Hellenes (the others being the Dorians from Dorus, and the Ionians from *Ion* son of *Xuthus*).

**Aerope** See *Atreus*.

**Aethra** Daughter of Pittheus and mother of Theseus. Her first lover was *Bellerophon*; she was later visited by Poseidon in the same night as she slept with *Aegeus*, as a result of which Theseus was born.

When Theseus abducted *Helen*, her brothers *Castor and Polydeuces* came to rescue her and took Aethra prisoner. She followed Helen to Troy as a slave. When Theseus died she committed suicide.

**Agamemnon** The most famous of the kings of Mycenae, son of *Atreus* and brother of *Menelaus*, King of Sparta. His kingdom comprised all the Argolid and many islands, as Homer tells us.

Both brothers married daughters of *Tyndareus*, Menelaus taking *Helen* and Agamemnon her sister *Clytemnestra*. He murdered her first husband, *Tantalus*, and their baby, and had by her four children of his own: *Iphigeneia*, Electra, *Chrysothemis* and *Orestes*. (These are the names found in Attic tragedy; for the first two Homer has Iphianassa and Laodice.)

When *Paris* abducted the beautiful Helen, thus starting the Trojan War (hers was 'the face that launched a thousand ships, / And burnt the topless towers of Ilium'), Menelaus called on Agamemnon to raise a Greek force. The troops gathered at Aulis, where a sign was given by the gods: a hare was torn by two eagles (according to Aeschylus' *Agamemnon*), which meant, in the interpretations of the prophet Calchas, that Troy would be taken but Artemis would oppose the Greeks. This she indeed did, being angry at Agamemnon, apparently because he had boasted that he was superior to her in hunting, or because he had neglected to sacrifice to her at an appropriate time. She prevented the Greek fleet from sailing by keeping the winds against them. Calchas then announced that Agamemnon must sacrifice his daughter Iphigeneia to appease the goddess. This was duly done: she was hoisted over the altar like a young animal, her saffron robes poured down to the sandy ground, and her eyes sank into her murderer's as the dagger fell... Thus Agamemnon gained his fair wind, but also the eternal hatred of his wife Clytemnestra.

An alternative version said that Iphigeneia was spirited away by Artemis, who substituted a stag on the altar at the last moment, and became a priestess of Artemis in barbarian Tauris. [Euripides, *Iphigeneia in Tauris*]

Agamemnon's distinguished career as commander-in-chief at Troy was marred by the plague sent by Apollo because Agamemnon had seized Chryseis the daughter of Apollo's priest Chryses. To replace her Agamemnon helped himself to *Achilles*' concubine *Briseis*, thus precipitating the quarrel which is the subject of the *Iliad*.

After the eventual victory of the Greeks Agamemnon returned home, accompanied by a new concubine, the prophetess *Cassandra*, to find his wife's vengeance awaiting him. In the meantime she had taken as her lover *Aegisthus*. According to the *Odyssey*, Aegisthus and his henchmen murdered Agamemnon at a feast. In the magnificent conception of Aeschylus, Clytemnestra herself welcomes the returning king, and tempts him to anger the gods by entering the palace treading on purple robes like an oriental potentate. Then, as he takes the ritual bath of the returned wanderer, she envelops him in a net and strikes him dead with an axe.

Agamemnon's son Orestes fled to Phocis, to return when he grew up to take his revenge. Electra and Chrysothemis remained in ignominy and slavery at Aegisthus' tyrannous court.

According to Pausanias, the kings of Mycenae were buried within the walls of the citadel. It was by digging here that Heinrich Schliemann in 1876 uncovered the grave circle with its magnificent golden grave goods including the funerary mask which he hailed as 'the face of Agamemnon'. The identification is unsubstantiated and romantic, but unforgettable.

**Agave** Daughter of Cadmus, King of Thebes, and his wife Harmonia, Mother of *Pentheus*. When the latter spied on the mysteries of the *Bacchae*, he was torn in pieces by the women and Agave bore his head back in triumph to Thebes, believing it to be that of a lion. When she recovered her senses she fled from Thebes to Illyria.

Her murder of her son was said to be Dionysus' revenge on her because she spread the rumour that her sister *Semele* had had a liaison with a mortal, so that Dionysus was not the son of Zeus but of a man.

**Ajax 1.** Ajax the Greater, son of Telamon and ruler of Salamis; married to Tecmessa. He was the bravest, after *Achilles*, of all the Greeks at Troy. He fought *Hector* in single combat and played a central part in the Battle at the Ships. After Achilles' death he treated Achilles' son *Neoptolemus* as his own. He also demanded the arms of Achilles, destined by *Thetis* for the bravest of the Greeks. But the Trojan prisoners named *Odysseus* not Ajax as the bravest, and he was awarded the arms. Ajax went mad and slaughtered the Greeks' flocks under the impression that he was killing the Greeks themselves, and on recovering his senses and realizing what he had done, he committed suicide. A long dispute then ensued over his right to burial after what he had done. Another account, which conflates this Ajax with his namesake, says that the dispute was over, not the arms of Achilles, but the Palladium (statue of Athena).

From his blood a flower sprang up which bears on its petals the letters AI (an exclamation of grief as well as the initial letters of the name Ajax, Aias in Greek). (But see also *Hyacinthus*.) His tomb on Salamis was an object of veneration to straightforward Dorians who, like Pindar, disapproved of the trickeries of Odysseus. [Homer, *Iliad*; Sophocles, *Ajax*].

**2.** Ajax of Locri, son of Oileus. He is one of the main Greek warriors at Troy, joining in the battle at the ships, the fight for Patroclus' body, and the funeral games for Achilles. On the capture of Troy he committed sacrilege against Athena by seizing *Cassandra* from her place of sanctuary by the statue of Athena, and carrying off the latter as well as the girl. On his return home Athena sent a storm to drown him: Poseidon rescued him but was then overruled, and destroyed with his trident the rock on which Ajax had taken refuge.

Three years after the return of the heroes, a series of bad harvests in Locris was attributed by the Delphic oracle to the anger of Athena at their hero. As expiation she demanded two Locrian maidens every year. The first to be sent were killed by the Trojans. The custom continued in historic times, but by now the girls were simply made, on arrival at Troy, to run the gauntlet from the beach to the temple. If they escaped death by beating they spent the rest of their lives, unmarried, in the shrine of Athena.

**Alcestis** The daughter of Pelias, King of Iolcus, and wife of Admetus, King of Pherae. See *Admetus*.

**Alcinous** King of Phaeacia, the paradisaic land (often identified with Corfu) visited by *Odysseus* on his return from Troy to Ithaca [*Odyssey* 6-8, 13]. He had given refuge to *Jason* and *Medea* when they were pursued by the Colchians; and he looked after Odysseus after his final shipwreck. It was his daughter *Nausicaa* who first encountered the naked and exhausted Odysseus on the beach and brought him safely into town. Subsequently Alcinous provided a ship to convey Odysseus, in an enchanted sleep, back to his own island of Ithaca. The ship was turned into a rock by Poseidon on its return journey, and the rock is often identified with Pondikonisi (Mouse Island) south of the Canoni peninsula.

**Alcmaeon** Son of *Amphiaraus* and Eriphyle, brother of Amphilochus. Eriphyle, bribed by *Polynices'* son with the robe of Harmonia, urged the brothers to lead a second expedition against Thebes to avenge their father and the sons of the *Seven against Thebes*. After conquering Thebes, Alcmaeon received a command from the Oracle at Delphi to kill Eriphyle. Then, like *Orestes*, he was driven mad and pursued by the *Erinyes* (Furies) of his mother. He was purified by Phegeus of Psophis and married his daughter Arsinoe, to whom he gave Harmonia's robe and necklace.

However, Alcmaeon did not recover from his madness and the territory became barren. He therefore went to seek a second purification by the River Achelous, and this was successful. He then married Achelous' daughter Callirhoe. The latter decided that she would like the necklace and robe for herself. Alcmaeon obtained these from Phegeus by telling him that the condition of his recovering his sanity was that he dedicate them at Delphi. As he was about to leave with his trophy, a servant revealed the truth and Alcmaeon was murdered by Phegeus' sons. Arsinoe's objections were silenced by shutting her in a box and selling her as a slave.

In due course Alcmaeon's sons *Acarnan* and Amphoterus killed those of Phegeus in revenge: they then settled the land north of the Achelous, which became known as Acarnania.

In Euripides' 'Alcmaeon' the hero met *Tiresias*' daughter Manto and had by her two children, Amphilochus and Tisiphone, whom he gave to *Creon* of Corinth to rear. Later he bought his daughter back as a slave, in a romance-like coincidence. Amphilochus became the eponym of Amphilochian Argos in Aetolia. [*Alcmaeonis*; Davies]

**Alcmena** Wife of Amphitryon and mother of *Heracles*. Zeus loved her and halted the sun for one day to extend his night with her; she then gave birth to twins, the mortal Iphicles and the divine Heracles. She accompanied Heracles on some of his labours and ended her life at Thebes living with his descendants. After her death she was transported to the *Isles of the Blest* where she married *Rhadamanthys*.

**Alcyone** Daughter of *Aeolus*, King of the Winds. She married Ceyx, son of the morning star. Both were transformed into birds, though the legends give conflicting reasons. According to Apollodorus, the gods, enraged by their marital bliss, or because they began to refer to each other as Zeus and Hera, changed them both into birds. Ovid [*Met.* 11] has a different story. Ceyx went on a voyage and was drowned. Alcyone in her grief was changed into a kingfisher and the gods allowed her husband to become a bird too, turning him into a gannet. Zeus then commanded that the seas should be calm for seven days before and after the winter solstice, while she was hatching her eggs: hence, 'halcyon days'.

Ten other heroines of lesser significance also bore this name.

**Alexander the Great** The historical Alexander was a king of Macedonia (356-323 BC) who conquered the Persian Empire and much of the land beyond as far as Central Asia and the Indus Valley. In the centuries following he became a figure of legend in Greek tradition (originating from Alexandria, the city he founded in Egypt), and his exploits were described in every language of medieval Europe and the Orient. The basis of the accounts is the Greek Alexander Romance, which probably dates from the third century BC. In this Alexander is made a son of Nectanebo, the last Pharaoh of Egypt. Taking his cue from Alexander's travels 'beyond the known world', the author brings Alexander into contact with weird and savage beasts and strange races of men — pygmies, lions with six legs, hairy women with wings, and so on; he meets the Queen of the *Amazons* and visits the legendary Queen Candace of Meroe. He marches through a land of perpetual darkness in search of the *Water of Life* — to which he is beaten by his cook, or his daughter; he explores the depths of the sea in a diving-bell and ascends to the heavens in a basket borne by four eagles. He visits the dwellings of the gods and the Oracle of King Sesonchosis of Egypt in the uttermost east. The leitmotif of all these adventures is Alexander's anxiety to learn the date of his death or to obtain immortality. He also meets a group of Indian Naked Philosophers or Brahmans, who request the latter boon from him. At last human-headed birds persuade him to desist from his impossible quest. He dies at Babylon, of poison.

Medieval Greece added further details to the portrait of the sage and seeker after universal knowledge (as did the Europeans of the age of chivalry, the Persians of early Islam, and so on, which are beyond the scope of this book). His daughter, who obtained the Water of Life, he turned into a mermaid and thus all the mermaids acknowledge him as father (or brother). He is thought in Macedonia to rule the whirlwinds. His name in modern Greek has been conflated into Megalexandros.

If caught by storms at sea, sailors may see the mermaids appear, and they will ask the sailors, 'Where is King Alexander the Great?' To which the correct answer is 'Alexander the Great lives and rules and keeps the world at peace.' The storm will then subside and the sailors may sail safely on. [*Greek Alexander Romance*; Abbott; P. Leigh Fermor, *Mani*]

**Alpheus** The god of the principal river of Elis, son (like all rivers) of *Oceanus* and *Tethys*. He fell in love with the nymph *Arethusa* and pursued her under the sea to the Sicilian island of Ortygia, where she rose as a spring. It was supposed that the waters of the Alpheus in fact flowed under the sea to the spring Arethusa at Syracuse — a pleasant place lined with papyrus plants.

**Althaea** Althaea married her uncle Oeneus, King of Calydon; she was the mother of *Deianeira* and *Meleager*. She caused the death of the latter, angry at his killing of her brothers, by burning a magical firebrand: when it was burnt out, his life ended. She then committed suicide. See *Meleager*. [Homer, *Iliad* 9]

**Amalthea** The nymph who nursed the infant Zeus on Crete and gave him a she-goat as wet-nurse. She gathered the *Curetes* around to sing and dance noisily, drowning out his cries so that his father *Cronus* would not discover him and kill him.

The child Zeus once gave Amalthea one of the goat's horns, promising that it would be miraculously filled with fruit: a 'cornucopia' or horn of plenty, sometimes also known as 'Horn of Amalthea'.

**Amazons** A race of women warriors dwelling beyond the River Thermodon in Scythia. They kept their men segregated on an island and mated only in order to produce children: male children were killed, or sent back to the men to bring up, while females were retained to become warriors. They were certainly believed to have a real existence, and are usually portrayed in fifth-century art in Scythian tunics and leggings.

Many heroes fought them, including *Bellerophon*. One of *Heracles*' labours was to capture the girdle of their queen *Hippolyta*; with him went *Theseus* who abducted the Amazon *Antiope*. The Amazons subsequently attacked Athens but were defeated by *Theseus* and his troops. The Amazons sent a contingent to fight at Troy under their queen *Penthesilea*: she was killed by *Achilles*, who fell in love with her even as he plunged his sword into her body.

The Amazons were said to have built the original Temple of Artemis at Ephesus. *Alexander the Great* was said to have conquered the Amazons and to have met their queen Thalestris; but she failed to seduce him, at least in some versions.

Later accounts derive their name by a false etymology of A-mazon, breastless, and claim that they cauterized one breast at birth to enable them to draw the bow more accurately.

Some of their customs may reflect practices of the barbarian races of north-eastern Europe and the Caucasus region, but their importance is mythical. Frequent representations of battles of Greeks versus Amazons encapsulate Greek nationalism against the barbarian forces of disorder. The fact that the Amazons are female stresses their otherness. Further, they articulate by contrast some of the polarities of male and female in classical Athens — warriordom versus marriage, promiscuity versus monogamy — and thus ratify the Athenian solution to the problem of women. [*Alexander Romance*; Henle; Tyrrell; G. C. Rothery]

**Ammon** The god of Thebes in Egypt, Amun, identified with Zeus by the Greeks. *Alexander the Great* claimed Ammon as his father, and was therefore represented on coins wearing the ram's horns that characterized the god. However, the *Alexander Romance* tells that

Alexander was actually the son of the last Pharoah, the wizard
Nectanebo, who came to his mother at night dressed up in a long
robe and ram's horns.

**Amphiaraus** A seer and warrior, father of *Alcmaeon* and Amphilochus. He killed his uncle Talaus of Argos and drove out *Adrastus*, thus
becoming king there. To patch up the quarrel, Amphiaraus married
Adrastus' sister *Eriphyle*, who was given the authority to arbitrate
in any disagreement between the cousins. When Adrastus was preparing the expedition against Thebes to restore his brother-in-law *Polynices* to the throne, Amphiaraus foresaw that the expedition would
fail and advised against it. But Polynices bribed Eriphyle with the
necklace of *Harmonia* to force Amphiaraus to join the expedition.
Amphiaraus went, but made his sons swear to kill Eriphyle in revenge.
At Nemea the death of *Opheltes* was interpreted by Amphiaraus
as an omen of failure. In the battle at Thebes, Amphiaraus killed
Melanippus but was then pursued by Periclymenus. Zeus threw his
thunderbolt and the earth opened and swallowed up Amphiaraus
with his chariot. Adrastus was in despair at the loss of his best fighter
'the eye of his army' and the expedition was defeated.
Amphiaraus however re-emerged from the earth near Oropos in
Attica, where he was revered in classical times as an oracular and
healing deity. His sanctuary, the Amphiareion, became an important place of pilgrimage especially for the sick. [Pindar, *Ol.6*, *Nem. 9*]

**Amphion and Zethus** The twin sons of *Antiope*, born to her after
she had been visited by Zeus and then married Epopeus of Sicyon.
Exposed at birth on Mt Cithaeron, they were brought up by
shepherds. Zethus became a warrior, Amphion a musician. Amphion
learnt his music from Hermes and increased the number of strings
on the lyre from four to seven.
After rescuing their mother Antiope from *Dirce*, they built the walls
of Thebes. Amphion's lyre had the magic power to make the stones
move of their own accord, while Zethus had to carry his share.
Amphion married *Niobe*, Zethus the nymph Thebe, after whom
Thebes was named.

**Amphitrite** Goddess of the sea, wife of Poseidon. *Theseus*, on his
way to Crete, dived into the sea to retrieve the ring which *Minos* had
thrown overboard as a challenge to him. While underwater he was
entertained at Amphitrite's court among the *Nereids*, who welcomed
him as a son of Poseidon; she gave him a wreath of roses which she
had received from Aphrodite at her wedding.
When Poseidon paid court to the nymph *Scylla*, Amphitrite turned
her into a monster.
Cult of Amphitrite is rare; her offspring include (sometimes) the
Nereids and *Triton*.

**Amphitryon** A grandson of *Pelops* by his mother, Amphitryon married *Alcmena* the daughter of Electryon, King of Tiryns and Mycenae. Electryon sent Amphitryon to retrieve from Elis some cattle stolen by the Teleboae or Taphioi, who lived on the Taphian islands off Acarnania; they had also killed Electryon's son. On his return Amphitryon accidentally killed Electryon (Hesiod in the *Aspis* says it was deliberate). Electryon's brother Sthenelus became king and exiled Amphitryon.

Amphitryon decided to avenge Electryon's son and went to Thebes to get help from King Creon. Creon agreed on condition that Amphitryon rid Thebes of a vixen sent by Hera to ravage Termessus. The vixen was in fact uncatchable: but Zeus turned both it and the hound which Amphitryon sent after it, into stone.

In the subsequent expedition to the Taphian islands, the daughter of King Pterelaus of the Teleboae, Comaetho, fell in love with Amphitryon and betrayed her father by plucking out the single golden hair that made him immortal (cf. the story of Scylla and Nisus: *Scylla 2*). Amphitryon conquered the Teleboae but executed Comaetho for her treachery.

When he returned to Thebes he found that Zeus had preceded him and spent the night with Alcmena; in fact he had held the sun still for a whole day to extend his night of pleasure. Amphitryon's subsequent union with his wife resulted, as usual in such cases, in the birth of twins, and these were *Heracles* and Iphicles, half-divine and all-mortal respectively.

Amphitryon died in battle with Heracles against the Minyans and his house and tomb were shown at Thebes in later generations. [Plautus, *Amphitryon*]

**Amymone** One of the daughters of *Danaus*. Sent to find water in arid Argos, she began to chase a deer. When she cast her javelin, she disturbed a satyr, who pursued her. Poseidon came to her rescue and frightened the satyr away by hurling his trident at him. Then he lay with Amymone, after which he removed his trident from the rock and the spring of Lerna gushed forth. See also *Danaids*.

**Anchises** A Dardanian king, descendant of Tros the eponym of Troy and nephew of Laomedon. When Zeus tired of Aphrodite mocking other gods and goddesses whom she had caused to fall in love with mortals, he made her fall in love with Anchises. She appeared to Anchises on Mt Ida in the guise of a mortal and they made love. When he discovered what he had done he was frightened, but Aphrodite promised to get the nymphs to rear his son, the fruit of this union, to the age of 5, and Anchises was to say the boy was the son of a nymph. This son was *Aeneas*.

When Anchises gave away his secret after drinking too much one day, Zeus struck him with a thunderbolt and left him lame in one leg. (Most mortal men who had intercourse with goddesses were maimed in some way — as were Tithonus and Adonis — for which a Freudian explanation involving the fear of castration by the more powerful woman would not be hard to find.) That is why Aeneas had to carry him on his back when they fled from the flaming ruins of Troy after the Greek sack; he travelled with Aeneas as far as Sicily. The Arcadians, however, said that he was buried at the foot of Mt Anchision in Arcadia. [Homer, *Iliad*; *Homeric Hymn to Aphrodite*; Vergil, *Aeneid*]

**Androgeos** Son of *Minos* and *Pasiphae* of Crete. His death while fighting the Bull of Marathon was suspected by Minos to be a piece of Athenian treachery, and was the cause of the yearly tribute of seven youths and seven maidens which Minos demanded from the Athenians, and whom he fed to the *Minotaur*.

**Andromache** Daughter of Eëtion, King of Thebe near Troy, which was sacked by *Achilles* in the early stages of the *Trojan War*. She married *Priam*'s eldest son *Hector* and their son was *Astyanax*, murdered by Achilles' son *Neoptolemus* at the Fall of Troy. Andromache then became Neoptolemus' concubine. When Neoptolemus married *Hermione*, the latter treated her badly. Alternatively, Andromache now (or after Neoptolemus' death) married Hector's brother *Helenus*, who had fled to Epirus, and bore him a son: her descendants became rulers of Epirus. [Homer, *Iliad*; Euripides, *Andromache Troades*]

**Andromeda** Daughter of Cepheus, King of Ethiopia, and *Cassiopeia*. The latter offended the goddesses of the sea by claiming that she was more beautiful than they: so Poseidon sent a sea-monster which was to be appeased only by the offering of Andromeda. Luckily *Perseus* flew by and saw her chained to her rock. Falling in love on the spot, he slew the monster with his sickle. Then he had to overcome Andromeda's former suitor, *Phineus*, before marrying her and taking her with him on his further adventures.

This story is often localized at Joppa, where part of the alleged monster was exhibited in historical times. (See, for example, Herman Melville, *Moby Dick*, Ch. 82.) Perseus's rescue of Andromeda is a popular scene in painting from Pompeii to Titian. [Ovid, *Met.*]

**Antaeus** A giant king of part of Libya, who used to wrestle with strangers. If he was ever thrown, the contact with his mother Earth renewed his strength. He roofed a temple with the skulls of those he had defeated. Eventually *Heracles* learnt his secret and defeated him by lifting him clean off the ground and crushing him in a bear-hug. [Pindar, *Isth*. 4]

**Anteros** Son of Aphrodite and Ares and brother of *Eros*, a personification of the 'love returned'. His altar at Athens was erected by the friends of one Timagoras, who was in love with a beautiful boy, Meles. Meles asked Timagoras to jump off the Acropolis to prove his devotion. He did, and was killed: Meles in remorse did likewise.

**Antigone** A daughter of *Oedipus*. When the latter went into exile, Antigone accompanied the blind man as his guide and helper. After Oedipus' death she returned to Thebes.

When her brother *Polynices* was killed fighting on the side of the *Seven against Thebes*, King *Creon* forbade him to be buried. Antigone's defiance of this order is the subject of Sophocles' play *Antigone*. It raises a profound tension of loyalties between polis and family, which must have been familiar to democratic Athens with its high emphasis on civic responsibility. Antigone was betrothed to Creon's son *Haemon*, but when Creon ordered her to be immured as a punishment, she hanged herself in her cave and Haemon committed suicide alongside her.

A different tale was told in Euripides' *Antigone*. Creon handed her over to Haemon for punishment, but he had her smuggled away and she later bore him a son. When Creon refused to forgive them, Haemon killed both himself and Antigone. [Sophocles, *Antigone*, *Oedipus at Colonus*; Euripides, *Phoenissae*]

**Antilochus** Son of *Nestor* and an important leader at Troy. He died defending Nestor against *Memnon*. After his death he dwelt, like other heroes on the White Island; see *Islands of the Blest*.

**Antiope 1.** A queen of the *Amazons*, who became the wife of *Theseus*.
**2.** Daughter of Nycteus of Thebes (or of the River Asopus). Her beauty attracted Zeus, who made her pregnant. She fled her father's anger and married Epopeus, King of Sicyon. Nycteus killed himself for shame and required his brother, King *Lycus* of Thebes, to punish her. At Eleutherae she gave birth to twins (as usual when a woman had a divine and a mortal lover), who were exposed on the mountain.

Imprisoned by Lycus, she was cruelly treated by his wife Dirce (perhaps she was jealous: in some versions Antiope had earlier been married to Lycus) until she was one day miraculously freed. Dirce was about to have her tied to the horns of a wild bull as a last punishment, when two young men turned up and recognized Antiope as their mother. These were *Amphion* and *Zethus*. They inflicted on Dirce the punishment she had planned for Antiope.

Dionysus, who favoured Dirce, drove Antiope mad until she was cured by Phocus, son of Ornytion. She then married him, and the two were buried together at Tithorea in Phocis.

**Aphrodite** Goddess of love and feminine beauty. Her name was explained by the Greeks as deriving from *aphros*, foam: when *Cronus* castrated his father *Uranus* he threw the severed genitals into the sea, and from the foam they created, Aphrodite was born. She floated ashore either on Cythera or at Paphos on Cyprus. A more conventional, Olympian, genealogy made her the daughter of Zeus and Dione.

In origin she seems to be an Anatolian goddess, her name perhaps cognate with the Semitic Astarte/Ashtaroth. This impression is strengthened by her connection with *Adonis*, the Semitic Tammuz. The oriental element is continued in the association with her cult of sacred prostitution, for example at Corinth; the trait is reflected in the myth of the daughters of Cinyras who became her votaries. In Syria she was worshipped, in Roman times, in the form of a fish as the Syrian Goddess. The Greeks recognized her oriental nature and Herodotus said that her oldest shrine was at Ashkelon.

She rapidly became humanized by the Greeks and is important in legend as the goddess awarded the golden apple by *Paris*: the displeasure of the other two goddesses caused the Trojan War.

She was married to the lame fire-god *Hephaestus*, but is more commonly associated with *Ares*, with whom she had a long-standing affair. One day, according to the bard Demodocus in Homer's *Odyssey*, Hephaestus trapped them in bed together with an unbreakable net, and then summoned the Olympians to come and see, while gales of 'inextinguishable laughter' seized the gods.

Her children by Ares include Fear, Panic and Harmony; by Dionysus she had *Priapus* and by Hermes *Hermaphroditus*. She also had two mortal lovers, *Adonis* and *Anchises*. She helped young lovers (like *Melanion*) but punished those who rejected love (like *Hippolytus*).

She was identified by the Romans with Venus, and thus the Julian family could claim descent from her through her grandson *Aeneas*.

The first nude female statue was Praxiteles' Aphrodite of Cnidus, which became famous and drew visitors from all over the world to see it. One man fell in love with it and contrived to be shut up in the temple at night. His attempt to copulate with the statue left a permanent mark on her thigh to blemish the whiteness of the marble. [Ps.-Lucian, *Affairs of the Heart*]

**Apollo** One of the 12 Olympian gods, son of Zeus and Leto, Apollo's mythology suggests that he is in fact a relatively late arrival in the Greek pantheon. At one time he was regarded as a borrowing from Near Eastern mythology. He has no obvious counterpart in other Indo-European pantheons. He is apparently not found in the Linear B texts of Mycenaean Greece, but he was associated especially with the Dorians and is the embodiment of the Hellenic qualities of clarity and reason. His name may be connected with that of the Hittite god Apulunas, or may be cognate with the Spartan word *apella*, or with the Latin root *pellere*, to drive away (i.e. to drive away plague). It may also be connected with *polios*, gleaming; some of his titles, such as Phoebus and Lycius, seem to be connected with the idea of light and his identity as a sun-god (distinct, however, from the sun-god Helios). Lycius may, however, be connected with the word *lycos*, wolf: see *Werewolves*.

Though his cult was spectacularly localized at Delphi on the slopes of Parnassus, he was thought to spend the winter months away, feasting with the Hyperboreans, while Dionysus reigned at Delphi.

Apollo and Artemis were born to Leto on the island of Delos. Hera, jealous of Zeus' latest amour, chased Leto from place to place, preventing her from giving birth, until at last the floating island of Delos put down roots of adamant in the depths of the sea, and she rested thereon, under a palm-tree, where she gave birth. Delos became one of the two chief centres of Apollo's cult.

When he grew up, Apollo went to seek a place on mainland Greece to establish a sanctuary. First he came to Telphusa in Boeotia, but the nymph of the place (also called Telphusa) did not want to be disturbed by the crush of pilgrims and sent him off to Crisa. Here he came to the sanctuary of Mother Earth, and killed the serpent *Python* — a clear symbol of the expulsion of the old earth-matriarchal religion (as conceived by the Greeks) by the new Olympian regime of light. After this hard struggle he realized that Telphusa had been playing tricks on him; he returned and pushed her over a cliff, and made himself a shrine there too. Then he set off and waylaid some sailors from Pylos, rushing onto their ship in the form of a dolphin. He made them bring him to Crisa, which he then renamed Delphi (after the dolphin), and the sailors became his first votaries. His first temple here was built by the heroes *Trophonius* and Agamedes.

The *Oracle* of Apollo at Delphi was renowned throughout the Greek world, and its prophecies became the stuff of legend as well as the regular responses to the daily cares of men.

Besides prophecy Apollo had many other attributes. We first meet him, in the *Iliad*, as a god of plague, Apollo Smintheus (mouse-god); his archery — which he shares with his sister Artemis — represents his sending of the arrows of disease. By a natural extension he became also a healer, with the title Paian or Paieon, healer, a trait magnified by his son *Asclepius*. Because wounds and diseases were often treated by incantation, he became also a god of music and song, and hence of prophecy. The shooter with the bowstring plays also on the strings of the lyre. The Muses, at home on Helicon, were often relocated on Parnassus because of their association with the god of song. As Apollo Aguieus he was also a god of the roads.

His skill with the lyre, with which he is often portrayed in art, derived from his purchase of the instrument from his baby brother Hermes, who invented it. *Marsyas* the satyr challenged him to a contest, Marsyas playing the flute. King *Midas* was the judge. When he awarded the prize to Marsyas, Apollo flayed Marsyas alive and turned Midas' ears into ass's ears.

Apollo and Poseidon hired themselves as day-labourers, for no explained reason, to King Laomedon when he was building the walls of Troy. These were thus impregnable to any human foe (hence the stratagem of the *Wooden Horse*, to induce the Trojans to take down their own walls).

His lovers included *Cassandra*, the *Sibyl*, *Daphne*, *Hyacinthus* and *Creusa* (see *Ion*).

**Arab** In modern Greek folklore, an evil spirit in the form of a black man, who lives in a well, smoking his pipe in the depths. J. C. Lawson associates this belief with the old-fashioned custom of sacrificing a Muslim or a Jew at the sinking of a new well (cf. the Europe-wide custom of immuring a sacrifice in a new bridge: see *Bridge of Arta*).

**Arachne** A Lydian woman whose skill in weaving and embroidery was so great that the Nymphs themselves used to admire them. Her head was turned and she boasted that her skill excelled that of the goddess Athena. Athena then challenged her to a competition; seeing that Arachne's work was indeed better, in her jealousy she destroyed Arachne's work and the girl hanged herself. Athena turned the pendent girl into a spider, doomed to go on weaving for ever (hence *Arachnidae* for the genus of spiders). [Ovid, *Met.*]

**Arcadia** A region in the central Peloponnese whose inhabitants claimed to be 'born before the Sun and Moon', in other words autochthonous, like the Athenians and other regional Greeks. They were credited with the invention of amoebean singing (singing in turn), and their land thus became an important literary landscape in the pastoral tradition. The god Pan was at home in Arcadia, as was the mysterious Lycaean Zeus. (See *Lycaon*.)

**Arcas** Son of *Zeus* and *Callisto*. When Callisto was killed (or transformed into a bear), Arcas was brought up by *Maia* (or *Lycaon*) and then became the king and eponym of *Arcadia*, to whose inhabitants he taught the arts of civilization. He is represented, with other heroes, on the east pediment of the Temple of Zeus at Olympia. See also *Bootes*.

**Archemorus** See *Opheltes*.

**Ares** God of War, 'gold-changer of corpses' as Aeschylus calls him, Ares is the son of Zeus and Hera. His name probably derives from a root meaning 'scream', or the Greek word for revenge, and is often used in poetry as a synonym for war or battle. He is known already in Mycenaean Greek in the Linear B tablets. But unlike such personifications as Strife, he is fully humanized by Homer's time, a berserk giant with the voice of ten thousand men. He takes an active part in the fighting in the *Iliad*.

The Areopagus, Rock of Ares, in Athens is named for him, being the site of the first murder trial, when Ares had killed Poseidon's son Halirrothius. Otherwise the cult of Ares is exceedingly rare (found mainly in Scythia and Thrace).

His main endearing trait is his long-standing affair with Aphrodite, who produced by him the sons Love (*Eros*), Fear and Panic, and a daughter Harmonia, who married *Cadmus*. For the famous episode of Hephaestus trapping the two adulterers in bed, see *Aphrodite*.

His other offspring included *Penthesilea* (by Otrere), *Oenomaus*, and perhaps the whole race of *Amazons*. He owned the grove where the *Golden Fleece* was guarded by a dragon and the field which *Jason* ploughed with the fire-breathing bulls; the spring of Dirce at Thebes was guarded by another dragon which was perhaps his offspring.

**Arethusa** A nymph with whom *Alpheus* fell in love; she became a spring in Ortygia, near Syracuse, where Alpheus' waters were thought to emerge from the earth after travelling under the sea from Elis.

**Argonauts** The heroes who sailed with *Jason* on the ship Argo to fetch the *Golden Fleece* from Colchis. The story of this voyage is referred to as familiar material in the *Odyssey*, and probably reflects the earliest colonizing ventures of the seventh-century Greeks in the Black Sea.

Jason was the son of Aeson, King of Iolcus, whose throne had been usurped by *Pelias*. When he claimed the throne of Iolcus, Pelias tricked him by telling him of an oracle demanding that Pelias appease the shade of *Phrixus* and bring back the Golden Fleece — a perilous task since King Aeëtes of Colchis had learnt that he would rule only as long as the Fleece remained in Colchis. It was hung on a tree in a grove sacred to Ares and guarded by a dragon which never slept.

Jason agreed to undertake the quest and employed *Argus* to build a ship, the *Argo*, the largest ever seen. Its prow contained a speaking beam, made from one of the prophetic oaks of Dodona and installed by Athena. Jason then enlisted heroes from all over Greece to join him in the quest: the total number named in different sources is over 60, but the following are agreed upon by most: *Heracles*, *Orpheus*, the *Dioscuri*, Zetes and Calais, *Peleus* and *Telamon*, *Idas and Lynceus* (who acted as lookout), *Admetus*, Periclymenus, *Augeas*, *Argus*, Tiphys (or Ancaeus) as steersman, Idmon and *Mopsus* (seers), *Theseus* and *Pirithous* (not in Apollonius Rhodius), *Amphiaraus*, *Laertes*, *Deucalion* and *Meleager*.

Their route went first via Lemnos. Here the women had been punished by Aphrodite for refusing to honour her: she had afflicted them with an unpleasant smell (perhaps a reflection of Greek anxieties about menstruation, or of the fumes of the then active volcano of

Lemnos). Their husbands had abandoned them for other lovers from the Thracian mainland, and the wives had then murdered the husbands, their lovers, and for good measure all the other men on the island. The women were thus quite pleased to see some new men arriving, and the island was in due course repopulated by the offspring of the Argonauts. Jason himself married *Hypsipyle*, their queen, and had two children by her.

On Samothrace they were initiated into the Mysteries of Samothrace.

Near Cyzicus they were hospitably entertained by the Doliones and their king Cyzicus, but were then attacked by six-armed giants, descendants of Poseidon. After escaping these they sailed on, only to put in again on the other side of the isthmus: failing to recognize their friends the Doliones, they entered into battle with them, in which Cyzicus was killed. His bride Cleite hanged herself.

The wind now remained against them for 12 days, until Mopsus explained that they must propitiate the Great Mother, Cybele, whose shrine was on Mt Dindymus. Their noisy ritual, banging swords on shields, was said to be the origin of the Corybantic dance in her honour.

On the coast of Mysia they went ashore. While Heracles went to cut a new club, his boy lover *Hylas* went to draw water. The nymphs of the spring fell in love with him and drew him into their waters, and he never returned. Heracles, who went to search for him, got left behind when the Argo sailed on [Theocritus, *Idyll* 13]. In his anger he took a number of Mysians hostage and later settled them in Trachis: through the generations the Mysians continued an annual hunt for the lost Hylas (a rite clearly related to similar searches for *Adonis* and *Hyacinthus* in other places).

Next the Argonauts met the Bebryces under their king Amycus, son of Poseidon, who challenged them to a boxing match (he always did this to visitors, and always won). Polydeuces took him on and won, killing Amycus [Theocritus, *Idyll* 22]. The Argonauts then drove off the Bebryces.

Their next anchorage was at Salmydessus near the mouth of the Bosphorus, whose king *Phineus*, a prophet, had been blinded for revealing Zeus' plan for the world. He was harassed by two *Harpies* who snatched away all his food and befouled his table, so that he was almost starving. The Argonauts prepared him a meal and, when the Harpies swooped, Zetes and Calais, the sons of Boreas the North Wind, set off on their winged heels to chase them off, driving them all the way to the Echinades Islands off Acarnania. Phineus in gratitude explained to the Argonauts how they might safely pass through the Clashing Rocks at the northern end of the Bosphorus. Here they sailed through safely by sending ahead a dove: the rocks clashed and nipped its tail-feathers; as they drew apart, the oarsmen heaved and Argo rushed through, assisted by Athena who held back the rocks

for a moment and gave Argo a push through the undertow. After
that the rocks never clashed again.

Sailing safely past the mouth of the Thermodon, where the
Amazons lived, they reached an island sacred to Ares where they
were attacked by birds who fired their sharp feathers at them like
arrows: these they drove away by beating their swords on their shields.
Here they met the four sons of Phrixus who accompanied them as
far as Aea, the home of Aeëtes. Here Eros ensured that his daughter
*Medea* fell in love with Jason.

King Aeëtes set Jason a test: he must yoke two fire-breathing bulls
to a plough, plough a field and sow it with dragon's teeth. Medea
gave him a magic drug made from the blood of *Prometheus*, with
which, after praying to *Hecate*, he anointed his body and weapons.
The flame from the bulls' nostrils was thus unable to harm him.

After he sowed the seed (the remnant of the teeth of the dragon
killed by *Cadmus* at Thebes), armed men sprang from the ground.
Jason hurled a rock among them and, each thinking his neighbour
had struck him, they began to fight until they were all dead.

Medea then led the Argonauts by night to the grove of Ares and
put the dragon to sleep with another magical potion. Jason seized
the Fleece and the Argonauts made swiftly off.

The return route of the Argo is very variously reported. In one
version they went down the Phasis (Pindar) or the Tanais or Don
(Timaeus) to the River of Ocean and into the Red Sea; then they
carried Argo across the Libyan desert to Cyrene and thence to the
Mediterranean. Or they crossed the Black Sea to the Danube, via
which they reached the North Sea and thence the Pillars of Hercules,
from the Atlantic side.

According to Apollonius Rhodius they set off towards the Danube,
pausing at the mouth of the Halys to sacrifice again to Hecate. The
Colchian fleet meanwhile was in pursuit under the command of
Aeëtes' son Apsyrtus, and cut off the Argonauts at the mouth of
the Danube. Here Jason and Medea contrived to murder Apsyrtus
in a temple of Artemis. (A bloodthirstier version of this story is that
Medea had brought Apsyrtus with her: when she saw Aeëtes in pursuit, she chopped Apsyrtus into pieces and threw them onto the
waves. Aeëtes had to stop to gather the pieces and bury them, and
the delay enabled the Argonauts to escape.) The Argonauts then
sailed up the Danube and into the Adriatic (which was at that time
supposed to be possible).

Here a storm ensued which indicated the anger of Zeus; the ship
itself spoke and announced that the Argonauts must be purified by
*Circe* (Aeëtes' sister) for the murder of Apsyrtus. So the Argo sailed
up the Eridanus (Po) and on into the Rhone, northwards to the river
of Ocean again, and back to the Mediterranean and to Circe's home
on the island of Aeaea. Then, in a series of adventures clearly
modelled on the *Odyssey*, they passed the *Sirens* safely (Orpheus'

lyre drowned the sound of their singing) and passed *Scylla* and *Charybdis* and the *Wandering Rocks*. They were entertained by the Phaeacians, where men from Colchis arrived to demand Medea back. As she was however no longer a virgin, Alcinous decreed that she must stay with Jason. Being then stranded on the Syrtes they carried Argo across the Libyan desert, visited the Hesperides and were then shown the way to the sea by *Triton*, who gave *Euphemus* a clod of earth. On Crete the bronze giant *Talos* prevented their landing and hurled rocks at them, until Medea drove him mad and he scraped his ankle on a rock. Here his one vein ran close to the skin; it was torn open and he died. They were wrecked off Anaphe but saved by Apollo. Euphemus threw his clod of earth into the sea and it became the island of Thera. They then made their way home after a final stop on Aegina.

Pelias was murdered by his daughters after Medea had persuaded them she could restore his youth (she had performed this trick already on an old sheep by cutting it up and boiling it, and later did the same for Aeson). The Funeral Games of Pelias were magnificent. Jason and Medea, however, were driven out and came to Corinth. (See further *Jason*, *Medea*.)

In general this account by Apollonius Rhodius seems to represent a harmonized vulgate of the traditional adventures of Argo, and it contains a number of *aetia* or mythical explanations of cults, place-names and the like. It also makes a remarkably fine romance and provided the material for several Attic tragedies. A much briefer account is given in the *Argonautica* which goes under the name of *Orpheus* but derives from Apollonius.

In the early 1980s Tim Severin constructed a Greek bronze age galley and successfully recreated the journey of the Argonauts, with 20 rowers, point-to-point from Iolcus to Colchis (though eschewing the fantastical return journey!) [Apollonius Rhodius, *Argonautica*; Severin]

**Argus** Several heroes were named Argus, including the builder of the Argo. The most famous was Argus of the Hundred Eyes, who was given by Hera the job of keeping an eye on Zeus' mistress *Io* after Hera had turned her into a cow. He was killed by Hermes, and Hera took his eyes and placed them in the tail of her sacred bird, the peacock. [Ovid, *Met.*]

**Ariadne** Daughter of *Minos*, King of Crete, who fell in love with *Theseus* and helped him to overcome the *Minotaur* by giving him a skein of thread to guide him out of the *labyrinth* in which it lived. After this rite of passage (as it seems to be) Theseus took his newly won bride with him on the voyage back to Athens, but abandoned her on the island of Dia (Naxos). Their arrival here is perhaps represented on the François Vase. Here Dionysus found her and made

her his bride. After her death he placed her in the sky as the constellation Corona Borealis, the crown he had given her at her wedding.

In all probability Ariadne started life as a Cretan goddess, adopted
into Greek mythology: her name appears to mean 'all-holy'.

Her story was a popular one with later artists. Ovid composed a
*Letter* of Ariadne to Theseus; Titian painted her discovery by Diony-
sus (Bacchus); Hofmannsthal provided a libretto for an opera by
Strauss.

**Arimaspians** See *Aristeas*.

**Arion 1.** A Greek poet of *c* 700 BC, a native of Methymna on Lesbos.
On returning from a tour of Sicily he was about to be murdered by
the ship's crew for his wealth. He sang a last hymn to Apollo and
leapt into the sea, where he was rescued by a dolphin (Apollo's beast),
which brought him ashore at Taenarum. He made his way to the
court of Periander at Corinth; when the ship arrived here, Periander
had the sailors crucified for their attempted murder of Arion.
[Herodotus]
**2.** A divine horse, son of Poseidon and Demeter.

**Aristaeus** The son of Apollo and the nymph Cyrene. Spying the latter
wrestling with a lion on Mt Pelion, the god admired her and took
her to the region of Cyrene in Libya. There she gave birth to Aristaeus
[Pindar, *Pythian* 9], who became a minor deity of healing and also
the inventor of bee-keeping [Vergil, *Georgics*] and inventor of other
agricultural pursuits. He was father of *Actaeon*.

He was responsible for the death of *Orpheus*' wife *Eurydice*: pur-
suing her in lust, he chased her into the path of a serpent which
bit and killed her. He features also in the story of *Erigone*.

**Aristeas of Proconnesus** A historical figure probably of the seventh
century BC who described in a lost poem, the *Arimaspea*, a visit he
made to the northern regions of the world, inhabited by the one-
eyed Arimaspians, the gold-guarding griffins (which possibly have
some relation to the goldmines of the Altai Mountains) and the
Hyperboreans. Legend had it that he was sometimes to be seen in
more than one place at a time, and he may have been a practitioner
of the kind of shamanistic out-of-body experiences known to be
characteristic of Central Asia. His name was still known as that of
a magician in thirteenth-century Byzantium. [Herodotus; Bolton]

**Artemis** The virgin goddess of the chase, and moon-goddess, as she
is known from literature, is in cultic reality a more frightening creature.
She is one of the many forms of the primitive mother-goddess, with
special concern for the lives of women both before and after marriage.
Her name is found in Linear B tablets: she is close to the shadowy

*Britomartis* and Dictynna of Cretan mythology. In classical times she was especially associated with the rites of passage of girls into woman-hood; at Brauron girls between the ages of 5 and 10 would spend a period in her service, known as 'being bears for Artemis', before taking part in a procession at Athens to mark their arrival at maturity. She was also identified commonly with Eilithyia the goddess of childbirth, and known in this aspect as Locheia and Soödina. In Sparta under the name Orthia she was worshipped in rituals which included the violent flogging of youths, from which in some cases, in Roman times, they died. In Tauris her cult, of which *Iphigeneia* was a priestess, was said to involve human sacrifice; a similar claim was made for Artemis Triklaria of Patras. Closer to the Anatolian mother-goddess figure is Artemis of Ephesus, represented with a vast number of pendulous breasts (sometimes, however, identified as bulls' scrotums). She is commonly, as Artemis Agrotera, a goddess of the wild. On Delos she was worshipped at an altar of counter-clockwise-turning goats' horns.

In mythology she is the sister of Apollo, daughter of Zeus and Leto; for the story of her birth see *Apollo*. Her birth on Ortygia (later Delos), which means 'quail island', suggests that she may, like Athena, have been thought to appear in bird form. As a goddess of the wild she is notable for her vengefulness, as in the cases of *Actaeon* and *Callisto*. The metamorphoses of these persons into animals, as of her priestess *Iphigeneia* into a deer, hint at a therio-morphic aspect of Artemis herself, displaced onto her victims. She may be identified with the *potnia theron* of Minoan religion and is often referred to as potnia (Lady) of bears, horses, or bulls; she presides also over the growth of vegetable life.

Her vengefulness appears also in her shooting (with Apollo) of all the children of *Niobe*. The giants *Otus and Ephialtes* killed each other when trying to spear a deer which was perhaps Artemis herself, flee-ing from their lust. Another of her amorous victims was *Orion*. The only mortal to whom she is known to have been kind is *Hippolytus*, but she abandoned even him as he lay dying (for 'the gods may not look on death.')

Her association with the moon — perhaps a function of her virgin purity — is a late development and incompatible with the existence of *Selene* (cf. Apollo and Helios).

**Asclepius** A healing god whose name may be related to the word *ascalaphos*, a lizard. Certainly he was commonly conceived of in the form of — or, later, accompanied by — a snake, and when his cult was imported to Athens the poet Sophocles acted as host to the god while the temple was being built; that is, he looked after the snake. Asclepius originated from Trikka in Thessaly and became the patron deity of two notable healing sanctuaries, Epidaurus and Cos.

In legend he was the son of Apollo by *Coronis* and was brought

up by the centaur *Chiron* who taught him the healing arts. His skill
was such that he even raised a man from the dead (usually *Hippolytus*); but Zeus in anger at this hurled his thunderbolt at Asclepius
and killed him. Apollo then killed the *Cyclopes* who had made the
thunderbolt and was punished by being made to serve the mortal
*Admetus* for a year. Asclepius became the constellation Ophiuchus,
Serpent-holder. His sons *Machaon* and *Podalirius* became the found-
ing fathers of medicine.

Despite his death, Asclepius achieved divine status. His role as a
saviour god made him, in the Christian era, a particularly dangerous rival to Christianity.

**Asopus** The god of the River Asopus, the name of two Greek rivers,
one in Sicyonia and one in Boeotia. The god was son, like all river-
gods, of *Oceanus* and *Tethys*, and married Metope, daughter of
Ladon. His children include *Aegina* (on whose island of the same
name there was another River Asopus in antiquity).

**Astyanax** The son of *Hector* and *Andromache*, murdered while still
a child by the Greeks when they captured Troy. He makes a memor-
able appearance in the *Iliad* as a babe in arms, frightened by the
nodding plume on his father's helmet.

**Atalanta** A huntress heroine, variously daughter of Iasus of Arcadia
or of Schoineus of Tegea. Exposed in infancy by her father (who
wanted a son) she was suckled by a she-bear and brought up by hun-
ters. *Jason* refused to take her on the Argo, but she joined in the
Calydonian boar-hunt, when *Meleager* fell in love with her.

In due course her father learnt of her existence and wanted her
to marry; but she wished to preserve her virgin freedom as huntress,
and even killed two centaurs who tried to rape her. So she devised
a test: she would only marry the man who could beat her in a foot
race. As she was the fleetest of foot of all mortals this seemed a safe
bet. Many suitors failed and were executed by Atalanta.

Finally came a young man of Arcadia (or Boeotia) *Melanion* (or
Hippomenes), who had prayed to Aphrodite for help: she had given
him three of the golden apples of the *Hesperides*, and he dropped
these one by one as they raced. Atalanta was so enchanted by their
beauty that she stopped to pick them up in turn, and thus lost the
race. They married, and their son was Parthenopaeus.

Ovid, however, says that Melanion forgot to thank Aphrodite for
her help, and lay with his wife in a shrine of Zeus, for which Aphrodite turned them both into lions (which mate, the Greeks believed,
not with one another, but only with leopards). [Hesiod fr. 21b and
3, Ovid, *Met.*, Propertius I.1]

**Ate** The personification of the 'moral blindness' which pitches a man into disaster, she was mythologized as the daughter of Zeus or of *Eris* (Strife or Discord). This concept is central to the understanding of Greek religion. She was thrown out of heaven by Zeus, and so dwells among men; but when she descends on a man to destroy him, her externality does not absolve him from responsibility for the actions committed under her influence. Ate is the key to the Greek concept of the tragic hero, destroyed by forces unleashed by himself but which he is powerless to forestall. The most famous example is *Agamemnon*'s anger at *Achilles* in the *Iliad*, for which he wrongly blames, not himself, but 'Zeus and Fate and the Fury who walks in darkness, who put wild Ate into my heart'. (19, 84-6). [Lloyd-Jones]

**Athamas** A king of Orchomenus. By his first wife Nephele he had two children, *Phrixus* and *Helle*. He then took a second wife, *Ino*, a daughter of *Cadmus*, who bore him two sons, Learchus and *Melicertes*. But Ino began to plot the death of Nephele's children. She ruined the seed corn by roasting it, so that the crops failed. When the king sent to Delphi to find out what to do to appease the gods, she bribed the messengers to say that the god had ordered the sacrifice of Phrixus. Just as the king was about to carry out the sacrifice, a ram with a golden fleece appeared and flew off with Phrixus and Helle on its back. (See further *Phrixus Helle*.)

Zeus had sent the infant Dionysus, born from the ashes of Ino's sister *Semele*, to live with Athamas and Ino. This angered Hera, who drove the couple mad: Athamas shot Learchus, mistaking him for a deer (or lion cub), and Ino jumped with Melicertes into the Saronic Gulf. His body, washed ashore, was given a funeral by Athamas' brother *Sisyphus*, who thus founded the Isthmian Games. Ino became a sea-deity known as Leucothea, and Melicertes became known as the hero *Palaemon*.

Athamas was exiled and settled eventually in Thessaly where he took a third wife, Themisto. Euripides (*Ino*), however, places this marriage at home. Ino meanwhile, in Euripides' version, had become a bacchant on Mt Parnassus and Athamas brought her home. Themisto plotted to kill Ino's children but was tricked by the nurse and killed her own. Athamas and Ino then went mad and killed their own children, as before.

Athamas in his old age was nearly sacrificed as a scapegoat by the people of Achaea in Thessaly; but Phrixus' son Cytissorus rescued him (Herodotus 7. 197; Heracles according to Sophocles' lost *Athamas Crowned*). Thereafter he returned to Orchomenus and was given sanctuary by King Andreus (Pausanias 9, 34, 5-9).

**Athena** A virgin warrior-goddess, embodiment of wisdom and protectress of Athens (and other cities). She was born from Zeus' forehead after he had swallowed his wife, the Oceanid *Metis*, whose name means 'cunning', to prevent her producing a son who would overthrow him. Athena's exit was effected by a blow from Hephaestus' axe.

Her name is pre-Greek. She is referred to in Linear B tablets as Atana potnia, and is probably a specialized form of the mother-goddess. Her most common title is Pallas, perhaps related to the word *pallax* (cf. modern Greek *pallikari*, a young brave) and therefore meaning maiden or female brave. (For the legendary origin of this name, see below.) Another common title is Tritogeneia, unexplained but perhaps derived from a supposed birth beside one of the Lakes called Tritonis. In Athens she was worshipped as Polias (of the city), Poliouchos (protector of the city), Parthenos (virgin) and Promachos (defender). In Homer she is regularly given the epithet *glaukopis*, which is often translated as grey-eyed but may in fact mean owl-faced, alluding to a bird-avatar of the goddess. She is always represented in art wearing armour, including a shield with a Gorgoneion, and draped in the aegis, a magical weapon consisting of a goatskin edged with the Gorgon's snaky locks. (Thus she sometimes also has the epithet *gorgopis*, gorgon-faced.)

She plays a leading role in the *Odyssey* (often in disguise) as adviser to the cunning Odysseus whose wiles are due to her wisdom, and is important also in the *Iliad* where she fights on the side of the Greeks. A notable scene is her restraining Achilles in his anger with Agamemnon by tugging his hair — a famous case of 'double motivation' of action: is she an outside figure or is she Achilles' 'conscience'? She gave help to many of the major heroes in their tasks, including *Perseus* (after he killed the Gorgon she invented flute-playing from the sound of the Gorgon-sisters' keening), *Heracles* and *Bellerophon*; she was less kind to *Arachne*, but helpful to *Orestes* in acquitting him finally of his guilt for the murder of *Clytemnestra*.

Her association with Athens began with a contest in the reign of *Cecrops* between her and Poseidon for the land: Cecrops awarded it to her. Hephaestus tried to rape her but his semen spilled on the Acropolis and produced a child *Erichthonius*.

Pallas features in her mythology in more than one way. She killed a giant of this name and used his flayed skin as a shield (the Palladium). According to Apollodorus, who seems to be trying to tidy up the tradition, she also had a friend, *Pallas*, daughter of *Triton*, whom she killed by accident. She then made a wooden image of Pallas and wrapped it in the aegis; this Palladium was worshipped in the citadel of Troy. It was one of the most important prizes which the Greeks seized from the conquered city.

**Atlantis** The legend of the lost island of Atlantis is known from Plato's dialogues *Timaeus* and *Critias*: he claimed to have derived it from the writings of Solon who got his information from the Egyptians. It took the firm of a circular island, larger than Asia and Libya together, divided by concentric belts of water, with a palace of the king on the central island. Plato located it beyond the Pillars of Hercules (Straits of Gibraltar) in the Atlantic Ocean. The people of Atlantis were eventually conquered by the Athenians, and then an earthquake caused the entire island to sink into the sea, causing massive floods which inundated most of the known world.

The circumstantial quality of Plato's description has induced many commentators to seek for a factual basis for the story. For centuries everyone was convinced that Columbus' New World was Atlantis. In 1882 Ignatius Donnelly published a book arguing that Atlantis had literally existed and was identical with the Garden of Eden and the origin of all mythology, the alphabet, and more, and its destruction equivalent to the worldwide story of the Flood (which in Greek myth, however, is associated with *Deucalion* and has no connection with Atlantis). Other interpretations range from the wild reports of lost cities glimpsed on the floor of the Atlantic Ocean (Charles Berlitz) to the theory, now the dominant one, that the whole story recalls in amplified form the destruction of Thera (Santorini) in about 1450 BC by a tremendous volcanic eruption, larger than that of Krakatoa, which caused the abandonment of the Minoan town there and the inundation of the north coast of Crete. Atlantis therefore is in a sense Minoan Crete. (See especially P. Young Forsyth, Luce). A more recent theory presses the text heavily on the topography of Atlantis and identifies the lost land with a marshy region on the lower Guadalquivir in Spain (K. A. Folliot).

None the less many scholars remain sceptical and believe that Plato invented the entire tale as an elaborate allegory. It remains at least surprising that not a breath of Atlantis is mentioned in any other ancient source.

**Atlas** A Titan, son of Iapetus and brother of *Prometheus*. His name means 'much-enduring', and it was his task to support the sky upon his shoulders. (The giant who holds up the sky is also found in Hittite mythology, where he is called Upelluri.) This was his punishment for his part in the war of the Titans against Zeus. He was located in North Africa and identified with Mt Atlas. According to Ovid he was turned into stone by *Perseus* with Medusa's head. He also guarded the Gardens of the *Hesperides*. When *Heracles* was sent to fetch the Golden Apples of the Hesperides, he asked Atlas to bring them while he held up the sky for a while. Atlas tried to trick Heracles into relieving him permanently of his task by offering to deliver the apples to *Eurystheus* himself; Heracles agreed, but asked him to hold the sky for a moment longer while he changed his position. As soon as the sky was back on Atlas' back, Heracles snatched the apples and ran off as fast as he could, leaving Atlas still at his eternal task.

**Atreus** Son of *Pelops* and *Hippodameia*. He and his brother *Thyestes* killed Pelops' bastard son *Chrysippus*, thus setting in train an ances-

tral curse (the sins of the fathers visited on the children), which
endured for three generations. The two became joint kings of Midea.
Atreus married Aerope and had two sons, *Agamemnon* and
*Menelaus*. (In Hesiod they are his grandsons, sons of Pleisthenes who
were reared by Atreus.)

Aerope betrayed to Thyestes her husband's secret. He had promised
to sacrifice to Artemis his first lamb; but when a lamb was born with
a golden fleece, he hid the fleece away in a chest; Aerope stole this
and gave it to Thyestes. When the Mycenaeans were told by an oracle
to elect as ruler one of the kings of Midea, Thyestes suggested they
choose whoever could produce a fleece of gold. Of course he won
the throne. Atreus, feeling he had been tricked, proposed a second
test; the kingdom should belong to whichever king could cause the
sun to run backwards. Atreus won, became king and banished
Thyestes.

He then invited him to a banquet, pretending a proposed reconciliation. In fact, he served to Thyestes a stew made from the flesh
of Thyestes' children (just as his grandfather *Tantalus* had served up
*Pelops* to the gods). Thyestes was shown the heads and hands of his
children at the end of the meal.

The gods' anger at the horrible murder, however, brought famine
on Mycenae. The oracle told Atreus to bring back Thyestes to
Mycenae. At the same time Atreus had married Thyestes' daughter
Pelopia, thinking her to be the daughter of King Thesprotus, and
had a son by her, *Aegisthus*.

Agamemnon and Menelaus were sent to Delphi to find out where
Thyestes might be. By chance they met him there and brought him
back to Mycenae, where they imprisoned him. Aegisthus went to
kill him, but Thyestes recognized his sword as his own. Pelopia
revealed all and killed herself. Aegisthus, refusing to murder Thyestes,
took the bloody sword to Atreus and told him that Thyestes was dead.
When Atreus went to offer sacrifice in thanks, Aegisthus killed him.
[Seneca, *Thyestes*]

**Attis** A semi-divine attendant of the Mother Goddess *Cybele*, who
loved him and made him promise chastity. When he broke his
promise she drove him mad and he castrated himself under a fir-
tree (or was killed by a boar, like *Adonis* — so Pausanias). His cult,
representing death and the resurrection of new life, became especially popular under the Roman Empire. His priests, the Galli, castrated themselves and sought him in the woods in an annual ritual
(compare *Hylas*). [Catullus poem 63]

**Augeas** King of Elis; he took part in the expedition of the *Argonauts*.
His main claim to fame is the appalling filth which he allowed to
accumulate in his stables and cow-sheds, providing *Heracles* with
the fifth of his labours — to clean them. This he did by diverting

the River Alpheus through the cow stalls. Augeas then refused to pay Heracles the agreed price — one-tenth of his herds — and Heracles made war on him and the *Molionidae*, defeated them and made Augeaus' son Phyleus king.

**Autolycus** A legendary thief, son of Hermes (god of thieves) and Chione. He managed to steal a large part of the lands of *Sisyphus*, concealing the theft by magically changing the cattle's appearance. Sisyphus then marked the hooves of his remaining cattle, and thus identified the thief.

Autolycus married Amphitheia and was father of Anticleia, who married *Laertes* and gave birth to Odysseus. Autolycus gave Odysseus his name, and the child inherited his grandfather's cunning. It was while visiting Autolycus that Odysseus received the wound in his thigh from being gored by a boar. Autolycus was also father of Polymele, the mother of *Jason*. [Homer, *Odyssey* 19]

# B

Bellerophon slays the Chimaera

**Bacchae** The title of a play by Euripides concerning the female votaries of Dionysus, usually known as *maenads*.

**Bacchus** A title of Dionysus, adopted by the Romans as the name of their equivalent god. Hence *Bacchae*.

**Bassarids** Female devotees of Dionysus from the region of Mt Pangaeum in Thrace. Because *Orpheus* scorned their god and worshipped Helios-Apollo, Dionysus drove them to tear him apart. They share their name with the male Bassaroi of Thrace, who went in for human sacrifice and, in a delirium of cannibalism, devoured each other. The two groups instantiate the tension of favourable and unfavourable attitudes to human sacrifice. [Aeschylus *Bassarids*; Porphyry, *De Abstinentia*.]

**Battus** A descendant of the Argonaut *Euphemus* who had created and colonized Thera with a clod of Libyan soil given to him by *Triton*. (See *Argonauts*.) The child was named Aristoteles but nicknamed Battus because he stammered. The Delphic oracle told him that the could get rid of his stammer if he founded a colony in Libya. Battus ignored the apparently impossible demand, and for seven years no rain fell on Thera. Battus then set off on his mission, reaching the island of Platea, where he founded a first colony. But as the drought on Thera still did not end, the colonists moved to the mainland, first near Aziris and finally at Cyrene. Battus was cured of his stammer when, out in the desert, he met his first lion and screamed in terror.

Battus' descendants as kings were called alternately Arcesilaus and Battus, and all have some claim to historical reality. Arcesilaus IV was honoured in two odes of Pindar. [Pindar, *Pyth* 4, 5; Herodotus]

**Baubo** Wife of Dysaules of Eleusis and mother of *Iacchus* (an honorific title of Dionysus). When Demeter arrived at Eleusis, searching for her daughter, Baubo offered her soup. Demeter refused. Then, to cheer the goddess up in her misery and make her laugh, Baubo lifted up her skirts and displayed her pudenda. The trick worked and Demeter drank her soup. Baubo's trick has a historical analogue in the vulgar abuse traditionally shouted at those who took part in the procession to Eleusis along the Sacred Way. See also *Iambe*.

**Bellerophon** Son of King Glaucus of Ephyre (Corinth) — but possibly also of Poseidon. Bellerophon went to King Proetus of Argos to be purified after an accidental murder. Proetus' wife *Stheneboea* fell in love with him; being rebuffed, she accused Bellerophon to Proetus of attempted rape (compare the story of *Hippolytus*). Proetus sent the young man to King Iobates of Lycia bearing a secret message (the earliest reference to writing in Greek literature) that Iobates should kill the bearer. Iobates set Bellerophon a series of exceedingly dangerous tasks. But the gods helped him to capture the winged horse *Pegasus* and gave him a golden bridle. Riding on Pegasus, Bellerophon was able to kill the *Chimaera* by shooting it in the mouth from mid-air with an arrow tipped with lead. The lead melted in the fiery breath of the creature and burnt out its insides.

Next Bellerophon was sent to fight the Solymi, again successfully, and finally the *Amazons*, to equal effect. Iobates then set an ambush of his own soldiers to kill Bellerophon, but again he killed them all.

Realizing at this point that he was fighting against the gods, Iobates changed his tack, giving Bellerophon his daughter and half his kingdom. Stheneboea either killed herself or (according to Euripides) was taken by Bellerophon for a ride on Pegasus and pushed off from a great height.

However, Bellerophon overreached himself by trying to ride on Pegasus up to heaven itself. Zeus sent a gadfly to sting Pegasus, who reared and threw his rider, Bellerophon fell to earth and drifted sadly across the 'Plains of Wandering' until he died. [Homer, *Iliad* 6; Pindar, *Ol*. 13 and scholiasts]

**Boötes** The wagon-driver of the constellation of the Great Bear (*Callisto*), identified with Callisto's son *Arcas* or Arctophylax (Bear-keeper).

**Boreas** God of the North Wind. He abducted the Nymph Orithyia while she played on the banks of the Ilissus in Athens, and by her had two sons, Calais and *Zetes*, who took part in the expedition of the *Argonauts* and distinguished themselves by chasing away the harpies from the dinner-table of *Phineus*. They were later killed by *Heracles* because they advised the Argonauts to abandon him in Mysia.

**Briareus** One of the three *Hundred-Handers* (known in the language of men, according to Homer, as Aegaeon), sometimes son or son-in-law of Poseidon; his 'human' name suggests a god of the Aegean Sea. He awarded the Isthmus to Poseidon in his dispute with Helios, and gave the latter Acrocorinth.

Once he was about to roast and eat the viscera of a monstrous bull which lived in the River Styx, because an oracle had foretold that whoever did so would overthrow Zeus and rule in his stead. But a kite snatched the viscera in time and brought them to Zeus.

**Bridge of Arta** A famous folksong of modern Greece tells how the builders of the bridge at Arta were unable to make it stand. A bird alighted on the stones and told them it would only stand if the master-builder's wife were immured within it. Pretending to drop his ring in the foundations, the master-builder induced his wife to go down and fetch it; at once the masons began to pour rubble on top of her. As she was buried she cursed the bridge, swearing that it would never stand. The builders called on her to withdraw her curse, lest one day her brothers cross the bridge and be killed. So she recanted and prayed that the bridge should stand firm for ever, for her brothers' sake.

The tale recollects the custom, known throughout Europe, of immuring a woman or girl in a bridge to ensure its solidity. [Stoneman, *Literary Companion;* Lawson]

**Briseis** Daughter of Brises, a priest from Lyrnessus, carried off by *Achilles* who made her his favourite concubine at Troy. *Agamemnon's* demand that he yield her to him, as leader of the expedition, was the chief reason for Achilles' quarrel with Agamemnon and his withdrawal from the fighting. She was returned to Achilles after the reconciliation following the death of *Patroclus.* [Homer, *Iliad*]

**Britomartis** A Cretan goddess, also known as Dictynna, and identified with Aphaea, whose temple is on Aegina, *Minos* pursued her in love but she was rescued by Artemis, whom as a virgin goddess of the wild she much resembles. She acquired the name Dictynna either because she fell into a fisherman's net (*diktys*) after falling off a cliff in her flight from Minos; or because she invented hunting-nets; or because she was once caught in one. More probably the name is connected with Mt Dicte on Crete. Her name is borrowed by Edmund Spenser in the *Faerie Queene* for his chaste female knight, one of the types of Queen Elizabeth I in the poem.

**Busiris** A Libyan king with the habit of sacrificing all visitors to his lands. He was despatched by *Heracles*.

# C

A Centaur

**Cabiri** These deities originated in Phrygia and were worshipped especially on the northern Aegean islands of Samothrace, Lemnos and Imbros. They played an important role in the Samothracian mysteries, under the names of Axieros, Axiokersos, Axiokersa and Cadmilus, identified with the Olympian deities Demeter, Persephone, Hades and Hermes.

Their name appears to be related to the Semitic root *kbr* meaning 'great'. They were often known as the 'Great Gods'. Their number varied: as twins they were also identified with those other twin deities, the *Dioscuri*, and regarded as helpers of sailors in distress, to whom they appeared in the form of St Elmo's Fire. [Bengt Hemberg; S. G. Cole]

**Cadmus** The founder of Thebes. After the abduction of *Europa*, her father Agenor sent his sons (who included Cadmus) to find her. The brothers had no success and gave up. Cadmus went to the Delphic oracle, which told him to abandon the quest, and to follow a cow until it collapsed from fatigue, and there to found a city. This happened at the site of Thebes in Boeotia ('cow-country').

Cadmus sent his companions for water to sacrifice the cow to Athena. They were killed by a dragon. Cadmus then slew the dragon and, on Athena's advice, sowed its teeth, which sprang up and became the Spartoi (Sown Men). They menaced Cadmus, who threw stones in their midst; each thinking his neighbour was hitting him, they began to quarrel and killed each other, all except five, who became ancestors of the Thebans.

To atone for killing the dragon, Cadmus became a slave to the god Ares for eight years, and then married his daughter *Harmonia*. The gods attended the wedding and brought as gifts a robe woven by the *Graces* and a necklace made by Hephaestus. (See further *Amphiaraus*.) Their children were Autonoe, *Semele*, *Agave*, *Ino*, *Actaeon* and Polydorus, all of whom except the last met with disaster. In their old age their grandson *Pentheus* became King of Thebes. After his murder by his mother, Cadmus and Harmonia went to Illyria and were turned into snakes.

The citadel of Thebes was called Cadmeia after its founder.

**Caeneus** A *Lapith* chief. Born a girl, Caenis, she was raped by Poseidon and, as the boon customarily offered by gods after such enjoyment, asked to be made a man to avoid this happening again. Poseidon also made him invulnerable at the same time. In the battle of the Lapiths and Centaurs the centaurs, unable to harm Caeneus, bludgeoned him into the earth with clubs — as depicted on a bronze plaque at Olympia.

**Calais** See *Argonauts*.

**Calchas** A seer of Mycenae (or Megara) who accompanied the Greek fleet to Troy. He prophesied, when *Achilles* was 9 years old, that Troy would never be taken without his aid. It was he who divined the anger of Artemis which kept the Greek ships becalmed at Aulis, and revealed that *Agamemnon* must sacrifice his daughter *Iphigeneia* to obtain a fair wind. At Troy he revealed that Agamemnon's capture of *Chryseis*, daughter of Chryses, priest of Apollo, had caused the plague which afflicted the Greeks. Some say that he also explained to the Greeks how to capture Troy; but this is usually said to have been done by the Trojan seer *Helenus*, captured on Calchas' advice. He was involved in the plot which led to the death of *Palamedes*.

He was fated to die when he met a better diviner than himself. This turned out to be *Mopsus* of Colophon, who accurately stated the number of figs on a fig-tree. Calchas' defeat broke his heart and he was buried at Notium. The two seers were venerated as joint founders of several cities of Asia Minor, including Perge, Selge and Sillyum. [Homer, *Iliad* 1; Aesch. *Agam*.]

**Calliope** Leader of the *Muses*, her special areas are lyre-playing and epic-heroic poetry.

**Callirhoe 1.** Daughter of Achelous and wife of *Alcmaeon*.

**2.** A daughter of Ocean and mother of *Geryon*.

**3.** A daughter of the River Scamander and wife of Tros; mother of Ilus, Assaracus, *Ganymede* and Cleopatra.

**Callisto** A companion of Artemis, vowed like all her nymphs to chastity, who was raped by Zeus in disguise as Artemis. When her pregnancy became apparent, Artemis in her anger changed her into a bear, which was then shot, either by Artemis herself or by *Arcas*, the son she bore to Zeus, when she wandered into the sanctuary of Zeus Lycaeus. Zeus transformed her into the constellation of the Great Bear, and Arcas became Arctophylax, the bear's guardian. Hera made the sea-gods promise that they were never to let her rival enter their realm; and so the Great Bear never sets.

**Calydonian Boar Hunt** Artemis sent a huge boar to ravage Calydon, because its king, Oeneus, omitted to include her in his annual offering of first fruits to gods. Oeneus asked the Greek cities to send their heroes to help him hunt the boar, offering its hide as a prize to the killer. Those who participated include *Peleus*, *Amphiaraus*, *Meleager* and *Atalanta*. Meleager killed it and won the prize, presenting it to Atalanta with whom he was in love. His uncles, the sons of Thestius, quarrelled with Meleager over this, and this led to his death. [Ovid, *Met.* 8]

**Calypso** A nymph who dwelt on the island of Ogygia, where she looked after *Odysseus* when he was washed ashore after shipwreck. She fell in love with him and wanted him to stay, offering him ageless immortality, but after seven years he tore himself away to return to his wife. She is not referred to independently of her role in this story. [Homer, *Odyssey*]

**Candace** A queen of Meroe visited by *Alexander the Great* in disguise: but she recognized him because she had secretly had his portrait drawn. Though she wanted to kill him because he had executed King Porus of India, to whom she was related, she relented when she found out that he had saved her son Candaules from the Bebryces. In later versions of the *Alexander Romance* another of her sons is called Kargos, which seems to be a form of the modern Greek shadow puppet hero, *Karagiozis*. [*Alexander Romance*]

**Cassandra** A Trojan prophetess, daughter of *Priam* and *Hecuba*. Apollo fell in love with her and taught her the art of prophecy, but when she continued to refuse his advances he ordained that her prophecies would never be believed. Her prophecies include the information that *Paris* would bring destruction on Troy, for which reason he was exposed at birth.

At the fall of Troy she was raped at Athena's altar by *Ajax* the

Locrian and then taken as a concubine by *Agamemnon*. When she reached Mycenae she was murdered along with her master by *Clytemnestra*. [Homer, *Iliad*; Aeschylus, *Agamemnon*, Euripides, *Troades*; M. Davies, *Epic Cycle*]

**Cassiopeia** Wife of King Cepheus of Ethiopia. Because she claimed to excel the *Nereids* in beauty, Poseidon sent a sea-monster which was only to be appeased by the sacrifice of her daughter *Andromeda*. For the rest of the story see *Andromeda*. After death Poseidon placed her among the stars in a tilted-up chair.

**Castalia** The spring at Delphi, sacred to the *Muses*.

**Castor and Polydeuces** See *Dioscuri*.

**Cecrops** The first King of Athens, born of earth and therefore with a snake's lower portion. He had three daughters, Aglauros (sparkling water), Herse (dew) and Pandrosos (all-dewy). They acted as nurses of Cecrops' successor *Erichthonius*, also born of earth.

During his reign an olive-tree and a spring suddenly appeared on the Acropolis, and the Delphic oracle announced that Athens must choose as patron one of the gods whose respective symbols these were, Athena and Poseidon. Cecrops acted as arbiter in this contest, in which role he and Pandrosos are portrayed on the west pediment of the Parthenon. Athena received the women's votes, Poseidon the men's. The women outnumbered the men and Athena won the city, but the women were punished by being deprived of the right to vote in Athens thereafter.

The relation of this myth to the political position of Athenian women is strengthened by the detail that Cecrops also introduced the institution of marriage to Athens.

**Centaurs** Horses with men's torsoes, heads and arms (and, in early art, men's legs as forelegs). They are also known — in Homer — as Pheres, beasts. Centaur is in fact a general designation for many sorts of composite, and the horse-men are, strictly, hippocentaurs (compare onocentaurs, ass-centaurs; and see *kallikantzaros*).

The Centaurs have sometimes been explained as a misunderstanding by the Greeks of their first encounter with mounted warriors from the east. But horses were well known in Greece, and the image of the Centaur surely derives from the repertoire of Near Eastern beast-man combinations which are common figures on sixth-century pottery (also *Sphinx*, and others). The Centaurs, 'beasts' or wild men of legend, were then given the iconography of these creatures.

The origin of the Centaurs was from *Ixion*'s attempted rape of Hera: she substituted a cloud in her form, and the cloud gave birth to Kentauros (which can be etymologized as 'prick-air'). He then mated with the mares on Mt Pelion to produce the horse-centaurs. These brutal wild men armed themselves with clubs or branches of trees. By an interesting opposition, the wise and gentle *Chiron*, teacher of medicine and tutor to *Achilles* and *Jason*, was also a Centaur. See also *Pholus*. [Dumezil, *Le Problème des Centaures*; Paul Baur, *Centaurs in Ancient Art*; Page du Bois, *Centaurs and Amazons*]

**Cephalus** A son of Herse, daughter of *Cecrops*, by Hermes. He was loved by *Eos*, Dawn, who took him to her home in the east. Cephalus was, however, married to Procris, a daughter of *Erechtheus*; she was jealous of his fidelity and hid in the bushes while he was out hunting, to spy on him. Hearing him call out the name of Aura, she became very agitated, not realizing that this 'Aura' was simply the breeze on whom he called to cool his limbs. Seeing the bushes move, he threw his spear and killed his wife. [Ovid. *Met.* 7]

Cephalus was banished. He then went to *Amphitryon*, who asked him to use his inescapable hound Laelaps to rid the country of an uncatchable vixen. Zeus solved the logical impasse by turning both dog and vixen to stone.

Cephalus then joined Amphitryon's expedition against the Taphians, and settled down in their country, where he gave his name to the island of Cephalonia.

**Cerberus** The three-headed dog who guarded the entrance to *Hades*. *Heracles* entered the *Underworld* through the cave at Taenarum to bring back Cerberus as the eleventh of his labours: but *Eurystheus* was so frightened at the sight that he sent him straight back again.

Visitors to Hades were supposed to take honey-cakes (baklava?) to keep the dog quiet as they entered. (See *Psyche*.)

**Cercopes** The two (or more) Cercopes were dwarfish ruffians who inhabited Lydia and robbed and killed passers-by. Though they seem to recall pygmies or barbary apes (and the Romans said that the Pithecussae, Monkey Islands, off Naples were named after them) their location does not suit this interpretation.

They were defeated by *Heracles* when he was a slave of Queen *Omphale* of Lydia: he tied them by their feet to a pole and carried them off over his shoulder. In this position they got a good view of his hairy bottom, at which they made such outrageous jokes that Heracles was amused and let them go. Finally Zeus turned them into stone (or monkeys).

**Charon** The ferryman of the dead who carries souls across the River Styx to Hades. A small coin was placed in the mouths of the dead as his fee. In modern folklore he has become, as Charos or Charontas, the spirit of death himself, riding on his black charger across the mountains and plains, scooping up the young heroes and maidens and setting them on his saddlebow. Great heroes, such as *Digenis Akritas*, wrestle with him for mastery. [J.C. Lawson; Rennell Rodd]

**Charybdis** A whirlpool at the northern end of the Straits of Messina, to avoid which sailors had to steer dangerously close to *Scylla* on the opposite side. Both the *Argonauts* and *Odysseus* had to negotiate these treacherous waters; Odysseus lost his ship here but escaped himself by clinging to a tree in the cliff face until the sucking subsided. [Homer, *Odyssey* 12; Apollonius Rhodius]

**Chimaera** A fire-breathing monster with a lion's head and body, a snake for a tail and a goat's head growing from the middle of its back. It dwelt on Mt Chimaera in the Taurus, and seems to represent the volcanic fires which even today burn near its summit (and on which shepherds sometimes cook their food). Servius interpreted the monster as an allegory of the mountain with fire at its peak, lions and goats roaming its slopes, and snakes at its foot. It was killed by *Bellerophon*. [Hesiod, *Theogony*; Homer, *Iliad* 6; F. Beaufort, *Karamania* (1817); R. Stoneman, *Across the Hellespont* 171-4]

**Chiron** A *Centaur*, but not of the breed of the rest of the Centaurs who were descended from *Ixion* and the cloud. Chiron was the son of *Cronus* and *Philyra*, and, unlike his wild compeers, was noted for wisdom and the art of healing. He acted as tutor to several heroes, including *Jason*, *Achilles*, *Asclepius* and *Actaeon*. He helped *Peleus* escape from fierce Centaurs and taught him how to win the *Nereid*, *Thetis*. He was shot by Heracles when the latter was fighting the other centaurs in Arcadia, but, despite his pain, could not die, being immortal. Eventually he became the constellation Centaurus.

**Chrysaor** Son of Poseidon and *Medusa*, born from the severed neck of the latter when *Perseus* beheaded her. He was father (by the Oceanid *Callirhoe*) of *Geryon*, the three-headed giant whose cattle *Heracles* was sent to steal.

**Chryseis** Daughter of *Chryses*. When *Agamemnon* returned her to her father to halt the plague afflicting the troops at Troy, he took instead *Achilles'* concubine *Briseis*, thus precipitating the quarrel which is the subject of the *Iliad*. Her name is the same as that of Cressida, under which she developed a much greater role in the medieval versions of the Trojan story.

**Chryses** A priest of Apollo Smintheus, father of *Chryseis*, who by his prayers brought a plague on the Greek army at Troy when *Agamemnon* seized his daughter as war booty.

**Chrysothemis** Daughter of *Agamemnon* and *Clytemnestra*, the gentle foil to the tough *Electra* in Sophocles' play.

**Chrysippus** Son of *Pelops*, loved by *Laius*. The latter's rape of Chrysippus may be the cause of the ancestral curse on the house of Laius which issues in the events of the *Oedipus* saga. He was murdered by his half-brothers *Atreus* and *Thyestes* to prevent him inheriting the throne.

**Chthonian Gods** Gods of Earth. The Greek divine world is divided into the gods of Olympus, who are worshipped with burnt sacrifices at altars, and those of the underworld, including both some gods (especially Demeter) and all the *heroes*, who are worshipped with offerings poured into pits. Chthonian divinities are usually closely linked with ideas of death and regeneration. The sinister figures of the *Furies* or *Erinyes*, and the *Keres* are also spirits of Earth.

**Cinyras** A king of Cyprus, possibly originating from Cilicia, who married the daughter of *Pygmalion*. In an incompatible story his daughter by another wife, *Myrrha*, was made by Aphrodite to fall in love with her own father, because her mother had boasted of her beauty. Myrrha's nurse helped her to make love to Cinyras in darkness by a trick, and their son was *Adonis*. When Cinyras discovered what he had done he killed himself.

**Circe** An enchantress, daughter of *Helius* and sister of Aeëtes, King of Colchis. She lived on the island of Aeaea (said to be off western Italy, and sometimes identified with Malta). She had the power to change men into beasts. She turned Picus, who rejected her love, into a woodpecker, and when *Glaucus* came for a magic potion to make *Scylla* love him, Circe gave him instead one which turned her into a monster.

When *Odysseus* came to her island she turned his advance party into beasts; but Hermes gave Odysseus the magic plant moly which preserved him from her enchantments. He then persuaded her to turn his men back into their true forms. Odysseus remained a year with her, and is said by Eugammon of Cyrene to have had by her a son, Telegonus, who later killed Odysseus without recognizing him, and then married Penelope.

**Cithaeron** The mountain which separates Attica from Boeotia, named after a king of Plataea, which lies at its foot. Many of the legends of Thebes were localized on Mt Cithaeron, such as the exposure of *Oedipus* and the death of *Pentheus*.

**Cleobis and Biton** Two young men of Argos who, when there were no oxen available, dragged the wagon carrying their mother, priestess of Hera, from Argos to the sanctuary. On arrival they died of exhaustion and were honoured as heroes. [Herodotus]

**Clio** Muse of history and prophecy, sometimes also of epic poetry (compare *Calliope*). She is often portrayed in art — first on the François vase — with musical instruments. In statuary she often holds a book-roll. She was the mother of *Hyacinthus* and *Orpheus*.

**Clytemnestra** Daughter of *Tyndareus*, sister of *Helen*. The two women were called *lipesanores*, husband-deserters, by Hesiod. While *Agamemnon* was away at Troy she consorted with *Aegisthus* and together they killed Agamemnon on his return. Clytemnestra was in turn killed by her son *Orestes* when he grew up.

**Clytie** A nymph loved and jilted by Helios. When she revealed their secret to her next lover, he began to hate her and she turned into a heliotrope, thus following his course across the sky with her gaze, every day for ever.

**Cocytus** The River of Wailing, one of the four rivers of the *Underworld*.

**Coronis** Daughter of Phlegyas. She was loved and won by Apollo. While pregnant by him she made love to the mortal Ischys. The news was brought to Apollo by a crow, which in anger he turned from white to black. He then killed Coronis and Ischys, but rescued from her body on the pyre the infant, who grew up to be the healer-god *Asclepius*.
   The Epidaurians said instead that she bore Asclepius while visiting Epidaurus and exposed him on Mt Myrtion, where he was suckled by goats (so Pausanias). [Pindar, *Pyth.* 4, Ovid, *Met.*]

**Chthonian Gods** Gods of Earth. The Greek divine world is divided into the gods of Olympus, who are worshipped with burnt sacrifices at altars, and those of the underworld, including both some gods (especially Demeter) and all the *heroes*, who are worshipped with offerings poured into pits. Chthonian divinities are usually closely linked with ideas of death and regeneration. The sinister figures of the *Furies* or *Erinyes*, and the *Keres* are also spirits of Earth.

**Corybantes** See *Curetes*.

**Creon 1** King of Thebes, whose sister *Jocasta*/Epicaste married *Laius*, father of *Oedipus*. After Oedipus had defeated the *Sphinx* and unwittingly married his own mother, Creon exiled him. He acted as regent for Oedipus' two sons *Eteocles* and *Polynices*, until they quarrelled and Polynices was exiled. In the subsequent war of the *Seven against Thebes*, Creon's son Menoeceus was killed. Creon refused burial to

Polynices as a traitor and thus was constrained to execute Polynices'
sister *Antigone*, who insisted on burying him. His son *Haemon*,
Antigone's lover, killed himself too, and Creon's wife *Eurydice* then
hanged herself.

Creon also acted as host to *Amphitryon*. He was killed by *Lycus*
when the latter invaded Thebes and usurped the throne. [Sophocles,
*OC*, *OT*, *Ant*.; Euripides, *Phoenissae*].

**2** King of Corinth who reared *Alcmaeon*'s children Amphilochus
and *Tisiphone*. Creon's wife sold Tisiphone into slavery and Alcmaeon bought her unwittingly.

He also gave a home to *Jason* and *Medea* when they fled from Iolcus
(see *Argonauts*). Jason then fell in love with and married Creon's
daughter Glauce: in revenge, Medea sent Glauce a poisoned robe
and murdered her own children by Jason. In the cyclic epic, *Capture
of Oechalia*, she also murdered Creon. [Eur., *Medea*]

**Cressida** See *Chryseis*.

**Cretan Bull** Poseidon sent the bull from the sea to confirm *Minos*'
claim to Crete: Minos, however, failed then to sacrifice the bull to
Poseidon, so the god made Minos' wife *Pasiphae* fall in love with
it. She had *Daedalus* construct a wooden cow in which she could
lie to mate with it: their offspring was the *Minotaur. Heracles* caught
the bull as his seventh labour, and released it near Tiryns; it then
terrorized Attica and was again captured by *Theseus*.

**Creusa** Daughter of *Erechtheus*, who married *Xuthus* of Aeolia. Her
son, *Ion*, was claimed as the offspring of a brief union with Apollo,
thus enshrining the claim of the Ionians (who included the Athenians)
to divine descent. Tidily, Euripides makes her mother also of Dorus
(eponym of the other main race of Greeks, the Dorians). [Eur., *Ion*]

**Croesus** A historical king of Lydia (c. 560-46 BC) who became a
figure of legend. He was said to be the richest of all men. He was
also very pious and sent many dedications to Delphi as well as fund-
ing the Temple of Artemis at Ephesus. He tested the Delphic oracle
by asking it to reveal what he was doing at a particular moment;
when it answered, correctly, that he was boiling a hare and a tortoise
in a cauldron, he placed supreme confidence in its powers thereafter.

He was visited by Solon and claimed to be the happiest of men.
Solon countered with the very Greek remark that no man should
be called happy before he is dead. Croesus prepared to make war
on Persia: consulting the Delphic oracle, he learned that if he did,
he would destroy a great Empire. Unfortunately he did: his own.
The Persians defeated him and seated him on a pyre to be burnt alive.
He prayed, however, to Zeus, who sent a miraculous shower of rain
and so he was saved (Bacchylides 13). He was then transported to

the land of the Hyperboreans. Herodotus and Plutarch (*Life of Solon*) say rather that he told the Great King of his conversation with Solon, and the King was so impressed that he spared him. The latter version seems to have a distinctly Athenian colouring.

**Cronus** The chief of the *Titans*, the children of *Uranus* and *Ge*, Heaven and Earth. Uranus imprisoned the *Hundred-handers* and the *Cyclopes* within Ge, so at her instigation Cronus castrated his father with a sickle, thus unplugging the exit for the prisoners. The story is almost certainly modelled (by Hesiod himself?) on the similar Hittite myth of Kumarbi.

Cronus then reimprisoned the Hundred-handers and Cyclopes and had several children by his sister Titan *Rhea* — the Olympian gods Hestia, Demeter, Hera, Hades and Poseidon. As he swallowed all these as they were born, Rhea concealed the last one, Zeus, and gave Cronus a stone wrapped in swaddling clothes to eat instead. She then gave Zeus to the Cretan nymph Amalthea, who suckled him on goat's milk and got the *Curetes* to dance and clash their cymbals to drown the infant's cries.

When Zeus grew up he married Metis, and she caused Cronus to vomit up his other children. Zeus released the Hundred-handers and Cyclopes, who then helped the gods to overthrow the Titans, who were imprisoned in Tartarus. Incompatible with this cosmogony is the anthropogony in which Cronus ruled the *Golden Age* of mankind (and was identified by the Romans with Saturn), and later became king of *Elysium*. [Hesiod, *Theogony*]

**Crow** Turned by Apollo from white to black because it brought him the news of his lover *Coronis'* infidelity. The interview with the white crow is portrayed on a beautiful fifth-century plate at Delphi.

**Curetes** Cretan *daemones* who danced and clashed their cymbals to drown the cries of the infant Zeus (see *Cronus*). The name, cognate with *kouros*, youth, identifies them as attendants on the distinctive 'young Zeus' of Crete, the youthful consort of the Great Mother. They are closely allied to the Corybantes who attended the Asiatic mother-goddess, *Cybele*.

**Cybele** An Anatolian mother-goddess, also known as Cybebe. Her cult was centred on Pessinus in Phrygia and at Mt Dindymus in Mysia (where the origin of its rites was attributed to the *Argonauts*). She wears a mural crown as protectress of her people, and as a goddess of the wild places, rides in a chariot drawn by lions. Her young male consort was *Attis* and her acolytes the Corybantes; in Roman times also the self-castrating Galli. The Greeks identified her with their own mother-goddesses, Demeter and Rhea: in some places, for example Piraeus, she was worshipped under her own name with Attis.

**Cyclopes** One-eyed giants who in Hesiod are the iron-workers of the gods. They were imprisoned in *Tartarus* by *Uranus* and *Cronus*, but released by Zeus, for whom they make the thunderbolts. In this role they appear for example in the legend of *Asclepius*. Their names are Brontes (Thunderer), Steropes (Lightener) and Arges (Bright).

But for Homer these one-eyed giants are a numerous tribe of savage pastoralists who live without laws, feeding on dairy products except when chance brings human flesh their way. They feature prominently in the adventures of *Odysseus*, who is imprisoned by the Cyclops *Polyphemus* (often referred to simply as 'the Cyclops'), who is a son of Odysseus' enemy Poseidon. A further tradition concerns Polyphemus' love for the nymph *Galatea*. One should not try to harmonize these disparate traditions: theology, folklore and romance do not inhabit the same mental worlds. [Homer, *Odyssey*; Eur., *Cyclops*]

**Cycnus 1.** A son of Ares killed in combat by *Heracles*. His story is given twice by Apollodorus, with different mothers for each version. The first time the two are separated by Ares, the second time Heracles kills him.
**2.** King of the Ligurians and friend of Phaethon, who mourned the latter's death constantly until he became a swan (and the constellation Cygnus).
**3.** A king of Colonae, son of Poseidon, who fought on the Trojan side against the Greeks. After being killed by *Achilles* he too was transformed into a swan.

**Cyrene** Daughter of the Lapith king Hypseus, she was one of those athletic maidens of Greek myth, much given to hunting and outdoor pursuits. Apollo fell in love with her when he saw her prowess in wrestling with a lion on Mt Pelion. Taking advice from *Chiron*, he lay with her ('swift is the doing, and short the road, when a god sets his mind to a thing' — Pindar, *Pyth.* 9) and carried her over the sea to Libya, where she became the eponym of the city of Cyrene and gave birth to *Aristaeus*. [Hesiod fragments 215-17; Pindar, *Pyth.* 9]

# D

Dionysus transforms the boat's mast into a vine

**Dactyls** A group of *daemones*, born on Mt Ida (hence Idaean Dactyls), probably the Phrygian mountain. They are associated with Rhea or Cybele the Phrygian mother-goddess; also with one of her Greek analogues, Adrasteia. They were regarded as inventors of metallurgy and of certain musical genres, as well as being masters of sorcery and amulets. (Their name means 'fingers'. According to one tradition they were named from the marks made when their mother, Rhea, pressed her fingers into the earth while giving birth to them.) Pausanias says there were five of them and located them on Cretan Ida, identifying them with the *Curetes* who protected the infant *Zeus* from *Cronus*. Their names were Heracles (not the great hero), Epimedes, Idas, Paeonius and Iasus.

**Daedalus** The inventor of sculpture and other mechanical and engineering arts; his name is a masculine form of the word meaning an idol or carved image, and as an adjective means 'cunningly contrived, artistic, intricate'.

He was a descendant of the Athenian king *Erechtheus* and son of Eupalamus, whose name means 'Skilled with his hands'. He killed his nephew and apprentice, Perdix (which was also the name of Daedalus' sister), when he boded to be a better artist than Daeda-

lus himself, and then fled to Crete. Here *Minos* commissioned him
to build the wooden cow in which *Pasiphae* was to mate with the
*Cretan Bull*.

His most famous act is the construction of the *Labyrinth* to house
the unholy offspring of this union, the *Minotaur*. According to Pliny
he modelled it on the so-called Egyptian Labyrinth, the temple of
Amenemhet III. In Homer he is said to have built a dancing-floor
in the form of a maze for *Ariadne*; the dance is then the dance of
the hero *Theseus* as he threads his way into the Labyrinth to kill the
Minotaur, aided by the ball of thread which Ariadne had given him
along with the instructions from Daedalus on how to penetrate the
maze.

Daedalus was then imprisoned by *Minos*, with his son *Icarus*, in
the Labyrinth. Daedalus planned their escape by constructing wings
for them both out of wax and feathers. Though Icarus flew too near
to the sun and crashed, Daedalus escaped safely. Minos tracked him
down by asking all the kings he met to thread a snail shell: when
the King of Sicily, Cocalus (Shell), managed this, Minos knew that
Daedalus had been this way. But Minos was then murdered by Cocalus, in some accounts by having boiling water poured over him in
his ceremonial bath (Sophocles, *Kamikoi*). Daedalus went to Sardinia
where his track is lost. Daedalic is used as a technical term to describe
the stiff statuary of the seventh century BC, with its strong southern
and Cretan influence.

**Daemon** A spirit or divinity. The term is especially used of gods when
the speaker is uncertain what particular god is at work. Thus Socrates
referred to the inner voice that prompted his actions as his daemon
or daimonion.

More commonly the word is used in the plural to refer to the groups
or collectives of superhuman beings such as *Dactyls* or *Curetes*, who
are rarely individualized. Many daemones had particular habitats,
such as *Nymphs* in rivers and *Nereids* in the sea.

In later antiquity, Neoplatonic philosophy gave the daemones an
important role as mediators between the spheres of men and God
— the gods themselves being too individualized to suit this mystic
purpose.

Christianity took the next step by declaring all the pagan gods to
be *daemones*. The word now acquires the connotations of the modern
word demon. Demons dwelt in groves and rivers as of old; they also
dwelt in statues and pagan temples, and a prime motive in destroying pagan works of art was to extirpate the demons dwelling in them.
[Socrates, *Apology*; Michael Psellus, *De operatione daemonum*;
A. Brelich].

**Danae** Daughter of Acrisius, King of Argos. Warned by an oracle
that her son would slay him, Acrisius shut her up in a bronze tower

(perhaps one of the beehive tombs of Mycenaean Greece, which were lined with bronze plates). None the less Zeus penetrated the defences in a shower of gold (easily allegorized by later writers!), and she gave birth to *Perseus*. Acrisius set the pair of them adrift in the sea in a wooden chest: they were washed up on the island of Seriphos and welcomed by King Polydectes. The latter fell in love with Danae and, to get rid of Perseus, sent him off to fetch the Gorgon's head. After Perseus had accomplished his mission (see *Perseus*) and killed Polydectes, Danae returned to Argos to live with her mother.

**Danaids** The 50 daughters of *Danaus* of Argos, by 10 mothers. Danaus' brother, *Aegyptus*, demanded them as brides for his 50 sons, but they concealed daggers in their wedding dresses and killed their husbands on their wedding night — all except Hypermestra. Danaus then remarried them by offering them as prizes in a foot race. They were condemned in Hades to fill everlastingly a vessel that could not be filled, probably as punishment for their crime. (The action can be interpreted as everlastingly carrying out the bride's ritual bath, of which they had deprived themselves.)

They may be in origin water-nymphs, celebrated for bringing water to the arid region of Argos: this function is explicit in the myth of one of them, *Amymone*.

They were said to have brought the Mysteries of Demeter from Egypt and to have instituted her festival, the Thesmophoria.

**Danaoi** Originally the family descended from Danae, though better-known legends make them the race of *Danaus*. They comprise part of the dynasty of Mycenaean Midea and Tiryns, the subjects of saga deriving from Mycenaean times. The term is used more generally in Homer and other authors to apply to the Greek troops at Troy. [West, *Hesiodic Catalogue of Women*].

**Danaus** The eponym of the *Danaoi*, brother of *Aegyptus* the eponym of the Egyptians. His family relationships, which include also the eponym of the Phoenicians, Phoenix his nephew, represent a mythological treatment of early Mediterranean history and ethnography.

Aegyptus and Danaus quarrelled, Danaus fleeing to Argos. Aegyptus then wished to marry his 50 sons to Danaus' 50 daughters (see *Danaids*), but they murdered their husbands on their wedding night. Lynceus, who was spared by his bride Hypermestra, then killed Danaus (in one version) and became king. In another version Danaus arranged a marriage for his daughters as prizes in a foot race (for the motif compare *Pelops*, *Atalanta*, etc).

**Daphne** A nymph of Arcadia or Thessaly. Leucippus, son of King Oenomaus of Elis, dressed as a girl in order to go hunting with Daphne, whom he loved. One day the girls stripped to swim, discovered his secret and killed him. Then Apollo, who was in love with her, raced after her. Unable to escape, she prayed to *Gaea*, who turned her into a laurel. The laurel (Greek *daphne*) then became sacred to Apollo.

A suburb of Antioch called Daphne, where there was a famous temple of Apollo, was regarded as the site of this event.

The theme is popular in art (see, for example, the painting by Pollaiuolo and the statue by Bernini) and is the subject of Strauss' opera (libretto by Hofmannsthal). [Ovid, *Met*. 1]

**Daphnis** A Sicilian demigod, son of Hermes and a player of the syrinx, which Pan taught him. His fidelity to his love Nomia was blighted by the daughter of the King of Sicily, who made him drunk and thus seduced him. Nomia blinded him and Daphnis then killed himself. Vergil *Eclogue* 10 has a very beautiful account of Daphnis' death and the mourning for him.

**Dardanus** Son of Zeus and Electra, the daughter of Atlas. He came originally from Samothrace and was the brother of *Iasion*. He was welcomed to the Troad by Teucer, son of the River Scamander. He was regarded as an ancestor of the Trojans (also known as Dardanians). He built the citadel of Troy and introduced the cults of the Samothracian gods and of Cybele. He also brought the statue of Athena, the Palladium, from Arcadia to Troy. [*Iliad* 20]

**Deianeira** Daughter of *Oeneus*, who married *Heracles* after he won her in a battle with the River Achelous. He entrusted her to the centaur *Nessus* to carry across the river; Nessus tried to rape her and Heracles shot and killed him with one of his poisoned arrows. Nessus as he died gave Deianeira some of his blood, which was infected with the poison, and told her that it could be used as a love charm. When Heracles later planned to abandon Deianeira for *Iole*, Deianeira dipped a cloak in this blood and sent it to Heracles to try to win him back. But the poison caused Heracles instead to die in agony, and he had himself immolated on a pyre on Mt Oeta.

Sophocles' Deianeira, in *Trachiniae*, gentle and helpless, is one of the most affecting female characters in Greek tragedy.

**Delphi** A site on the southern slope of Mt Parnassus, overlooking the plain of Crisa and the Gulf of Corinth. In classical times it was regarded as the centre of the world: Zeus sent two eagles to fly from each horizon, and this is where they met. The spot was marked by a navel-stone or *omphalos*. Apollo made the place his own cult centre, and it became one of the two most important Panhellenic shrines in Greece (with Olympia). Its administration was a source of constant friction between the different Greek states. The Delphic *Oracle* was internationally famous. Like other oracles it normally dealt with questions like 'Where shall I erect an altar to be best pleasing to the gods?' or 'Shall I marry so-and-so?' In legend the oracle was credited with giving ambiguous riddling advice like that given to *Croesus*. Oracles were delivered in hexameter verse by the priests who interpreted the inspired raving of the *Pythia* or prophetess, who sat on a tripod in the temple of Apollo. By Plutarch's day (second century AD) the oracles were given in prose.

It is the most magnificent of all Greek sites and in antiquity its treasures were unequalled. The Emperor Nero removed 500 bronze statues from Delphi but made scarcely any impact on its overall appearance. Time, looters and Christians have disposed of the rest. [P. Hoyle, *Delphi*]

**Demeter** Goddess of agriculture and nutrition, whose name means 'Earth Mother' according to a common ancient interpretation. Her titles, such as Karpophoros, fruit-bearing, emphasise her role. Homer refers to her union, at the wedding of *Cadmus* and *Harmonia*, with Harmonia's brother *Iasion* in a ploughed field — evidently a form of fertility rite transferred to the legendary plane. Demeter was widely worshipped, and in 1801 E. D. Clarke recovered from Eleusis a statue which he believed to be of Demeter (it was actually a Caryatid from her temple), amid much protest from the locals who believed that its presence, in the middle of their dung-heap, secured the fertility of their fields. She was worshipped in specific aspects such as Demeter Erinys at Onkeion, or Black Demeter (with a horse's head) at Phigaleia. The myth attached to the latter cult is that Poseidon tried to rape her; she disguised herself as a mare, but Poseidon turned himself into a stallion, and she subsequently gave birth to the horse Arion and then concealed herself at Phigaleia.

She seems to have her origins in Mycenaean times, and in mythology was one of the children of Cronus and Rhea. Her sons by Iasion were Plutus (Wealth) and Philomelus, the inventor of the wagon (who became the constellation Boötes).

Demeter is best known for her role in Eleusinian myth, as mother by Zeus of *Persephone*. After Hades carried her off at Enna, Demeter wandered through the world to seek her: 'the peaks of the mountains and the deeps of the sea rang with her immortal cries', but Demeter could not discover her whereabouts until on the tenth day it was revealed by *Helios*. Demeter refused to give up her daughter and return to Olympus. She came instead to Eleusis where she sat down by the well Callichoron and wept. Here she was found by the daughters of Celeus, King of Eleusis, and brought to his home. Celeus' wife Metaneira welcomed her and gave her a drink of kykeon (barley-meal and pennyroyal mixed with water), and *Iambe* eventually induced her to smile by her antics. Demeter was appointed nurse to Metaneira's son *Demophoon*. But when the goddess tried to make him immortal by placing him on the fire, Metaneira discovered her and cried out in alarm. Demeter then revealed her identity and demanded the establishment of the Eleusinian rite, in honour of Demophoon; 'and the boy grew like a god'.

But when the temple was finished Demeter 'ordained the cruellest of years for men...No seed sprouted in the rich soil, for bright-crowned Demeter lay hidden; oxen in vain dragged the bent ploughs through the fields, and white barley was scattered in vain on the ground.' At last Zeus sent Hades to bring back Persephone from the dead, and put an end to her mother's sorrow and the blight on the land, but as Persephone had eaten some pomegranate seeds in Hades, she could only return for part of each year, and so the earth only brings forth crops in the summer season.

Before she left Eleusis, Demeter taught *Triptolemus* the art of agriculture, and lent him her dragon chariot, with which he travelled over the earth teaching the remaining peoples of the world how to grow and harvest the crops.

Besides the Eleusinia, the other major Athenian festival of Demeter was the women's festival of the Thesmophoria. [*Homeric Hymn to Demeter*; Ovid, *Met*; Eur., *Helen* 1301-68]

**Demogorgon** 'The dread name of Demogorgon' [Milton, *Paradise Lost* II 264-5] is given only by an ancient commentator on one line of Statius' *Thebaid*, and is probably a mistake for Demiourgos, creator-god. Its resonance has given it a long life in English poetry, notably in Spenser and Shelley.

**Demophoon 1.** A son of *Theseus* and *Antiope*, brother of *Acamas*. **2.** Son of King Celeus of Eleusis. Demophoon was nursed by *Demeter*, who placed him on the fire to make him immortal, until discovered by his mother Metaneira. Demeter then demanded the institution of a festival for her at Eleusis in honour of the boy: 'Yet will he forever have undying honour because he lay on my knees and slept cradled in my arms.' The festival seems to have taken the violent form of a mutual stoning by the people of Eleusis. It is common for a major festival to be established in memory of a child hero (compare *Opheltes*, *Melicertes*). [*Homeric Hymn to Demeter*; Mylonas, *Eleusis*]

**Deucalion** The Greek Noah. Son of *Prometheus*, he married Pyrrha, daughter of *Epimetheus* and *Pandora*, and was ruler of Phthia. He was warned by Prometheus of the impending Flood, a legend common to all Near Eastern peoples (the story of Utnapishtim in the epic of Gilgamesh, Ziusudra in Sumerian legend, Noah in Genesis) and awkwardly displaced to the high and mountainous terrain of Central Greece. His 'ark' drifted for nine days before running aground on Mt Parnassus. To repeople the earth, he and his wife were told by the oracle of Themis to throw over their shoulders the bones of their mother. Pyrrha understood that Mother Earth was meant; as they cast her stones over their shoulders, at Opous, those thrown by Deucalion became men, those thrown by Pyrrha women. These were the Leleges, a people of Eastern mainland Greece. This legend explained, to Greek ears, the similarity of the words for people (*laos*) and stone (*laas*).

**Digenis Akritas** The 'Twice-born Border Lord', one of the most famous heroes of medieval Greek legend, whose story is told in several verse narratives (Russian as well as Greek) and is the subject of the Acritic cycle of folk-songs. Many medieval buildings are known as castles or tombs of Digenis.

In the narrative poem Digenis is the grandson of a Cappadocian prince, Andronicus Ducas and his wife Anna; their daughter Irene was carried off by the Emir Mousour, Prince of Syria, and their son was Basil Digenis Akritas. The epithet 'twice-born' refers to his parentage, half-barbarian and half-'Roman'. An Akritas is a warden of the border lands, and this title dates the legend's origins to the historical circumstances of the ninth century. Like Achilles, Digenis is a precocious hunter, and when he is grown up he becomes a scourge of highwaymen; he falls in love with Eudocia, the daughter of an Emir called Ducas, steals her away and continues his pacifying activities. He entertains the Emperor Basil, who appoints him Lord of the Borders.

His adventures recall at more than one point those of Alexander in the *Alexander Romance*. They include the blinding of his cook (as Alexander curses his cook Andreas), a fight with a fire-breathing serpent (one of Alexander's adventures in the Karaghiozis shadow-puppet cycle) and a lion, a fight with an Amazon queen, Maximo, on the banks of the Euphrates (like Alexander again), and the building of a palace and a garden on the Euphrates. He dies of illness, a theme elaborated in the folk-song describing his struggle with *Charon*, and the narrative ends with his death and the building of his tomb. [*Digenis Akritas*, ed. and tr. by John Mavrogordato; and by Denison B. Hull]

**Diomedes 1.** Son of *Tydeus* and of Deipyle daughter of *Adrastus*. He took part in the expedition of the *Epigoni* against Thebes. He plays an important role in the *Iliad*: he wounds two gods, Aphrodite and Ares, and is the centre of a notable scene when he exchanges his armour with his hereditary guest-friend *Glaucus* of Lycia, who is fighting on the other side.

In the Epic Cycle he often worked with *Odysseus* — in the murder of *Palamedes*, the bringing of *Philoctetes* from Lemnos, the capture of the Trojan spy Dolon and the theft of the Palladium from Troy.

On his return from Troy he found his wife Aegialeia had been unfaithful to him, so he sailed away to Italy, where he and his companions were turned into birds. He received cult as founder of a number of South Italian cities.

**2.** A king of the Bistonians of Thrace, son of Ares and *Cyrene*. *Heracles'* eighth labour was to tame his man-eating horses, which he did by feeding their master to them; after which they never touched meat again.

**Dionysus** The god of wine, vegetation and the life-force; of ecstasy and anomie. This very un-'classical' god was long regarded as an outsider and latecomer to the Greek pantheon: the Greeks themselves so regarded him, putting his origin in Nysa in Asia or Ethiopia, where he was nursed by bees and whence he arrived accompanied by panthers. They also regarded him, rather like Heracles, as a god who had begun his life as a mortal, and he had a tomb at Delphi. In fact, he may be of Thracian origin; but a single Linear B tablet from Pylos referring to 'di-wo-nu-so-jo' (the genitive form of the name in Mycenaean Greek) suggests that he belongs after all to the oldest stratum of the Greek gods. He is certainly firmly enshrined in the mythology of Thebes. *Cadmus'* daughter *Semele* conceived a child by Zeus; when she demanded to see the god in his full majesty, he blasted her with a thunderbolt and snatched the foetus from her ashes, placing it in his thigh until it was ready to be born. He then gave it to Hermes, who gave it to Ino (or the nymphs of Nysa) to rear. An alternative (Orphic) version of his birth was from the union of Zeus and Persephone in the form of snakes.

The fullest source for the rites of Dionysus is Euripides' *Bacchae*, in which the *maenads* or bacchants, women devotees of the god, race across the mountains in an ecstatic frenzy, seizing small wild animals, tearing them apart and eating the raw flesh. In this way the maenads sacramentally incorporated the power of the god himself, whom they addressed as Axie Taure, glorious bull. The maenads dressed in fawnskins and carried *thyrsoi*, which were vine branches topped by a pine cone and wreathed with ivy. Many of his myths reflect this Dionysiac trait of 'losing the wits' and of tearing or being torn apart.

In this play Dionysus also shows his power as the god of miraculous and fruitful transformations: not only does he appear in the form of a bull and break open the prison of the bacchants, but the ground flows with milk and honey. Another myth concerns his capture by Tyrrhenian pirates who had promised to bring him to Naxos: when they altered course he caused the mast of their ship to turn into a vine in fruit; panthers and other wild beasts appeared on the deck, and the sailors leapt into the sea where they were transformed into dolphins. (The scene is portrayed on several Attic vases, notably a beautiful plate by Exekias, and on the Monument of Lysicrates in Athens.)

Dionysus was also honoured in tragic choruses. The meaning of the word tragic is disputed, but seems to be related to *tragos*, goat, and suggests a festival including a procession of mummers in animal costume. In Athens this kind of performance developed into the dramatic form we know as tragedy; plays were performed at the two festivals, Lenaea and Dionysia, of which Dionysus was patron. Dionysus is regularly accompanied in art by ithyphallic satyrs and sileni, and these figures formed the chorus in the satyr plays performed as a tailpiece to each tragic trilogy.

He is also sometimes identified, as Bacchus, with the Iacchus of the Eleusinian Mysteries, where his role as a god of life and rebirth makes him an appropriate participant.

Dionysus' mythology gives him a career as a hero before his divine status is established by his miracles. He was father by *Althaea* of *Deianeira*. His invention of the vine is important in Attic mythology — see *Erigone* — and he gave the daughters of King Anius of Delos the power to turn all they touched into wine, corn or oil. Hera punished him for the invention of wine by driving him mad, and he wandered with an army to Egypt, where he established the oracle of Ammon, and to India, where the pillars of Dionysus were a landmark for the legendary Alexander. In Phrygia he encountered King *Midas* (see *Midas*). He is important in the legend of *Ariadne*, rescuing her after her after her abandonment by *Theseus* on Dia or Naxos.

He also entered the *Underworld* to seek the shade of his mother Semele and restore her to life. He descended through Lake Lerna, asking the way from Prosymnus, who asked for sexual favours on his return. But Prosymnus was dead when Dionysus came back, so Dionysus planted a phallic stick on Prosymnus' tomb. In order to release Semele, Hades demanded a gift, and Dionysus gave him one of his favourite plants, the myrtle, which thereafter became associated with mourning.

The wandering Dionysus was particularly vicious to those who opposed the introduction of his rites to the city (which may reflect genuine historical resistance to the spread of his cult, or at least an acknowledgement that its wild, irrational quality was difficult to contain within the bounds of civic society). *Pentheus*, who opposed him at Thebes, was torn apart by maenads who included his own mother *Agave*; the Thracian king *Lycurgus* was driven mad and blinded, and then cut off his own leg mistaking it for a tree; the daughters of *Proetus* at Argos were driven mad, thought themselves to be cows and ran around the countryside naked, tearing children to pieces and eating them. Other groups of women were also driven mad by him for less clear reasons: the daughters of *Minyas*, changed into bats; the *Bassarids*; the women of Attica when he introduced the vine to Icarius (see *Erigone*). See also *Antiope*. His cult was gradually incorporated in the city festivals through drama, and at Delphi he shared the honours with Apollo, dominating during the winter months when Apollo was away feasting with the Hyperboreans.

He has a quite different role in Orphic doctrine, where he is murdered as a baby (also known as Zagreus) by the Titans: these seem not to be the Titans overthrown by Zeus but a race of pre-men (etymologically related to *titanos*, quicklime) who daubed themselves with gypsum as a disguise. After killing Dionysus they butchered his body and, in a reversal of normal sacrificial practice, first boiled and then roasted the meat. But Athena rescued the heart, from which the god was resurrected, and Zeus blasted the Titans with his thunderbolt. From the ashes the race of men were born. Orphic rites are an attempt to expiate the crime and achieve the dominance of the divine element in man constituted by his cannibalistic primal meal.

In classical art Dionysus is represented as a mature bearded figure, dressed in Phrygian costume. But in later centuries, because of his association as young god with the mother-goddess Cybele, he is youthful and beardless. [Nonnus; Détienne]

**Dioscuri** Castor and Polydeuces, the twin 'sons of Zeus' and Leda are important deities especially in Sparta (where many things, including the kings, went in pairs), where they were known also as the Anakes and worshipped in the form of a wooden structure in the shape of an H. They have strong links with similar twin gods of other Indo-European religions, notably the Asvins (horsemen) of Hindu mythology. They are closely associated with their sister Helen (born from the same egg) as the Asvins are with the Dawn Goddess. They are also known as protectors of sailors, to whom they appear in the form of St Elmo's Fire; they were identified with the constellation Gemini.

In mythology they were sons of Tyndareus the husband of Leda, and like all twins of mixed mortal and divine parentage one was immortal and the other not. They were notable athletes, Castor as rider and Polydeuces as boxer (he displays his prowess in the fight with Amycus, described in Theocritus, *Idyll* 22: see *Argonauts*). They rescued Helen after she was carried off by *Theseus*, but themselves carried off the *Leucippides* Phoebe and Hilaeira (light-names again), who were daughters of Leucippus, brother of Tyndareus and King of Messenia. But their cousins *Idas and Lynceus*, to whom the girls were betrothed, pursued them. Lynceus, with his preternatural sight (lynx-eyed) saw the twins hiding in a hollow oak on Mt Taygetus. Idas killed Castor with a spear; Polydeuces killed Lynceus; Idas then hurled a tombstone at Polydeuces; but Zeus killed Idas with a thunderbolt.

Polydeuces was the divine one of the pair. But such was his love for his brother that he did not wish to be immortal alone, and asked Zeus that they should be allowed to share alternate days of death below the earth and life on Olympus. Zeus granted his prayer, and 'opened the eyes, and loosened the voice, of bronze-belted Castor'. (Pindar, *Nem.* 10).

Homer knows, or admits, nothing of all this. From the walls of Troy Helen scans the Greek troops for her brothers, 'for she did not know that the life-giving earth already held them, at home in hollow Lacedaemon.' [Farnell; Rendel Harris]

**Dirce** The wife of King Lycus of Thebes and a loyal votary of Dionysus. Because of her cruelty to *Antiope*, the latter's sons *Amphion* and *Zethus* had her dragged to death behind a bull. Dionysus made a spring burst from the earth at the place where her body was gored. In historical times the spring Dirce was located either in Thebes or on Mt Cithaeron.

**Discord** See *Eris*.

**Dolon** A Trojan who entered the Greek camp as a spy, dressed in a wolfskin, at night. But *Diomedes* and *Odysseus* captured him, forced him to reveal the Trojan dispositions, and killed him. [*Iliad*]

**Dragon** As in modern folklore Greek dragons and serpents are the guardians of treasure. The most famous of these in ancient myth is Ladon, who guarded the apples of the *Hesperides* and which became the constellation Draco.

According to Artemidorus, dreaming of a dragon means that the dreamer will become wealthy.

A modern tale is that of Iannaki and the 40 dragons. Having killed, as he thinks, all of them, he and his mother take over their castle. But one survives, becomes the queen's lover, and together they plot to kill Iannaki. The queen feigns illness and sends Iannaki to fetch the Water of Life (or Immortality) from a garden where it is guarded by (more) dragons. Iannaki is, however, successful and the dragon's ploy is foiled. [J. C. Lawson]

**Dryads** *Nymphs* of the trees.

**Dryope** A daughter of Eurytus of Oechalia who was raped by Apollo. She was transformed into a lotus tree. [Ovid, *Met*. 9]

# E/F

Europa and the bull

**Echidna** A monster, half-nymph, half-snake, daughter of *Gaea* and *Tartarus* (usually). Her children by Typhaon were *Chimaera*, *Hydra*, Cerberus and Orthus; later the *Sphinx*, the Nemean Lion and the Crommyonian Sow. She was killed at last by *Argus* of the Hundred Eyes. [Hesiod, *Theogony*]

**Echo** A Heliconian nymph, punished by Hera for her endless chatter by the impediment of being able only to repeat the sentences of others. She fell in love with *Narcissus*, who spurned her; she faded away until only her voice was left. [Ovid, *Met.* 3]

**Electra, 1.** Daughter of *Agamemnon* and *Clytemnestra*, reduced to ignominy in her mother's household after the murder of Agamemnon. Surviving plays by all three Attic tragedians treat her story. She secretly tends the tomb of Agamemnon until the return of her brother *Orestes* from exile, and helps him to murder their mother. She later married Orestes' companion *Pylades*, [Aeschylus, *Choephori*; Sophocles, *Electra*; Euripides, *Electra*, *Orestes*; Seneca, *Agamemnon*]
**2.** Electra is also the name of a nymph of Samothrace, the faintest of the Pleiades.

**Eleusis** An Attic town on which the cult of Demeter centred. Founded in legend under King Celeus, the *Mysteries* of Demeter were one of the most important festivals of the Attic calendar. [*Homeric Hymn to Demeter*, Mylonas]

**Elpenor** The youngest of *Odysseus'* companions. Sleeping on the roof or window-ledge of *Circe's* house on Aeaea, Elpenor fell to his death. His ghost upbraided Odysseus, when he visited Hades, for not giving him a proper funeral, and Odysseus returned to Aeaea to do this. [*Odyssey*]

**Elysium, Elysian Fields** The home of the blessed dead, where they enjoy a happy and carefree life in eternal sunshine, unlike the miserable gloom that surrounds the flittering, whimpering shades in Hades. It is generally identified with the Islands of the Blessed, near or beyond the River Oceanus, though sometimes it is regarded as a region of Hades. It was ruled by Cronus — an extension of the idea of his ruling over the Golden Age — but also by the judge of the dead, *Rhadamanthys* [*Odyssey*, 4; Hesiod, *Works and Days*] Pindar describes how the virtuous dead 'travel to the tower of Cronus, where ocean-born breezes blow around the island of the blest, and sprays of gold flower from the earth and from the sea . . . with which they crown their heads, obeying the high decrees of Rhadamanthys . . . who sits beside the great father, consort of Rhea, throned on high.' [0.2; compare fragment 129] Initiates in the *Mysteries* thought to ensure themselves a direct passage to this blessed realm.

Sometimes the islands were identified with real ones: Pausanias mentions the White Island (*Leuce*) in the Black Sea where the dead Achilles, Patroclus, the two Ajaxes, Antilochus and *Helen* lived on after death. Plutarch (*De defectu oraculorum*) has Cronus sleeping eternally on an island in Britain, guarded by *Briareus*.

**Endymion** Though Endymion was King of Elis, his legend is associated with Mt Latmus in the Troad. He fell into an eternal sleep as a pleasant alternative to death as punishment for an attempt, like that of *Ixion*, to rape Hera. Here he was seen by Selene, the Moon (whose Semitic name, al-Lat, seems to be echoed in the name of the mountain), who fell in love with him and managed to bear him 50 daughters without waking him up. The daughters were considered to represent the 50 months between each celebration of the Olympic Games in Elis. His tomb sanctuary can be visited outside Heracleia. [Keats, *Endymion*]

**Eos** Goddess of the Dawn and sister of the Sun and Moon. Her children included several winds and the Morning Star. Among her lovers whom she carried off were *Cephalus* and *Orion*. Her most enduring affair was with *Tithonus*, a prince of the Trojan royal family. She obtained from Zeus immortality for Tithonus, but forgot to ask for eternal youth as well. Over the millennia he shrank and became a croaking wreck; Eos locked him away to deaden the sound of his voice, and at last turned him into a cicada.

Her sons by Tithonus were *Memnon* and Emathion.

**Epicaste** See *Jocasta*.

**Epigoni** The sons of the *Seven against Thebes*, who marched again against Thebes to avenge their fathers, shortly before the Trojan War. The warriors were: *Alcmaeon* and *Amphilochus*, sons of *Amphiaraus*; Sthenelus son of Capaneus; Polydorus son of Hippomedon; Euryalus son of Mecistus; Promachus (or Tlesimenes) son of Parthenopaeus; Thersander son of *Polynices*; *Diomedes* son of *Tydeus*; and *Eteoclus* (no relevant father). Alcmaeon led the expedition because the Delphic oracle told them that this would ensure success. They fought a battle near Thebes at Glisas. Then the Thebans fled the city and the Epigoni razed it to the ground; which is why Thebes has no mention in the *Homeric Catalogue of Ships*. Thersander became King of Thebes. For Alcmaeon's story see *Alcmaeon*. [M. Davies]

**Epimetheus** Brother of *Prometheus* (Forethought); his name means Afterthought. He married *Pandora*, the first woman, and opened her box of evils, thus beginning the troubles of the human race. Their daughter was *Pyrrha*. [Hesiod, *Works and Days*]

**Erato** Muse of song and dancing.

**Erechtheus** King of Athens, son of Pandion and Zeuxippe and grandson of *Erichthonius*; brother of *Procne* and *Philomela*; father of three sons, including *Cecrops*, and four daughters, *Procris*, Chthonia, Orithyia and *Creusa*. After him is named the Erechtheum on the Acropolis, where he was worshipped with Athena Polias; he perhaps represents a form of Poseidon with whom Athena disputed the possession of Attica. He disappeared from life when the earth was opened by a blow of Poseidon's trident, after he had killed Poseidon's son *Eumolpus*, King of Eleusis, in battle.

His existence is perhaps motivated by a desire to tidy up the legendary chronology of Athens, with its two Cecropses and the similarly named Erichthonius.

**Erichthonius** A child born of the semen spilled by Hephaestus when he tried to rape Athena on the Acropolis. He was born in Cecrops' reign and brought up by Cecrops' daughters, Pandrosos and Herse. He was kept in a box; when they looked in it one day, the sight they saw (an infant with a serpent's tail?) so horrified them that they went mad and leapt off the north wall of the Acropolis. Erichthonius was then brought up in Athena's shrine and became king. He instituted the Panathenaea.

**Erigone** The daughter of Icarius, who lived in Attica in the days of King Pandion. When Dionysus gave him the gift of wine, the country people, on drinking it, thought they had been poisoned, and killed him. Erigone hanged herself in grief. Plague — or drought — followed. *Aristaeus*, in response to the instructions of Apollo, instituted a festival in which dolls were hung from trees, like Erigone. Her name, 'spring-born', the common association of swinging and fertility, and the motif of drought, all combine to make this story a clear reflection of a spring fertility ritual, not unlike the story of the barrenness of the land ensuing on Demeter's grief and the subsequent introduction of agriculture.
   According to Ovid, Dionysus was Erigone's lover.

**Erinyes** The avenging spirits of the dead, also known (the Latin form) as Furies, who pursue parricides. They were born from the drops of blood of the castrated *Uranus* which fell on the Earth, and were thought of as hideous hags, black in colour and with eyes oozing pus (their portrayal on stage in Aeschylus' *Eumenides*' was said to be so horrendous that several women in the audience had miscarriages).
   Their names are sometimes given as Allecto, Tisiphone and Megaera, though they are more often indeterminate in number.
   Their best-known myth is their pursuit of *Orestes* for his murder of Clytemnestra; they drive him mad, and his pollution is inescapable until a trial at Athens in which Athena decrees Orestes free of pollution on the grounds that the son is not kindred to his mother, but only to his father. She then renamed the Erinyes 'Eumenides', the Kindly Ones, and gave them a home under the Areopagus and made them guardians of civic order in Athens.
   Elsewhere they had cult with the Graces, and had the usual connection of chthonian spirits with the fertility of the earth.

**Eriphyle** The wife of *Amphiaraus*. See also *Alcmaeon*.

**Eris** The personification of Discord, mother, according to Hesiod, of a number of other unpleasant creatures including *Ate*, Labour, Forgetfulness, Famine, Strife, Murderous Quarrel and others. She was the 'wicked fairy' who, in fury at not being invited to the wedding of *Peleus* and *Thetis*, hurled among the guests a golden apple inscribed 'for the fairest'. The three goddesses who claimed it, Aphrodite, Athena and Hera, asked the Trojan prince Paris to judge the contest, and thus began Athena's undying hatred for Troy. [Hesiod, *Theogony*]

**Eros** God of Love, according to Hesiod born with Gaea and Tartarus from Chaos. This principle of attraction (along with its opposite, repulsion) lay at the root of much pre-Socratic cosmology, being particularly important in the theories of Empedocles. Eros received cult as a god in various localities. Later he was conceived of as the son of Aphrodite (her attendant in Hesiod). He represents (in Plato for example) the erotic bond of man and boy rather than that of man and woman, his mother's province.

His personification as a 'literary' god in romantic narrative is not found before the Hellenistic period (Apollonius Rhodius, Vergil); and the handsome youth of earlier art now degenerates into a winged *putto* (or a multiplicity thereof, *erotes*). The best-known story about him, the tale of Cupid and *Psyche*, is known only from the third-century AD writer Apuleius.

**Erotocritos** The hero of an epic poem of the same name composed by Vintzentzos Kornaros of Crete between 1600 and 1640. Crete was under Venetian rule at this time. Though the plot is pure medieval romance, borrowed from the French writer Pierre de la Cypède, and taking the form of a Greek equivalent to Ariosto, the characters and atmosphere are entirely Greek, while the language of the poem is a precious document of Greek of the period.

Erotocritos, son of the king's counsellor Pezostratos, falls in love with Aretousa, daughter of King Heracles and Queen Artemis of Athens. He declares his love by nightly lute-serenades outside her window. Her melancholy grows, until her father arranges a tournament at which the winner is to be crowned by herself. The tournament and its heroes are described at enormous length. Of course Erotocritos wins, and is emboldened to ask for Aretousa's hand; but instead he is banished in disgrace, and the girl and her nurse are imprisoned until she shall consent to the husband of her father's choice. Eventually Erotocritos returns in disguise to fight for the king against a besieging enemy. He then dares again to ask for Aretousa's hand, and this time is, happily, successful. [Kornaros, tr. Stephanides]

**Erysichthon** A Thessalian who cut down a grove sacred to Demeter; she punished him with perpetual hunger, and he devoured all his possessions. His daughter Mestra sold herself as a slave to buy him food, then changed shape and did so again — and again. But nothing could satisfy Erysichthon's hunger and he ended by consuming himself. [Callimachus, *Hymn* 6; Ovid, *Met*. 8]

**Eteocles** Son of *Oedipus*. The latter cursed his two sons for refusing him sanctuary after he blinded himself. As a result they were perpetually at odds. Eteocles broke his oath to rule jointly with his brother *Polynices*, and banished the latter. Polynices then assembled the expedition of the *Seven against Thebes*; in their unsuccessful assault on Thebes, both brothers were killed.

**Eumaeus** The swinehead of the royal family of Ithaca, *Odysseus* and his father *Laertes*. He welcomed Odysseus on his return to Ithaca in disguise, and in his hut Odysseus first revealed himself to his son. The description of Eumaeus' hut is a masterpiece of genre, and has led to numerous attempts to locate it precisely on Ithaca. [*Odyssey*; Rodd]

**Eumenides** See *Erinyes*.

**Eumolpus** A son of Chione, daughter of Boreas, by Poseidon. Chione threw the new-born infant into the sea to conceal her shame, but Poseidon rescued it and took it to Ethiopia, where the king in due course gave the lad one of his daughters as wife. But Eumolpus assaulted his sister-in-law and was banished to Thrace; here his son plotted against the Thracian king, and Eumolpus was banished again, and came to Eleusis. He was a founder, with Celeus, of the Eleusinian Mysteries, and purified Heracles after his murder of the Centaurs, and initiated him. Subsequently Eumolpus became King of Thrace, and sent an army to help Eleusis when Athens declared war on the town. In the fighting he was killed by *Erechtheus*.

**Euphemus** A son of Poseidon with the ability to walk on the water, he sailed with Argo, as deputy helmsman, and when the Argonauts were stranded in Libya Triton gave him a clod of earth, which he lost overboard in a shipwreck; it was washed up on the island of Thera (Pindar, *Pyth*. 4); or, he threw it overboard because of a dream and it *became* the island of Thera (Apollonius Rhodius). This event was the reason for the subsequent foundation by Therans under *Battus* of the colony of Cyrene in Libya; the soil returned to its home. This complicated tale was clearly invented as a foundation myth of the far-flung Greek colony on the African shore.

**Europa** Daughter of King Agenor of Tyre (or Sidon). Zeus fell in love with her, carried her off disguised as a white bull, and brought her to Crete. Their three sons were *Minos*, *Rhadamanthys* and *Sarpedon*. Zeus made for her the bronze giant *Talos* and the watchdog Laelaps. Then she married Asterion and their daughter was Crete. She seems to be another form of the Cretan mother-goddess and should be distinguished from (though she was later merged with) the Oceanid whose sister was Asia (later also Libya and Thrace) and who became eponym of the continent of Europe.

**Eurydice** 1. A Thracian nymph, married to *Orpheus*: after *Aristaeus* caused her death Orpheus descended to Hades to fetch her back, but lost her again because he was unable to keep his promise to the gods of the *Underworld* not to look behind him as he led her to the upper world.

**2.** Wife of King *Creon* of Thebes, and mother of *Haemon*, who hanged herself after Haemon committed suicide over the body of *Antigone*.

**Eurystheus** King of Mycenae or Tiryns, son of Sthenelus and Nicippe daughter of *Pelops*. Sthenelus usurped the throne, which should have gone to Electryon, whose grandson was *Heracles*. Hera prevented Heracles from inheriting by causing Eurystheus to be born first. After Heracles killed his wife and children in madness, the Delphic oracle ordered him to perform 12 labours at Eurystheus' behest. On the labours, see *Heracles*. A popular scene in vase-painting is Eurystheus hiding in an oil-jar, terrified at the sight of the Erymanthian boar which Heracles has just brought safely in.

 After Heracles' death and deification Eurystheus was killed in battle by Heracles' son *Hyllus*, fighting for Athens against the Argives; or by Alcmene after being captured by Hyllus.

**Euterpe** One of the Muses, in late authors the patroness of flautists.

**Fates** See *Moirae*.

**Furies** See *Erinyes*.

# G

Medusa the Gorgon

**Gaea, Ge** Goddess of Earth. She was born, with Tartarus and Eros, from Chaos, and is mother of *Uranus* and Pontus. She also married Uranus, and bore the *Titans*, *Cyclopes* and *Hundred-Handers*. Because Uranus hid the last in her body, she persuaded the Titan *Cronus* to castrate her husband and allow them to emerge. Such a violent separation of Earth and Sky is paralleled in Polynesian myth; and in the Babylonian *Enuma Elish* (the Creation myth), Apsu and Tiamat, the sweet and bitter waters, are similarly torn apart by Ea. The drops of blood that fell on Ge engendered the *Erinyes, Giants* and *Meliae*.

Other children of Ge include *Typhoeus* who, like the Giants, fought against the gods of Olympus; *Tityus*; the horse Arion (in some versions; cf. *Demeter*); *Echidna*, by Tartarus; and *Antaeus*.

She was not abolished from existence by the rise of the next generation of gods under Zeus. She helped the Seasons (Horae) to nurse *Aristaeus*, and was responsible for the death of *Orion*. Like earth-goddesses in other traditions (for example Wagner's Nordic Erda) she had oracular powers; her oracle at Delphi was given by her to *Python*. [Hesiod, *Theogony*]

**Galatea** A sea-nymph, daughter of Nereus and Doris, loved by the

*Cyclops Polyphemus*. Because she spurned him for his ugliness and loved *Acis*, Polyphemus killed Acis by hurling rocks at him; these became the Cyclopian rocks off Acireale in Sicily.

**Ganymede** A Trojan prince, son of Tros or Laomedon. Zeus fell in love with his beauty and sent his eagle (or, descended in the form of an eagle) to carry Ganymede off to Olympus to be the gods' cup-bearer. Zeus sent the boy's father a pair of horses (or a golden vine) as compensation. The Roman form of his name is Catamitus, hence 'catamite'. [*Homeric Hymn to Aphrodite*]

**Gello** A female demon who carries off and devours young children. She is first mentioned by Sappho, as a maiden who died early and thereafter attacked and caused the death of infants. Gelloudes (the plural) are mentioned as a class of demons by Michael Psellus (eleventh century AD) and Leo Allatius (seventeenth century AD). The latter tells a story of Saints Sisynius and Sinydorus, who tried to capture one. She transformed herself into various shapes (a trait borrowed from the marine deities whom one form of her name recalls (Gialoú — from *gialós*, shore). Finally they captured her in the form of a goat's hair entangled in the king's beard. They then forced her to reveal her 12½ names, thus removing her power. These names are Gulou, Mora, Byzou (bloodsucker), Marmarou (stony-hearted), Petasia (winged one), Pelagia (sea-creature), Vordona (swooping like a hawk), Apletou (insatiable), Chamodracaena (earth snake), Anavardalaia (Soaring), Psychanaspastria (soul-snatcher), Paidopniktia (child-strangler), Strigla. [Psellus, Allatius, J.C. Lawson]

**Geryon** The triple-bodied king of the island of Erytheia off Cadiz, son of *Chrysaor* and Callirhoe. Heracles' tenth labour was to capture his cattle from the herdsman Eurytus and the two-headed dog Orthos (brother of *Cerberus*). He sailed there in the bowl of the Sun. Living in the far west, Geryon seems to be a 'herdsman of the dead' and Heracles' task a parallel to the descent into Hades (cattle, which emblematize life, being thus torn from the realms of death). [Pindar fr. 169; Stesichorus *Geryoneis*; Croon]

**Giants** A race of beings born from *Gaea*, engendered by the blood that dropped from the castrated *Uranus*. Their home was Phlegra, probably in Thrace though the Phlegraean fields were later located near Mt Vesuvius, and the giants given connections, like the *Cyclopes* and *Typhoeus*, with volcanic fire. They were normally conceived of as human in form with legs that ended in snakes' tails — as on the great Altar of Pergamum, now in the Antikenmuseum in Berlin.

The Giants made war on the gods of Olympus at the instigation of Gaea, who was angry at Zeus' refusal to give them a plant which would make them invulnerable. They attacked with rocks and burning branches. The gods learnt that they could only overcome the Giants with the aid of a mortal, and *Heracles* carried out this role.

Their king was Porphyrion, the eldest of them Alcyoneus whom Heracles despatched. Others were Enceladus, killed by Athena; Mimas, blasted by Zeus' thunderbolt; Ephialtes, blinded by Apollo and Heracles; Hippolytus, killed by Hermes who was wearing Hades' cap of invisibility; Agrius and Thoas, killed by the Fates using bronze clubs. In Apollodorus, Athena flung the island of Sicily on Enceladus, and Poseidon threw part of Cos on Polybotes; the fragment became the island of Nisyros.

The Giants were not infrequently confused with the Titans, who made a similar assault on Olympus. [Hesiod, *Theogony*]

**Glaucus 1.** Son of *Sisyphus*, King of Ephyre (Corinth). His wife *Eurynome* bore to Poseidon a son *Bellerophon* whom Glaucus reared as his own. He was eaten by his own horses after losing a chariot race to *Iolaus*, and his ghost continued to haunt the Isthmus for generations.
**2.** A descendant, grandson of Bellerophon, who appears in the *Iliad* as leader of the Lycians, with *Sarpedon*, and, on discovering that *Diomedes*' grandfather Oeneus once entertained Bellerophon, exchanges his golden armour for Diomedes' bronze. When he died, Apollo had his body brought by the winds to Lycia.
**3.** A sea-god (his name means sea-green) who started life as a fisherman but was transformed by a herb he ate into a merman. He loved *Scylla*, but *Circe* loved him and turned Scylla into a sea-monster. He was a friendly patron of sailors and had the gift of prophecy; he had an oracle with the *Nereids* on Delos.
**4.** A son of *Minos*, who drowned in a jar of honey in childhood. The Curetes said that he could be revived by whoever could find the best analogy for a cow belonging to Minos which changed its colour (red, white, black) three times a day. *Polyidus* hit on the blackberry; then, being enclosed with Glaucus in a chamber tomb, he succeeded in reviving Glaucus with a magic herb, and taught him divination. As prophecy is a common property of sea gods, there may be some merging of identity with Glaucus (3).

**God** The conventional translation of the Greek word *theos*; thus the word is used of all the Olympian deities. Gods in this sense are a kind of aristocracy of creation, not unlike men in their passions and behaviour, but infinitely more beautiful and powerful; and they are immortal. Between gods and men are two other races, the *daemones* and the *heroes*. Later the word came to be used, usually in the form *ho theos*, the god, to refer to a supreme divinity. This usage is found as early as Plato. More often in Neoplatonic philosophy other abstractions — such as The One — filled this purpose; then Christianity appropriated the old Greek term for the single Christian God.

**Golden Age** Under the reign of *Cronus* there existed a Golden Race of men who lived free from care and enjoyed eternal youth and banquets. They all died as if falling asleep, without pain. They had no need to work because the land produced its fruit spontaneously. They vanished from earth with the coming of the Olympian rule of Zeus. (The myth clearly relates, though awkwardly, to the role of the Olympian Demeter in teaching men the necessity of agriculture. It also recalls the life of Adam in Paradise before he was driven out to earn his bread in the sweat of his brow.)

The Golden Race was succeeded by those of Silver, Bronze and Iron (our own). This scheme of Ages and Metals shows striking similarities with Near Eastern accounts including Persian, Jewish, Indian and Babylonian myths, and it seems likely that Hesiod, who recounts it, had it from such a source. [Hesiod, *Works and Days* 106-21 with West's notes]

The myth became a moral commonplace in Hesiod himself and in later diatribes on the endless decline of mankind in beauty, morality, privilege and strength, and on the duty of work. The Romans placed this age under the rule of Saturn (=Cronus). A similar life is led by the blessed dead, under the rule of Cronus, in the *Elysian Fields*. [Lovejoy and Boas]

**Golden Fleece** The fleece of the ram sent by Poseidon to substitute for *Phrixus* when his father *Athamas* was about to sacrifice him. It flew off with Phrixus and his sister *Helle* on its back and bore Phrixus to Colchis, where he sacrificed it to Poseidon and hung its fleece in a grove sacred to Ares. The expedition of the *Argonauts* was mounted to bring it back to Greece.

**Gorgon** The Gorgons were three daughters of the sea-deities Phorcys and Ceto, named Stheno, Euryale and *Medusa*, who dwelt by the River of Ocean. Their hair was of snakes and they had vast grinning mouths and tusks, and golden wings. Their look had the power to turn men to stone, a trait central to the story of *Perseus* and the Gorgon (see *Medusa*).

The grinning, hideous masks of Gorgons, Gorgoneia, were commonly used as apotropaic images to ward off evil spirits. A large and famous one is that on the temple of Artemis on Corfu, excavated by W. Dörpfeld assisted by Kaiser Wilhelm II, who wrote a book about Gorgons. The origin of the figure is much disputed, and they have been interpreted as spirits of the thunder, of the sun, of the winds, and so on. Like many of the monsters of Greek myth, their iconography derives from Near Eastern art. (A particularly implausible view of their origin was that they were a poor attempt at portraying lions.)

There was a Gorgoneion on the south face of the Acropolis rock in Athens; medieval travellers reported that it had the power to foretell the embarkation of invading fleets from the distant south.

In modern folklore, though a Gorgon is still a metaphor for an ugly, or a depraved woman, the Gorgons have double fish-tails and are in fact mermaids, beautiful and deceitful; they have adopted many of the traits of the ancient *Nereids*. [Wilhelm II; Martoni; Myrivilis]

**Graces** 'Charites' in Greek. The three Graces were daughters of Aphrodite by Zeus (or of Helius by Aegle — Onomacritus), and their names were Aglaea, Thalia and Euphrosyne. They had cult notably at Orchomenus where they were worshipped in the form of three meteorites. But they attain their highest significance as associates with the Muses in the poet's craft; the Muses give the matter, but the Graces add that 'grace beyond the reach of art', pure inspiration, seductive charm. Pindar's *Olympian* 14 is a beautiful invocation of the Graces of Orchomenus: 'if anything sweet or delightful warms the heart of any mortal man, whether he has beauty, or skill, or the light of victory shining upon him, it is your gift.'

**Graeae** Two (or three) ancient women, daughters of Phorcys and Ceto, who lived in the western regions towards Ocean, where the sun never shone, and had one eye and one tooth between them. Perseus tricked them into relinquishing both to persuade them to tell him what equipment he needed to overcome the Gorgons. They told him that he had to obtain from a group of nymphs a pair of winged sandals, a bag called a *kibisis* and Hades' cap of invisibility. In an alternative version, the Graeae were guards on the road to the Gorgons, and by stealing the single eye and throwing it into Lake Tritonis Perseus managed to sneak past them safely and unannounced. Aeschylus (*PV*) describes them as having the form of swans.

**Griffin** A beast with a lion's body and the head and wings of an eagle, known in all Near Eastern artistic traditions. Variants may have snake heads, scorpion tails, bird's feet, etc. *Aristeas* described in his poem the gold-guarding griffins of the Arimaspians. Though appearing in art from Geometric times onward, both as independent figures and as decorative motifs, for examples as handles or spouts, they have no role in Greek mythology; they sometimes accompany gods (especially Apollo, Dionysus) as watchdogs.

# H

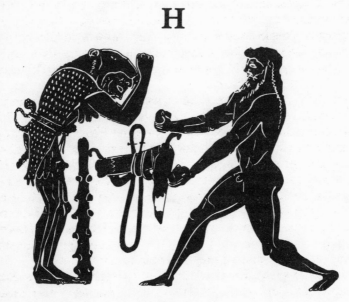

Heracles and Atlas

**Hades** One of the three sons of *Cronus* (the other two are Zeus and Poseidon), who in the division of the world won the *Underworld*, the world of the dead, which was known as the 'House of Hades' and by metonymy itself also called Hades. He had no cult except, remarkably, in Elea. His only myth is the rape of *Persephone* or Kore while gathering flowers. This event was often located on the 'fair field' of Enna in Sicily. During the fifth century his place is usurped, under the influence of Eleusinian myth, by the very similar Pluton ('the wealthy one'), under which name he enters Roman mythology. In the rare artistic representations he carries a sceptre or a key, and in Eleusinian dedications is portrayed enthroned beside Persephone.

**Haemon** Son of *Creon*, King of Thebes. According to Apollodorus he was one of the Theban youths killed by the *Sphinx* for failing to answer her riddle; but in Sophocles' *Antigone* he is alive after *Oedipus'* triumph and disaster, and is the lover of *Antigone*. On her execution by Creon he killed himself.

**Harmonia** Daughter of Ares and Aphrodite, and wife of *Cadmus*, King of Thebes. Her wedding presents included a necklace made by Hephaestus, and a robe; see further *Alcmaeon*.

She bore Cadmus a son, Polydorus, and four daughters: *Ino*, Autonoe, *Semele* and *Agave*. After the tragic deaths of all their daughters, Cadmus and Harmonia left Thebes for Illyria and were changed into snakes by Ares.

**Harpies** Winged female demons. In art they are often shown as winged women rather than bird-bodied women like the Sirens. According to Hesiod their names were Aello and Ocypete. Later sources add Celaeno. The names mean storm, swift-flyer and black cloud. They are, with *Iris*, the fine-haired daughters of Thaumas and Electra daughter of Ocean.

Unlike the musical Sirens whom they resemble in appearance, they are foul beasts, best known in the Argonautic legend of King *Phineus*: they descended on his table every time the blind king sat down to eat, snatching the food and befouling the table service, until driven away by the sons of the North Wind to the Echinades islands.

The most famous harpies in art may not be harpies at all — the creatures on the 'Harpy Tomb' from Xanthus in the British Museum, shown bearing away the souls of the dead to Hades. Their discoverer, Charles Fellows, saw in them the 'ravishing Harpies' who bore away the daughters of *Pandarus* 'to serve the Furies, who hate constantly'. But they seem closer to *Keres* in their function.

The harpies were mothers to *Achilles'* two talking horses, *Xanthus* and Balius, by Zephyrus, and also to the horses of the *Dioscuri*.

**Hebe** 'Youth', daughter of Hera, engendered parthenogenetically by the goddess' eating of lettuce (a traditionally anaphrodisiac plant, like Hera's sacred tree the agnus castus). She was a cupbearer of the gods and became the wife of *Heracles* after his deification.

**Hecate** A goddess whose origins are in Asia Minor: she displays various characteristics of other mother-goddesses and is especially close to Artemis as rearer of children. She is characteristically worshipped at gateways and junctions of three roads. The dog is her creature and is offered to her in sacrifice: she is associated with the world of ghosts and, particularly in later periods, the special deity of witches and sorceresses. She is sometimes represented with three heads or faces. In mythology she is a Titan who preserved her honours after Zeus' triumph: the torches she carried as a goddess of the dead were once used in the battle of the gods and giants to kill Clytius.

Her rites are described in some detail by Apollonius Rhodius in his account of the witch *Medea*.

**Hector** The eldest son of *Priam*, King of Troy, and leader of the Trojan army against the Greek invaders. His wife was *Andromache* and their son *Astyanax*.

He is one of the most prominent characters in the *Iliad*, fighting a duel with *Ajax*: his simple soldierly courage makes him a foil to the pettish *Achilles*. After Hector with Apollo's help had killed Achilles' friend *Patroclus*, Achilles returned to battle, killed Hector, and dragged his body around the walls of Troy, tied by its heels to his chariot. He then preserved the body in his tent. Priam eventually came secretly to Achilles' tent and played on Achilles' human sympathies, as a result of which the latter agreed to return the body. The *Iliad* ends with the magnificent funeral of Hector.

**Hecuba** The second wife of *Priam*, King of Troy: she came from the region of the River Sangarius on the south coast of the Black Sea. Her 19 children include many of the best-known of Priam's 50 sons and daughters: *Cassandra*, *Creusa*, Deiphobus, *Hector*, *Helenus*, Laodice, *Paris*, Polydorus, *Polyxena*, *Troilus*.

Hecuba was made *Odysseus*' slave after the fall of Troy. When they stopped on the return from Troy at the Thracian Chersonese, Hecuba discovered that its king, Polymestor, had murdered her son Polydorus. She blinded him and killed his children, whereupon she was turned into a dog and was buried nearby at a place thereafter called Cynossema (Dog's Grave).

Nicander put her metamorphosis into a dog immediately after Priam's death: after she scratched Polymestor's eyes out, the citizens stoned her: a stone lodged in her throat and she could thereafter only bark. The association with the dog suggests some assimilation to the goddess *Hecate*.

In the *Iliupersis* Apollo brought her safely to Lycia (Hector was in this poem the son of Apollo).

She is a prominent character in Euripides' *Troades*, and *Hecuba*. [Ovid, *Met.*; Pindar, *Pa.* 8]

**Helen** The daughter of *Leda* and *Tyndareus*, King of Sparta, born from the same egg as the twins Castor and Polydeuces (the *Dioscuri*). Worshipped as a goddess at Sparta, in the rest of Greece she was, rather, a legendary figure. Her beauty caused her to be seized first by *Theseus* and carried off to Attica; but while he and *Pirithous* were away in Hades, her brothers came with an army and took her back. She was then courted by numerous suitors including *Idomeneus* and *Odysseus* (who was, however, more interested in her cousin *Penelope*). Odysseus advised Tyndareus to make all the suitors swear to defend her final choice, which was *Menelaus*. Theocritus' 18th *Idyll* is a wedding song for the pair, hinting at Helen's role as a goddess of womanhood (and dawn?) at Sparta. The couple had a daughter, Hermione.

It was Helen's seizure by the Trojan prince *Paris* while staying in their house which occasioned the war of the Greeks against Troy. The sworn suitors had to honour their pledge to fight for her. And thus the beauty of one woman's face 'launched a thousand ships/And burnt the topless towers of Ilium'.

Helen was generally regarded as a willing partner in the elopement, as much in love with beautiful young Paris as he with her. However, she became lonely in Troy and was regarded by its inhabitants with hostility as the cause of the war. So it is not surprising that she helped the Greeks in the last stages of the war, refusing to give away Odysseus when he entered Troy in disguise. She did, however, in one legend try to trick the soldiers in the *Wooden Horse* by addressing each in the voice of his own wife: but Odysseus persuaded them not to answer, and so their presence was not revealed to the Trojans.

An alternative version which sought to exonerate Helen from the charge of fickleness had it that a 'phantom' Helen went to Troy while the real one was spirited away to Egypt for the duration of the war. The Egyptian version, which was originated by Stesichorus as an 'apology' for an earlier poem in which he had made her a flighty woman, and had been blinded by the gods as a punishment, was the basis of Euripides' *Helen* as well as the opera by Strauss and Hofmannsthal, *Die Ägyptische Helena*.

In the traditional version, on being reunited with Menelaus at the end of the war, her beauty overcame him and he dropped the sword with which he was about to transfix her in revenge. On their way home together they stopped at the mouth of the Nile where Helen was taught the secrets of healing herbs — 'that nepenthes, which the wife of Thone [Polydamna], in Egypt gave to Jove-born Helena'. [Milton, *Comus*]

Several versions of her death were current. In Euripides' *Orestes* she is translated just as Orestes is about to murder her. According to the Rhodians she was driven out of Sparta by Menelaus' sons and took refuge with Polyxo, widow of *Tlepolemus*: but Polyxo got her maids to dress up as Erinyes and hang Helen from a tree. She was then worshipped as a goddess. A south Italian tradition placed her on the White Island with other blessed heroes of the Trojan War, where she was married to *Achilles*. The traditional version gave Menelaus and Helen a peaceful death in Sparta after which they were buried at Therapnae and became guardian gods of the city: the shrine (Menelaion) may be visited near Sparta to the south-east.

**Helenus** A Trojan seer, son of *Priam* and *Hecuba*. When captured by Odysseus he revealed to the Greeks how Troy could be taken: the *Palladium* must be captured, *Pelops*' bones must be brought to Troy, and *Philoctetes* must be persuaded to come from Lemnos with his bow. Helenus quarrelled with his brother Deiphobus because the latter was awarded *Helen* as wife after *Paris*' death.

After the fall of Troy *Neoptolemus* took Helenus on his ship as far as Epirus, where the seer founded the city of Buthrotum, and gave him his concubine *Andromache*, formerly the wife of Helenus' brother Hector. According to Vergil he prophesied to Aeneas the foundation of Rome.

**Heliades** The daughters of *Helius*, sisters of *Phaethon*, who wept at his death and were transformed into poplar trees. See also *Hyades*.

**Helicon** A mountain in Boeotia, home of the *Muses*, whose especial haunt was the grove of the River Termessus or Permessus, below the spring *Hippocrene*.

**Helius** The Sun, son of the Titans *Hyperion* and *Theia*. He was absent from the casting of lots by the gods for shares in the earth, and so was allotted no special region. To make up for this, Zeus allotted him the newly arisen island of Rhodes, of which he became the patron. The Colossus of Rhodes was a bronze statue of Helius. His portion is an appropriate one as Rhodes claims to receive more hours of sunshine per year than any other place in the Mediterranean.

The nymph Rhode bore him seven sons, one of whom had three sons, Lindus, Ialysus and Camirus, after whom the three major cities of Rhodes were named. He married Perseis, a sea-nymph, who bore him Aeëtes (see *Argonauts*), *Circe* and *Pasiphae*. He was also father of the *Graces* by Aegle. He seduced Leucothoe by disguising himself as her mother: when her father buried her alive in punishment he transformed her into the frankincense bush. *Clytie*, who had revealed his act out of jealous love for Helius, turned into a heliotrope.

His best-known son was *Phaethon*, to whom he lent his chariot, with disastrous effect.

He lent *Heracles* the bowl in which he travelled daily across the sky, to enable the hero to reach the far west in the course of his labours.

Helius is an unusually literary member of the Greek pantheon: his cult is insignificant, and he was often assimilated to Apollo. His lack of cult suggests perhaps the lack of enthusiasm of the Greeks for cult of natural objects. But it must be remembered that the philosopher Anaxagoras was prosecuted for impiety because he stated that in his opinion the sun was a large fiery stone, about the size of the Peloponnese.

**Helle** The sister of *Phrixus*, and daughter of *Athamas* and Nephele. She was carried off with Phrixus on the Golden Ram. As it flew from Orchomenus to Colchis, Helle fell into the sea and was drowned, or became a bride of Poseidon: the region of the sea where she fell was named the Hellespont (Helle's Sea).

**Hellen** The eldest son of *Deucalion* and *Pyrrha*, and eponym of the Hellenes, Greeks. Father of Dorus, Aeolus and *Xuthus*.

**Hephaestus** Son of Zeus and Hera, or of Hera alone, god of fire and the blacksmith of the gods. His cult was practised especially on the

volcanic island of Lemnos, on which he fell after Zeus threw him
out of heaven in anger at Hera's bearing him without her husband's
aid. It took Hephaestus a whole day to fall from heaven, and afterwards he was permanently lame. (This may reflect the fact that smiths
in antiquity were often lame men, unable to move fast but with corres-
pondingly over-developed upper limbs.) Alternatively he is said to
have been thrown out of heaven by Hera because of his lameness,
and he fell into Ocean and was cared for by *Thetis* and the Oceanid
Eurynome.

Hephaestus was not only a smith but a master craftsman. He made
a golden throne for Hera, but when she sat on it she was bound fast.
He refused to return home to Olympus, until Dionysus made him
drunk and brought him back; he then released Hera.

His other creations included robot tables which went wherever the
gods wanted them; the armour of Achilles, ordered by Thetis; and
the first woman, *Pandora*. He also enabled the birth of *Aphrodite*
from Zeus' head by splitting it open with an axe.

His official wife was Aphrodite (sometimes Aglaea, one of the
*Graces*), though Aphrodite spent most of her time with other male
gods, notably Ares. A splendid tale in the *Odyssey* tells how
Hephaestus trapped Ares and Aphrodite in bed together with a magic
net, and the gods gathered to watch their discomfiture, shaking with
unquenchable laughter.

His lust for Athena resulted in the birth of *Erichthonius*; and when
*Achilles* fought the river *Scamander* in the *Iliad* Hephaestus dried
the waters up with a great flame to save Achilles from drowning.

**Hera** Several of the earliest temples in the Greek world were dedicated to Hera (notably those at Samos, Olympia, Perachora and above
all Argos). At Argos she vied with Poseidon for mastery of the land
and her primacy was decreed by the river-gods of the region; Poseidon
took his revenge by drying up the springs. Hera has sometimes been
explained as a Mycenaean palace goddess, though her name has not
been found in the Linear B tablets. Many have seen her as a relic
in the Olympian religion of a pre-Olympian goddess of Mother Earth,
ruler of the enclosing folds of the nurturing hills; her tempestuous
marriage to Zeus marks her absorption into the Indo-European system where the male sky-god is dominant. In mythology she is Zeus'
sister, daughter of Cronus, as well as his wife. Her epithet in Homer,
*boöpis*, cow-faced, is consonant with the regular sacrificial use of
cows in her cult. In cult she is above all the goddess of marriage,
fulfilled womanhood, Hera Teleia ('the fulfilled').

In Homer she is a difficult and obstreperous wife to Zeus, goaded
by his authoritarianism and womanizing, but she is kind in general
to few, not even her own son *Hephaestus*.

Several attempts were made on her virtue: by the *Giant* Porphyrion,
and by *Ixion* and *Endymion*.

Above all Hera persecuted her husband's lovers: *Leto*, *Io*, Semele and the daughters of *Proetus*. When *Tiresias* settled an argument between Hera and Zeus about which of the sexes gained the more pleasure from sexual intercourse, by saying that the woman enjoyed it nine times as much, she blinded him.

She was hostile above all to the hero who bears her name, *Heracles*, Glory of Hera. Once her hostility to him reached such a pitch that Zeus bound an anvil to her ankles and hung her out of heaven by her wrists.

She did, however, support *Jason* and the *Argonauts* throughout their travels. She and Athena opposed the Trojans because *Paris* had awarded the prize of their beauty contest to Aphrodite, and she once helped the Greeks by persuading Zeus to lie with her on Mt Gargarus while Poseidon was egging on the Greeks.

She scarcely figures in mythology outside the poems of Homer.

**Heracles** Heracles is the Greek hero *par excellence*, an idea expressed by Pindar in the remarkable formulation *heros theos*, 'hero god'. Heracles is the mortal son of Zeus and *Alcmena* who by his deeds finally won a place on Olympus and marriage to Hera's daughter *Hebe*. His name, unlike those of the gods, is a human one in form (compare Herodorus, Pericles) and means 'Glory of Hera' — paradoxically in view of that goddess' noted and incessant hostility towards him.

At one time scholars considered him to be a 'Dorian' interloper, but it is clear that his adventures belong to the Mycenaean tradition and period.

Heracles was conceived by *Alcmena* after a visitation by Zeus when her husband *Amphitryon* was away at war with the Taphians. When the nine months had passed, Zeus boasted that on that day a son would be born of his line who would rule over the lands of Greece. Hera, angered at her husband's continual philandering, decided to thwart him; she sent Eleithyia, goddess of childbirth, to delay Heracles' birth while she ensured that the son of the Tirynthian king Sthenelus should be born on that day. This son, *Eurystheus*, who was also of Zeus' line through *Perseus*, grew up to be King of Tiryns and Mycenae (see below).

Alcmena was in pain from the delay to the birth. To relieve her, her servant Galanthis rushed in and startled Eleithyia, whose attention lapsed, allowing the birth to take place. Eleithyia turned Galanthis into a weasel. Alcmena bore twins, the half-divine Heracles and the all-human Iphicles. Very soon Heracles gave proof of his exceptional powers. Hera sent two snakes to attack the child in its cradle; but the babe, new-born though he was, 'raised his head and made first trial of battle, gripping both snakes by their throats, one in each unshakeable hand...The life-breath fled from their hideous coils.' [Pindar, *Nem.* 1].

The young Heracles was taught wrestling by *Autolycus* and archery by Eurytus, King of Oechalia: the bow and arrow came to be his characteristic weapon (one normally scorned by the Greeks as a coward's weapon). His lyre lessons ended when he killed his teacher. Soon he visited King Thespius of Thespiae and rid his land of a lion which had been terrorizing Mt Cithaeron — but not before sleeping with Thespius' 50 daughters on 50 successive nights. One refused, and was condemned to remain a virgin; she became a priestess in his temple. According to Apollodorus it was the skin of this lion which Heracles thereafter wore, though this is more usually said to have been the Nemean lion's.

Heracles championed Thebes by mutilating the heralds sent to collect the tribute due to the Minyan king of Orchomenus, and then made Orchomenus tributary to Thebes. He married Megara, daughter of King *Creon* of Thebes; on returning from the war Heracles found that Creon's throne had been usurped by *Lycus*. After killing Lycus, Heracles was driven mad by Hera, and killed his own children and, in some versions, his wife also.

To punish him for this crime, the Delphic *oracle* ordered him to perform 10 labours for King *Eurystheus*, promising him immortality if he accomplished them. Two were discounted by Eurystheus so he had to perform 12 in all.

These 12 labours are the most famous part of the saga of Heracles, and the subjects of innumerable representations in art — most notably the series of metopes from the Temple of Zeus at Olympia (the first full cycle) and those of the Temple of Hephaestus (Theseion) at Athens (see Brommer). The order became canonical by the sixth century BC, though many are known from art or literature as early as the eighth century BC. They carried Heracles neatly to all four quarters of the known world from his centre in the Argolid.

1. The Nemean Lion. This lion, son of Orthus and *Echidna*, lived in a cave on a hill at Nemea, which was still shown to travellers in the eighteenth century. Because its pelt was impenetrable to weapons, Heracles strangled it with his bare hands, skinned it with its own claws, and wore its pelt as his symbol ever after. The lion became the constellation Leo.

2. The Hydra of Lerna. Another offspring of either *Typhon* or *Echidna*, it was a huge serpent with seven heads which lived in the malarial marshes of Lerna (it is perhaps a symbol of those noxious airs). Heracles found that every time he lopped off one of its heads, two more grew in its place. At the same time the Hydra's companion, a large crab, kept nipping at Heracles' toe. So he called his nephew *Iolaus* to help: Iolaus cauterized each stump with a firebrand as Heracles lopped the head off, and so the monster was finally killed. Heracles dipped its arrows in its

gall to make them more deadly. The crab became the constellation Cancer. However, Eurystheus would not allow this as a bona fide labour because of the help Heracles had from Iolaus, and so another had to be added to the cycle.

3.  The Erymanthian Boar. A savage creature which dwelt on Mt Erymanthus in Arcadia. On his way to despatch it Heracles was entertained by the *Centaur Pholus*; the other Centaurs came and tried to steal their wine; Heracles drove them away but Pholus accidentally poisoned himself with one of Heracles' arrows in the fight. When Heracles brought the boar back alive to Eurystheus, the king was so frightened that he hid in a large sunken oil jar and refused to emerge until Heracles had taken the beast away again.
    At this point the series of labours was interrupted by Heracles' participation in the expedition of the *Argonauts*. (See also *Hylas*.)

4.  The Ceryneian hind. A deer with golden horns sacred to Artemis. Heracles pursued it for a year before he finally caught it while crossing the River Ladon, and brought it back alive to Tiryns.

5.  The Stymphalian birds. These birds with bronze beaks and claws, and feathers as sharp as arrows which they fired at their pursuers, haunted Lake Stymphalus. Heracles nevertheless managed to start them from their coverts and shot them down as they flew overhead.

6.  The Augean Stables. The cattle sheds of King Augeas of Elis had not been cleaned for so long that they were choked with dung. Heracles cleared them in a day by diverting the River Alpheus through them. He cunningly offered to charge Augeas a fee for this disagreeable work; but Augeas refused to pay him. None the less, Eurystheus, learning that Heracles had proposed to do the work for hire, discounted this labour also; and so the total rose to 12.

7.  The Cretan Bull. The first deed outside the Peloponnese carried Heracles south to Crete to capture this bull, the father of the *Minotaur*. Heracles brought it back to Tiryns and released it again, whereupon it began to terrorize the district around Marathon, until Theseus despatched it.

8.  The Horses of Diomedes. This next deed took Heracles north to Thrace, where the Bistonian king *Diomedes* had four horses which fed on human flesh; Heracles cured them of this by feeding them their own master, and then freed them on Mt Olympus. On his way to Thrace, Heracles visited *Admetus* and fetched his wife *Alcestis* back from Hades.

9.  The Girdle of the Amazon. The *Amazons* lived to the north-east
    on the southern shore of the Black Sea. Heracles took with him
    on this expedition *Theseus* and *Telamon*. The Amazon queen
    *Hippolyta* agreed to give him her girdle; but the Amazons
    attacked the Greeks and Hippolyta was killed. Theseus also
    helped himself to the Amazon *Antiope* at this time.

    On the way back the party stopped at Troy. Apollo and Poseidon
    had built the walls of Troy for King *Laomedon* but the king had
    refused to pay them. Poseidon sent a monster to ravage the land,
    which could only be appeased by the sacrifice of Laomedon's
    daughter Hesione. Heracles rescued Hesione and killed the
    monster; but Laomedon refused Heracles' reward also, thus
    storing up trouble for himself later.

10. The Cattle of Geryon. Now Heracles had to travel to the far west
    to steal the cattle of the three-headed king *Geryon*, which were
    guarded by the herdsman Eurytion and his dog Orthus. *Helius*,
    the Sun, lent him the bowl in which he travelled daily across the
    sky, to make the long journey to the west.

    On reaching the goal of his journey he erected the Pillars of
    Hercules at the straits of Gibraltar to mark his achievement;
    according to some versions he cut through an isthmus here to
    allow the waters of Atlantic and Mediterranean to mingle. He
    killed the herdsman and his dog and made off with the cattle;
    when Geryon pursued him he killed him too. [Stesichorus,
    *Geryoneis*]. He then travelled back along the north coast of the
    Mediterranean.

    Near Marseilles he was attacked by Ligurians. He beat them
    off with stones, which still lie scattered on the plains around Mar-
    seilles. He travelled down through Italy and despatched the giant
    Cacus who lived in a cave near the site of the future Rome (a
    Roman story). One of the cattle escaped near Rhegium and fled
    to western Sicily, where King Eryx commandeered it. Heracles
    fought with Eryx and killed him. He then made his way back
    to Tiryns.

11. The Apples of the Hesperides. (The order of the final two labours
    is sometimes reversed; both symbolize in one way or another a
    journey beyond the world of the living to that of the dead.) The
    location of the Garden of the Hesperides was not easy to dis-
    cover. Heracles consulted the sea-god *Nereus* to find the way.
    The sea-god, as is the way of sea-gods, forced Heracles to wrestle
    with him before he would divulge the secret, and changed him-
    self into many different forms; but Heracles held on and finally
    Nereus gave away the secret. To reach the land beyond Ocean,
    Heracles followed a somewhat bizarre route which led him to
    the Caucasus, where he released the Titan *Prometheus* from his
    bonds, and then to the North African coast. In the course of

this journey he had several adventures. He was nearly sacrificed by King Busiris of Egypt, but killed him at the eleventh hour. He had a wrestling match with the giant *Antaeus*, which again he won.

At the edge of the world he came upon the giant *Atlas* at his usual task of holding up the sky. Heracles persuaded Atlas to go and fetch the apples for him, while he would hold up the sky in the giant's absence. When Atlas returned with the apples, he saw an opportunity to be rid of his tedious task for ever, and suggested that he should carry the apples to Eurystheus himself. 'Very well,' said Heracles, 'but just hold the sky a moment while I shift my position.' The foolish giant did so; Heracles snatched the apples and made off with all speed back to Tiryns, leaving Atlas still at his eternal task.

12. Cerberus. Heracles' last task was to fetch the watchdog of Hades, the three-headed Cerberus, from the *Underworld*. In preparation for the descent, Heracles first had himself initiated in the Eleusinian Mysteries by *Eumolpus* or Musaeus. He then descended through the cave at Taenarum, guided by Hermes. In Hades, he released *Theseus* from his bonds but could not move *Pirithous*, killed one of Hades' cattle, and persuaded him to let him take Cerberus. When he reached Tiryns with the hound Eurystheus was, as usual, so terrified that he ordered Heracles to take the creature straight back again. And so ended the 12 labours.

After the conclusion of his labours Heracles heard that Eurytus of Oechalia was offering his daughter *Iole* as a prize in an archery contest. Heracles won it but Eurytus refused the prize, so Heracles stole his cattle instead. Eurytus' brother, Iphitus, thinking Heracles innocent of the theft, invited him to help search for the cattle. Heracles flung him from the roof and killed him; for this crime he was afflicted with a disease. Despite being purified by Deiphobus at Amyclae, he remained ill and asked the advice of the Delphic oracle. When the Pythia refused to speak to him, Heracles stole the god's tripod and fought with Apollo for it. Zeus broke up the fight with a thunderbolt. The Pythia then informed Heracles that he must be sold into slavery for three years to expiate his crime, and must give the price to the sons of Iphitus.

So Heracles became slave to Omphale, the Queen of Lydia. While serving her — in some versions dressed throughout the period as a woman — he captured the *Cercopes* and killed the aggressive farmer Syleus who forced strangers to work in his vineyard; he also killed a snake which was terrorizing the lands around the River Sangarius, and in this guise is portrayed in the constellation Ophiuchus (snake-carrier).

Once freed from slavery, Heracles set out to take revenge on the kings who had insulted him. First he collected a Greek army and led an expedition against Troy, accompanied by *Telamon* (the attack is depicted on the east pediment of the temple of Aphaea on Aegina). He killed Laomedon and seized Hesione, who became mother of *Teucer* by Telamon. She obtained the release of her brother Podarces by a gift to Heracles, and Podarces took the new name of Priam (from *priamai*, to buy).

Heracles' ships were then driven by foul winds, sent by Hera, to Cos, where the hero captured the city of the Meropes. The gods then summoned Heracles to help them in the war against the *Giants*, and by his aid they won.

Heracles now raised an army against Augeas, but was defeated, mainly because of the participation on Augeas' side of the twin warriors the *Molionidae*, sons of Actor. He later shot them at Cleonae, and a second expedition against Augeas was successful. After dethroning Augeas, Heracles established the Olympic Games in celebration. Pindar encapsulates the mood of this episode in a beautiful ode devoted to it, in which he writes: 'The radiance of the moon's beautiful eye made evening shine. All the precinct rang with music.' [*Ol.* 10]

He then killed Neleus and his sons, including Periclymenus, who disguised himself as an eagle; and attacked Hippocoön of Sparta with the help of Cepheus of Tegea. He seduced Cepheus' daughter Auge and she bore *Telephus*. Cepheus and his sons were killed, but Heracles managed to kill Hippocoön.

Now Heracles travelled to Calydon, where he fell in love with *Deianeira*, the daughter of King Oeneus. He fought Achelous for the girl and won her, but then exiled himself from Calydon because he accidentally killed Oeneus' cupbearer by an angry blow. While the couple were crossing the River Evenus, the *Centaur Nessus* tried to seize Deianeira; Heracles shot him with a poisoned arrow, and as Nessus died he gave Deianeira some of his poisoned blood, pretending that it would act as a love charm if Heracles should ever be unfaithful to Deianeira.

Heracles' further adventures in the north included his battle with *Cycnus*. Then, leaving Deianeira in Trachis, he went to win back Iole from Eurytus, who had insulted him. When Deianeira learnt of his new love, she smeared a robe with Nessus' philtre and sent it to Heracles. But it was no love charm, but a deadly poison which seared the hero's skin and flesh. Dying in slow agony, he took his son *Hyllus* and had him build a pyre on Mt Oeta. Heracles ascended it, but no one could be persuaded to light it until *Philoctetes* agreed to do so; Heracles gave Philoctetes his bow and arrows in thanks. The fire enveloped Heracles and he ascended to Olympus, a god at last. Here he was reconciled to Hera and married her daughter *Hebe*.

Cult of Heracles was widespread in Greece, and unlike other heroes (for obvious reasons) he had no tomb in a specific place: rather he had a special type of heroön, especially common at Sicyon, consisting of 'a quadrilateral stone basis supporting four pillars at the corners, the front ones surmounted by a pediment and the space between them unroofed'. (Farnell). But he had few festivals and none of the cultic status of the Olympian Gods.

As a god Heracles was identified in antiquity with the gods Melqart of Tyre and Sandan of Tarsus, in both of whose cults a ritual burning of images on a pyre was involved. But this does not argue an origin as an oriental god, but rather an assimilation of the Greek deity to Eastern cults. His images are found as far east as Persia.

**Heraclidae** The sons of Heracles. After his death they were driven from their homes in Tiryns and Thebes by *Eurystheus*, and came to Marathon. *Theseus* then helped them to make war on Eurystheus, who was killed; but they were driven out of the Peloponnese none the less. The Delphic oracle gave them the obscure instruction to try again at the third harvest. A second attempt after three years failed; *Hyllus* was killed and they retreated to Doris. Hyllus' great-grandsons then surmised that they were the third harvest referred to by the Pythia; they invaded the Peloponnese, killing *Orestes'* successor Tisamenus. Temenus won Argos, Cresphontes Messenia, and the sons of Aristodemus Laconia. They gave Elis away and left the Arcadians their own land. The whole myth is designed to explain the ethnic composition of the Dorian Peloponnese — ethnography through myth. The 'Dorian Invasion', which brought the new wave of Greeks to succeed the Mycenaeans, was known to the Greeks as the return of the Heraclidae. (Scholars however now incline to see this movement not as an invasion but a gradual seepage.)

**Hercules** See *Heracles*.

**Hermaphroditus** Son of Hermes and Aphrodite, reared by nymphs on Mt Ida in Phrygia. Near Halicarnassus in Caria he was seen by the nymph Salmacis, who fell in love with him. When he bathed in her spring she enfolded him in her arms and prayed to the gods that they might never be parted. Their two bodies became one. Thereafter, through Hermaphroditus' horrified curse, all men who bathed in the spring Salmacis became hermaphrodites. [Ovid, *Met.*]

**Hermes** The name of this god is related to the word *herma*, a pile of stones. His most common representation in antiquity is the herm, a plain pillar with protruding male genitals, and sometimes a bearded head atop it, which stood at street corners and doorways. He is thus, as cairn or marker post, a delimiter of space and in that sense intermediary between conflicting or separate parties. (Monkeys often guard their territory by surrounding it with a series of males as sentries, seated upright with erect penises displayed.) He acts as conductor of the souls of the dead to Hades, *psychopompus*, and is the god both of trade and of trickery. In literature his main role is as messenger of the gods. He is the patron of all forms of communication and was identified with the Egyptian scribe-god Thoth. A silence in conversation — where we say 'angels are passing overhead' — was remarked by the Greeks with 'Hermes is passing.'

This rich complex of associations gave him a rich character in Greek mythology. He was son of Zeus and the Pleiad Maea, goddess of midwives. She bore him on Mt Cyllene in Arcadia. The new-born babe immediately invented the lyre from the shell of a tortoise which he killed. Having taught himself to play it, he then set off to steal the cattle of Apollo, dragging them backwards to mislead pursuers by their reversed hoofprints. They were said to have been hidden by him in a cave at Pylos (Nestor's Grotto), where rock formations resemble the hides of cattle hung up to dry. Apollo set off in pursuit but could not find the cattle until Hermes confessed his trick. Hermes also showed him the lyre he had made, and Apollo was so enchanted that he let Hermes keep the cattle in exchange for the instrument.

When Hermes grew up and became herald of the gods his symbol was the caduceus, a wand with two snakes around it, and he is often shown with winged cap and sandals too.

> To his feet his fair wing'd shoes he tied,
> Ambrosian, golden, that in his command
> Put either sea, or the unmeasur'd land,
> With pace as speedy as a puft of wind.
> Then up his rod went, with which he declin'd
> The eyes of any waker, when he pleas'd
> And any sleeper, whom he wish'd diseas'd.

[Chapman's Homer, *Odyssey* 5]

He fought in the war of the Gods and Giants wearing Hades' cap of darkness — which he later lent to *Perseus* — and saved Zeus from Typhon who had stolen the god's tendons. He killed *Argus*, and rescued Dionysus from the corpse of his mother. His amours include: Herse, who bore *Cephalus*; Aphrodite, who bore *Hermaphroditus*; and Clytie, who bore *Myrtilus*. He was also father of *Pan*, possibly by *Penelope*.

His function as mediator and helper is well portrayed in his missions to *Odysseus* in the Odyssey, both to tell him to leave *Calypso* and to protect him from *Circe*. He appears in Aeschylus' 'Prometheus Bound' as Zeus' factotum but is otherwise not common in literature. [*Homeric Hymn to Hermes*; L. Kahn]

**Hero and Leander** Hero was a young woman of Sestos, priestess of Aphrodite, who was loved by Leander, a young man of Abydos:

he nightly swam the Hellespont to visit his beloved. She hung out a lamp to guide him, but one night it blew out in a storm and he was drowned. Byron emulated his feat, and only caught a chill. The story is the subject of a poem by Musaeus, and is popular in Renaissance and later painting (one of the most dramatic representations is by Rubens).

**Heroes and Hero-Cult** Greek religion places in the hierarchy between *gods* (*theoi*) and men not only the *daemones* but also the heroes, the ancient glorious dead of mortal race. They received cult like gods, but in the form of libations at an eschara or low altar and not burnt sacrifice on an ordinary altar. Scholarship has divided over the origins of the heroes: 'faded gods' or glorified men? What seems clear is that no one explanation will do for all heroes. The Italian scholar Angelo Brelich wrote an important study of the phenomenology of Greek heroes showing their diverse but often repeated traits and roles: they may be warriors (Achilles), seers (Mopsus, Calchas), athletes (Theagenes, Cleomedes of Astypalaea — see Paus. 6,9), healers (Machaon or the historical Hippocrates), founders of cities (Mopsus, Heracles, for example at Abdera), founders of races (Ion, Dorus) or 'culture' heroes (Talthybius for heralds, Eumolpus for a caste of priests); but all function at crucial points of the interaction of human affairs with the divine. Thus very many are honoured as founders of cities or shrines. In practice all the non-divine characters of Greek mythology may be regarded as heroes. The origin of classical cult of the heroes may often be seen in the identification of Mycenaean tombs, from the eighth century on, as tombs of heroes. Some certainly historical characters also became heroes (Theagenes), and some might be anonymous (the dangerous 'hero of Temesa', a kind of ghost). [Farnell, Brelich]

**Hesione** Daughter of *Laomedon*.

**Hesperides** These nymphs, whose number and parentage are variously given, though their name means Daughters of Evening, guarded the golden apple-tree on an island in the far west beyond the river of Ocean. The hundred-headed snake Ladon helped them to guard the apples, until he was killed by *Atlas*, acting for Heracles, when he was carrying out the last or penultimate of his labours. They are portrayed in a remarkable painting by Frederic Leighton, 'The Garden of the Hesperides'.

**Hestia** The goddess of the Hearth, daughter of Cronus and Rhea, and patroness of the household. Though important in cult (mainly private), she has no mythology. [Hesiod, *Theogony*; *Homeric Hymn to Hestia*]

**Hippocrates** A physician of Cos (c. 460-367 BC), and founder of rational medicine; by the third century he was receiving cult at the sanctuary of Asclepius. In the middle ages there was a legend on Cos that his daughter appeared every six or eight years in the form of a dragon, weeping for release from her torment, which could be effected by a kiss. [Mandeville *Travels*; Buondelmonti]

**Hippocrene** A spring on Mt Helicon created by *Pegasus* with a stamp of his hoof. The *Muses* danced alongside its waters. It lies some way above the well-known Grove of the Muses on Mt Helicon.

**Hippodamia** Daughter of *Oenomaus*, King of Pisa (Olympia), who became the wife of *Pelops* after he won her in a chariot race with her father.

**Hippolyta** Queen of the Amazons, whose girdle Heracles brought back as his ninth labour. He killed her in the process. None the less she was sometimes regarded as the wife of *Theseus*, perhaps by confusion with her sister Antiope whom Theseus carried off when he accompanied Heracles on this expedition; and hence she was the mother of *Hippolytus*.

**Hippolytus** The son of *Theseus* and *Antiope*, he was brought up in Troezen. When Theseus married *Phaedra*, Phaedra fell in love with her stepson, but he was a votary of Artemis, devoted to hunting and committed to chastity. In anger at his rebuff, Phaedra wrote a letter to Theseus accusing Hippolytus of attempting to rape her. Theseus believed her, banished his son and cursed him: Poseidon responded by sending a bull out of the sea which overturned Hippolytus' chariot as he fled along the shore, and killed him. The story is the plot of Euripides' *Hippolytus*.

Hippolytus had a cult at Troezen where girls about to marry dedicated a lock of hair to him. He symbolizes, perhaps, an aspect of virginity, a kind of arrested development in youth, a state which must be honoured but left behind in order to reach maturity. According to the Troezenians he became the constellation Auriga, the Charioteer.

**Hippomenes** Another name for *Melanion*. See *Atalanta*.

**Horae** Minor goddesses representing the Seasons.

**Hubris** Presumptuous or violent behaviour which brings on a man the anger of the gods: personified as a goddess in poetry. Excess breeds hubris, said Solon: power leads to pride. So in Aeschylus' *Persians* the failure of Xerxes' expedition against Greece is the punishment by the gods of his hubris, not least in scourging the Hellespont for its disobedience to him. Once a man falls into hubris, *Ate* takes away his wits and his doom is sealed. 'Ancient hubris gives birth to an avenging daemon...arrogant boldness...black Ate' [Aeschylus, *Agamemnon* 762 ff]. The gods' punishment of hubris is a keynote of the Greek theory of divine justice and central to the theology of tragedy. [Lloyd-Jones, *The Justice of Zeus*]

**Hundred-Handers** Three sons of *Uranus* and *Gaea*. Their names are *Briareus* (or Aegaeon 'in the language of men'), Gyges and Cottus. Besides their 100 hands they had 50 heads apiece. Cronus imprisoned them with the *Cyclopes* in Tartarus; Zeus released them to help in his war on the *Titans* and then reimprisoned them. Briareus also helped Zeus crush a mutiny of the other gods. [Hesiod, *Theogony*]

**Hyacinthus** The son of King Amyclas of Sparta. *Thamyris*, the first lover of boys, fell in love with him. So too did Apollo, but one day when they were playing discus Apollo accidentally killed him. (Perhaps Zephyrus, also in love with the boy, blew the discus astray in jealousy.) The blood from his wound became the flower that bears his name, and on its petals may be seen the letters *aiai* (alas!) Hyacinthus had cult and an annual festival at Amyclae. He is evidently a 'dying god' of the seasons. [Ovid, *Met.*]

**Hyades** Daughters of Oceanus and a nymph, Aethra or Pleione (the latter case making them sisters of the Pleiades). They vary in number from two to seven. Their name implies that they are rain-nymphs. They were often said to have been the nurses of Zeus at Dodona, or of Dionysus at Nysa. When their brother Hyas was killed by a boar they died of grief and became the stars which by their setting in mid-November signal the season for seafaring to end, and for ploughing to begin. The poet Claudian confused them with the Heliades, sisters of *Phaethon*.

**Hydra** A serpent which dwelt in the marshes of Lerna. It had seven (or more) heads, and Heracles' second labour was to kill it; see *Heracles*. The Hydra seems to be a personification (if that is the right word) of the malarial miasmas of this marshy region, in which is situated one of the oldest complexes of buildings in mainland Greece.

**Hylas** Son of the Dryopian king Theodamas. *Heracles* killed Theodamas and made Hylas his squire and lover. He travelled with him on the voyage of the Argo, but when they went ashore in Mysia to draw water, the nymphs of a spring fell in love with Hylas and drew him into their waters, from which he never returned. Heracles searched everywhere for the boy and thus was left behind when Argo sailed on. The search for Hylas became an annual ritual in the region (a vegetation god rite?). There is an evocative painting of Hylas' end by the Pre-Raphaelite painter Waterhouse. [Apollonius Rhodius; Theocritus, *Idyll* 13]

**Hyllus** Son of *Heracles* and *Deianeira*, who built the pyre on which Heracles immolated himself: the dying Heracles instructed Hyllus to marry his concubine *Iole*. Hyllus fought with the Athenians against the Argives in the wars of the Heraclidae, and it was either he or *Iolaus* who killed *Eurystheus*. When he led the Heraclidae against Mycenae he was killed in the battle.

Apollonius, however, makes Hyllus son of Heracles by a Phaeacian nymph: he became the eponym of the Hylleis of northern Illyria.

**Hymen** Patron deity of marriage, personification of the *hymenaioi*, hymns sung at marriage. He has no mythology.

**Hyperboreans** A legendary race, the Dwellers beyond the North Wind. Apollo was thought to spend his three months' winter absence from Delphi with the Hyperboreans, and *Perseus* visited them in his search for the *Gorgons*.

Herodotus placed them beyond the Issedones, the one-eyed Arimaspians and the gold-guarding griffins, in Central Asia. *Aristeas of Proconnesus* seems to have described a visit to them in his lost poem *Arimaspea*. [Pindar, *Ol*. 3, *Pyth* 10]

**Hyperion** A *Titan*, husband of *Theia* who bore him Sun, Moon and Dawn. He is not clearly distinguished from *Helius* [*Homeric Hymn to Helius*]

**Hypsipyle** Queen of Lemnos. When the women of Lemnos murdered all the men on the island (see *Argonauts*) Hypsipyle rescued her father Thoas by setting him adrift in a chest. When the Argonauts arrived the men-starved women were pleased to see them: Jason married Hypsipyle and she bore him two sons.

But the women of Lemnos sold her into slavery and she was bought by the King of Nemea to be nurse to his son *Opheltes*, whose death she caused by disobeying an oracle which said that the child must not be placed on the ground until it could walk. She put it down to show the *Seven against Thebes* where they could find water. It was bitten by a snake, and at the child's grave the Nemean Games were founded. This adventure, and her punishment and release by Dionysus, were the subject of Euripides' *Hypsipyle*, in which Thoas is present with her as well as her son Euneus, who became the master of the guild of state musicians at Athens.

# I

Io guarded by Argus

**Iacchus** A deity honoured in the Eleusinian Mysteries and often identified with Dionysus who was also known as Bacchus. He seems to personify the sacred cry Iacche, memorably made the refrain of a processional ode of initiates in Aristophanes' *Frogs*.

**Iambe** Daughter of *Pan* and *Echo*, servant to King Celeus of Eleusis and *Metaneira*. When Demeter visited Eleusis in her search of *Persephone*, Iambe made her a cup of kykeon (a drink of water, barley and honey) and made bawdy jokes until Demeter was persuaded to smile, and accepted the drink. Her role in the legend is a doublet of that of *Baubo*. Her name is a feminine form of *iambos*, meaning lampoon: it was customary for bystanders to shout obscene abuse at those who took part in the procession along the Sacred Way from Athens to Eleusis, and Iambe's story is probably a mythological explanation (*aition*) for this custom. Dirty talk is a common part of fertility rituals like the Eleusinian Mysteries. [*Homeric Hymn to Demeter*]

**Iamus** The son of Evadne, a daughter of Poseidon, by Apollo. In fear of taking the child home, she had given birth in the woods, where it had been nourished by snakes with honey as it lay among the violets (Greek *ia*). The boy grew up to become a prophet. [Pindar, *Ol.6*]

**Iasion** Son of Zeus and Electra daughter of *Atlas*. He came from Samothrace to Thebes for the wedding of his sister *Harmonia* to *Cadmus*. On this occasion he lay with Demeter in a thrice-ploughed field, and their son was *Plutus*, Wealth. (*Odyssey* 5, 125-7). Zeus, however, killed Iasion for his presumption.

Diodorus Siculus made him the originator of the Mysteries of Samothrace, and then husband of *Cybele* and a god in his own right. He is yet another young consort god associated with a fertility goddess.

**Icarius 1.** The father of Penelope.
**2.** An Athenian whom Dionysus taught viticulture. When Icarius introduced the local peasantry to wine, they thought they had been poisoned and killed him. His daughter *Erigone* hanged herself in grief. Dionysus then drove the girls of Athens mad. The Athenians discovered from an oracle that this was a punishment for their murder of Icarius, and instituted an autumn festival of Icarius and Erigone which involved swinging (a common element of fertility rituals, which again this myth reflects).

**Icarus** The son of *Daedalus*. When Daedalus contrived their escape from their Cretan prison on wings made of feathers fastened with wax, Icarus in his excitement flew too near to the sun. The wax melted and he plunged to his death in the sea near the island subsequently called Icaria. He was buried here by *Heracles*. [Ovid, *Met.* 8]

**Idas and Lynceus** Sons of Aphareus, King of Messenia and cousins of the *Dioscuri*. They took part in the Calydonian boar-hunt and the expedition of the *Argo*. Idas stole Evenus' daughter Marpessa, whom Apollo loved. Evenus drowned himself in a river, which then took his name; Apollo fought Idas until Marpessa made her choice for the mortal.

Their conflict with the Dioscuri arose over the daughters of Leucippus to whom Idas and Lynceus were betrothed (what happened to Marpessa?) For this story see *Dioscuri*.

**Idomeneus** Son of *Deucalion* and King of Crete, he led 80 ships to Troy. On his return he was expelled by a usurper, Leucus, who had also stolen his wife (like *Aegisthus* in the case of the returning *Agamemnon*). Idomeneus left Crete and made a new home in southern Italy. A different account tells that Idomenus swore to sacrifice the first creature he encountered on his safe return home. It turned out to be his son. His carrying out of the sacrifice, however, angered the gods, and he was banished.

A variant version of the story is the plot of Mozart's opera *Idomeneo*.

**Ino** Daughter of *Cadmus* and *Harmonia*. She married *Athamas* and acted as nurse to her nephew Dionysus. Her jealousy of Athamas' children by his first wife is described under *Athamas*, *Phrixus*.

When Hera drove Athamas and Ino mad so that they killed their children, Ino took her son Melicertes and leapt into the sea off the Isthmus of Corinth. *Melicertes* was washed ashore and buried by *Sisyphus*. Under the name Palaemon he became the hero honoured in the Isthmian Games. Ino became the sea-goddess Leucothea. She and Palaemon were helpers to sailors in distress, notably Odysseus.

**Io** Daughter of the Argive river Inachus. Zeus fell in love with her. Inachus was warned by an oracle to banish her or else Argos would be struck by a thunderbolt. After Io was banished, either Hera in her anger, or Zeus to conceal the affair, turned Io into a cow. Hera begged Zeus to make her a gift of the cow, and set *Argus* of the hundred eyes to watch over her. However, Zeus sent Hermes to kill Argus, for which he earned the epithet Argeiphontes. Hera set his eyes in the tail of her bird, the peacock. Hera then sent a gadfly to torment Io. This stung her into wandering all over the world: through Dodona, the Bosporus (Cow's Ford), and even to the Caucasus where *Prometheus* was chained. She then made her way back to the Nile, where Zeus found her and fathered a child, who was called Epaphus, 'the touch (of the god)'. She was by this time restored to human form.

Hera now got the Curetes to kidnap Epaphus and took him to Syria where he was reared by the Queen of Byblus.

Io was often identified by the Greeks with the Egyptian goddess Isis. The daughters of Danaus traced their descent from her.

The tale of Io was told in the lost epic the *Danais*, and her wanderings are recounted by herself in Aeschylus' *Prometheus Bound*.

**Iolaus** Son of Iphicles, *Heracles*' brother. He helped him kill the *Hydra* by cauterizing the neck stumps as Heracles struck off the heads. Iolaus (or *Hyllus*) killed *Eurystheus* after Heracles' death. He was regarded as the first colonist of Sardinia.

**Iole** Daughter of Eurytus, King of Oechalia. Heracles won her as bride in an archery contest set up by her father, but he refused to let her marry Heracles because he had killed his previous wife in his madness. Heracles, however, made Iole his concubine later in his career, and thus caused Deianeira in her jealous grief to send him the poisoned robe which killed him. See *Heracles*. [Sophocles, *Trachiniae*]

**Ion** Son of Creusa, the daughter of *Erechtheus*, and *Xuthus*; he became the eponym of the Ionians. The Athenians made various attempts to fit him into their history in order to establish their primacy among the Ionians. In the traditional genealogy, Xuthus left Athens for the Northern Peloponnese and his son Ion became king of that region. He came to Athens to help lead the war against Eleusis, in conclusion of which he founded the Apolline festival of the Boedromia. Thus far Pausanias: Strabo says that Ion also organized Attica politically.

But in Euripides' *Ion*, Xuthus was King of Athens after Erechtheus, and Ion was actually the son of Creusa by Apollo. To keep her infidelity secret, Creusa abandoned the child; Hermes took it to Delphi where the boy was brought up as a temple servitor. When Xuthus and Creusa visited Delphi to consult the oracle about their childlessness, Apollo told Xuthus that the first person they met on leaving the temple would be his son. It was, of course, Ion, whom Xuthus assumed to be a bastard son of his own. Creusa was angry and plotted to kill Ion, but just in time learnt from the Pythia that Ion was actually *her* son; she went on to have two more sons by Xuthus, the eponymic Dorus and Achaeus. But the mythographers did not manage to include Ion in the Attic king lists. [Euripides, *Ion*]

**Iphigeneia** The eldest daughter of *Agamemnon* and *Clytemnestra*. Agamemnon sacrificed her at Aulis to appease the anger of Artemis and obtain a fair wind for Troy. [Aeschylus, *Agamemnon*; Euripides, *Iphigeneia in Aulis*] Artemis rescued Iphigeneia at the last moment and substituted a deer, transporting the girl to Tauris (the Crimea) where she became a priestess of Artemis and the ministrant of a rite involving the human sacrifice of all visitors to the land. [Euripides, *Iphigeneia in Tauris* for this and the following]

In due course her brother *Orestes* arrived in Tauris with his companion Pylades, to steal a statue of Artemis in the hope of curing Orestes of the madness resultant on his murder of his mother. After various adventures and narrow escapes, brother and sister recognized each other and escaped with Pylades to Attica.

Iphigeneia's links with Artemis are so close that she appears to be a by-form of the goddess. She received cult in Tauris (Herodotus 4, 103) and some Greek cities, and in Attic tradition her sacrifice was localized at Artemis' sanctuary of Brauron, a site dedicated to the rites of passage attendant on girls passing from childhood to adulthood.

**Iris** The messenger of the gods, who took the form of a rainbow (the Greek meaning of the word).

**Islands of the Blest** See *Elysium*.

**Itys** See *Tereus*.

**Ixion** A king of Thessaly, the first murderer (the Cain of Greek legend). He failed to pay his father-in-law Eïoneus the bride price for his wife, and when Eïoneus tried to collect it, flung him into a pit of fire. Because no man would purify him, Zeus invited him to Olympus, where he at once made an assault on Hera. But she deceived him with a cloud in her shape, with which he copulated: the son of this union was Centaurus (Prickair), who mated with the mares on Mt Belion to produce the race of *Centaurs*. As punishment for the attempted rape Ixion was chained for ever to a wheel of fire in the *Underworld*. [Pindar, *Pyth*. 2]

**Iynx** The daughter of Pan and *Echo*, a witch who cast an erotic spell on Zeus; Hera turned her into a wryneck. The wryneck was used in binding magic: it was stretched on a wheel and spun round at speed [Pindar, *Pyth*. 4,214] or it could be substituted by a wheel which spun on a string and replicated the whistling cry of the bird. Its use as an erotic charm is reflected in Theocritus, *Idyll* 2, and is still recalled in the word 'jinx'.

# J

Jason disgorged by a dragon

**Jason** The son of Aeson king of Iolcus and leader of the expedition of the *Argonauts*. *Pelias* usurped Aeson's throne, or was entrusted with it until Jason should come of age. Jason was brought up on Mt Pelion by the *Centaur Chiron*. Pelias was warned by an oracle to beware a man who should come to Iolcus wearing only one sandal. When Jason grew up he returned to Iolcus to reclaim his inheritance. On the way, he met an old woman trying to cross a river. He carried her across, losing one sandal in the mud as he went. The old woman was in fact Hera in disguise, and for this kindness she was Jason's supporter ever after.

Jason duly arrived at Iolcus wearing his single sandal and was recognized by Pelias as the man the oracle had warned him of. Jason claimed the throne, but Pelias told him that an oracle had commanded him to appease the ghost of *Phrixus* by bringing back the Golden Fleece. Pelias said that he was too old for the task and asked Jason to undertake it, expecting thus to see the last of him.

For the next stage of the story, see *Argonauts*. An uncanonical episode of the story of Jason is portrayed on a red-figure cup which shows Jason being disgorged by a dragon in the presence of Athena — perhaps the dragon which guarded the Golden Fleece, in which case Jason came closer to disaster than the usual versions allow. The help of *Medea* the daughter of the King of Colchis was crucial to the success of his quest.

On his return to Iolcus, Jason duly claimed the throne, and Medea contrived the murder of Pelias by a trick (see *Medea*). But Jason and Medea now left Iolcus, and lived for 10 years at Corinth as private citizens under King Creon. At this time Jason took part in the hunt for the Calydonian boar (see *Meleager*).

Presently Jason fell in love with Creon's daughter Glauce and divorced Medea. She sent Glauce a poisoned robe which killed her, and then murdered her children by Jason (see further *Medea*). Jason seems to have gone back to Iolcus to become king; he died in a curiously banal way, being struck by a rotting beam that fell off the Argo where it lay beached as a memento of his great expedition. [Euripides, *Medea*; Apollonius, *Argonautica*, *Orphic Argonautica*; Diodorus]

**Jocasta** The daughter of Menoeceus, the wife of *Laius*, King of Thebes, and the mother and wife of *Oedipus*; known in Homer as Epicaste. An *oracle* declared that she must have no son by Laius, and so they exposed the child on Mt Cithaeron. None the less the child grew up to defeat the *Sphinx*, murder his father and marry his mother. See *Oedipus*. Their sons were *Eteocles* and *Polynices*, their daughters *Antigone* and Ismene. In Sophocles' *Oedipus the King* Jocasta commits suicide on discovering Oedipus' identity. But in Euripides' *Phoenissae* she survives to commit suicide over the bodies of her sons, killed in the war of the *Seven against Thebes*.

**Judas Iscariot** The betrayer of Jesus is a common figure in modern Greek folklore and is thought to have been born on Corfu, the ancient name for which is Scheria. The name Iscariotes is still found among the modern inhabitants of the island. A legend known from two medieval manuscripts, which borrows heavily from the Oedipus story, tells that the mother of Judas dreamed that she would bear a son who would be the ruin of Israel. So when her son was born she set the child adrift in the sea. It was, however, rescued by some herdsmen who brought it back to the town and the child was adopted by the woman's husband, Robel. When he grew up Judas entered the service of King Herod in Jerusalem. After some years Robel bought a house in Jerusalem. Herod saw the fine orchards that Robel had and ordered Judas to go and steal him some fruit. In the course of this escapade Judas met Robel, whom of course he no longer recognized, and killed him. Herod then ordered Robel's wife to take Judas as her husband, which she did. In due course she told the story of her first child, and the secret was out. Judas went to Jesus to confess, and became one of his disciples; but he used to steal the alms they collected to send it to his wife. And thus his greed was the downfall of Jesus. [Edmunds]

# K

Heracles and a Ker

**Kale ton Oreon** The 'Beautiful one of the Mountains'; a *Nereid* in the modern Greek sense, perhaps conceived as their queen. According to the *Alexander Romance* she was the daughter of *Alexander the Great* whom he turned into a mermaid, or a Nereid, because she got to the Water of Life before him, so that she became immortal and he did not. [*Alexander Romance*; Psellus; Leo Allatius; Lawson]

**Kallikantzaros** A kind of hobgoblin, usually conceived as very large, black and hairy, with red eyes and goat's ears; kallikantzaroi have large tongues, tusks and sexual organs. They have clawlike fingers and goats' or asses' legs. They are particularly dangerous during the 12 days of Christmas, when they stop gnawing through the tree on which the world rests: while they are absent, it grows again. In this period they enter men's houses and befoul food, break furniture and brutalize wayfarers. To keep them at bay, householders keep a fire burning brightly, mark the house with a cross or bind it with red thread, or surround the windows with prickly leaves to keep them out.

Their name seems to be the same as that of the ancient *Centaurs*, though physically they more closely resemble the *Satyrs*. Professor Lawson was shown pictures of satyrs on Attic vases which his inform-

ants identified as kallikantzaroi. Their prevalence at the New Year
season can be paralleled in ancient rites also, and at this period mummers often circulate (or did until recently) dressed as kallikantzaroi.
(A connection with northern European mumming, and pantomime
horses, is not absurd.) It was believed in the seventeenth century that
children born during the 12 days of Christmas would turn into kallikantzaroi, and to prevent this their feet were scorched in the fire
to prevent claws growing. [Dumézil, Lawson]

**Karaghiozis** The hero of the modern Greek shadow-puppet theatre,
identical with the Turkish Karagöz (Black Eye). Performances of Karagöz are known from accounts of nineteenth-century Istanbul, but
there is no evidence for the Greek Karaghiozis before the War of
Independence. Despite this, the repertory of plays includes not only
comedies on themes of Ottoman times, but Greek traditional stories, notably the battle of *Alexander the Great* and the *dragon*.
   Karaghiozis is a cunning buffoon, a Hellenic Mr Punch, represented
as a hunchback with a multi-jointed left arm. His inseparable companion is the ruffian Hadjiavatis, and other characters include Mrs
Karaghiozis, the shepherd (wearing a fustanella), Barbayorgos, a Turkish dandy, the Vizier's buxom daughter, the Bey, the Jew, the gen-
tlemanly Stavrakas, and so on. Despite its bawdy nature, Karaghiozis
was and still is popular entertainment for children as well as adults.
The humour is Aristophanic in quality, and more than one modern
production of Aristophanes has used the imagery of Karaghiozis to
bring the classical plays into twentieth-century focus. [Richard Davey;
G. Ioannou]

**Kastro tis Orias** The 'Castle of the Beautiful One', usually localized
at the southern end of the Vale of Tempe, is the subject of a modern
Greek folk-tale which takes various forms. A Cretan song tells how
the Turks captured the castle by sending a soldier in disguise who
prevailed on the princess to open the gates: the story resembles that
of Nisus' daughter *Scylla* betraying her city to the enemy leader with
whom she falls in love. A variant recorded in Muntaner's *Cronaca*
(W. Miller p. 38) has the girl falling to her death to avoid the Frankish
conqueror of Araklovo in the Morea (Peloponnese). [Politis; Miller]

**Keres** Keres are black, winged demons, daughters, like the Fates,
of Night. In popular lore they were a kind of goblin or ghost: they
had to be placated at the annual festival of the Anthesteria in Athens
(rather like the Roman *lemures* at the Lemuria), and they were kept
at bay by smearing pitch on doorways, chewing buckthorn, and similar expedients. They are the source of diseases and most of the evils
that come to mortals, including old age, death, and crop-blights. In
Homer they reach a more literary level as spirits ('keres of death')
who control the destiny of the heroes (especially in the *Iliad*) and

descend on them as they die to tear their flesh and drink their blood. They are commonly associated with the *Fates* and receive cult with them. Plato assimilates them rather to the *Harpies*, from whom, indeed, they cannot always be distinguished in art, as both have the task of carrying off the souls of the dead. [Jane Harrison, *Prolegomena*]

**Kore** 'Maiden'. A title of *Persephone*.

# L

Theseus kills the Minotaur in the Labyrinth

**Labyrinth** The prison built at Knossos for the *Minotaur* by *Daedalus*. It had one entrance and was composed of many winding alleys and dead ends. *Theseus* penetrated it safely to kill the Minotaur by the aid of a clew of thread, which enabled him to find his way out again.

The word derives from the Cretan word *labrys*, a double axe, an important religious symbol in Minoan Crete, and suggests that the original Labyrinth may have been some sort of shrine connected with the bull-cult of Knossos.

This famous structure was portrayed on many of the coins of Knossos, and many have sought its remains. Some have supposed it to reflect the complex architecture of the Palace of Minos itself. In the Middle Ages it was identified with a complex system of caves in the hills near Gortyn, and this opinion held sway until the early nineteenth century, when it was finally determined that this was simply an old quarry.

Other structures also bore this name, notably the palace or temple of Amenemhet III in Egypt, and it came to be applied to some of the larger temples of the Greek world with their forests of columns (for example that of Hera on Samos).

The Labyrinth seems to reflect a form of dance or elaborate game, like the Game of Troy in Vergil's *Aeneid* — a danced representation of conflict and resolution — and its descendants are the Pilgrim's Ways of medieval cathedrals. [S. H. Hooke (ed.), *The Labyrinth*; Penelope Reed Doob, *The Idea of the Labyrinth*]

**Laertes** King of Ithaca and father of *Odysseus*, the subject of charming scenes in Homer's *Odyssey* where, though a king, he even tills his own fields.

**Laestrygonians** A race of savage giants whom *Odysseus* encountered in his wanderings. One of his men was eaten by them; Odysseus fled in his ship, but the giants harpooned some of his other ships and ate their occupants. [Homer, *Odyssey* 10]

**Laius** The son of Labdacus, King of Thebes, brought up at the court of *Pelops*, where he fell in love with Pelops' son Chrysippus, and subsequently carried him off to Thebes. This crime brought a curse on his house which was harshly visited on his son *Oedipus*, who unwittingly murdered his father before marrying his father's wife. See *Oedipus*.

**Lamia** A monster in the form of a woman with bestial, and non-matching legs (for example one of bronze and one goat- or ass-leg). Lamiae are dirty, gluttonous and slovenly in ancient and modern belief alike. Like *Gello* and the *Strigles* they are thought to strangle young children.
   Somewhat distinct from these is the pair of Lamiae in Apuleius' *Golden Ass*, who tear open a sleeping man's breast and take away his heart. The Lamia of Keats' poem is properly a *Vampire*. [Lawson]

**Laocoon** A Trojan priest who warned the Trojans that the Wooden Horse contained Greek soldiers. His advice was ignored even though he cast a spear at the horse to show by the reverberation that it was not hollow. When the horse had been dragged inside the city, Poseidon sent two sea-serpents which strangled Laocoon and his two sons. The scene is the subject of one of the most famous of all Greek sculptures, the joint work of three Rhodian sculptors — the subject and touchstone of G. E. Lessing's essay on the classical Greek style in art. [Vergil, *Aeneid* II; Lessing]

**Laomedon** King of Troy, who hired Apollo and Poseidon to build the walls of Troy. They were thus impregnable to outside human force; but Laomedon refused to pay the gods their hire and threatened to sell them into slavery. Poseidon then sent a sea-monster to ravage the land. The beast could only be appeased by the sacrifice of Laomedon's daughter Hesione. Heracles, however, passed by and rescued her. Laomedon then refused him any reward too, with the result that Heracles came back and mounted the first Greek expedition against Troy. That this was a late intrusion into saga is suggested by the fact that Heracles and his men did manage to penetrate Troy, though the myth of Laomedon suggests that the walls were intended to be unbreachable except by the stratagem of the *Wooden Horse*.

**Lapiths** A Thessalian tribe, descended from Lapithes who, according to Diodorus, was brother of Centaurus the ancestor of the *Centaurs*. Despite their consanguinity, Lapiths and Centaurs were hereditary enemies, and staged a particularly vicious battle at the wedding of Pirithous; this became a common motif of temple sculpture (for example the west pediment of the Temple of Zeus at Olympia). Pirithous then drove the Lapiths out of Thessaly to Doris; and from here they were expelled by the Dorian king Aegimius, with the help of *Heracles* and an army of Arcadians.

**Leda** The daughter of the King of Aetolia, who married *Tyndareus* during his exile from Sparta in his youth. Her children were *Helen*, *Clytemnestra, the Dioscuri* and three other obscurer figures. Zeus coupled with her in the form of a swan, and from the egg she laid Helen and the Dioscuri were born. The egg was preserved in a sanctuary of Helen at Sparta.

**Lethe** One of the four rivers of the *Underworld*, the River of Forgetfulness, at which the dead drank in order to forget their former lives. A spring of this name was close to the oracle of *Trophonius* at Lebadeia; those who consulted it drank first of this spring in order to forget their past, and then of another spring, called Memory, so that they would remember the visions that were presented to them when they entered the cave.

**Leto** A goddess of Asia Minor, also known in Etruscan (Letun), patroness of the fruitful earth, lady of the beasts and plants, with cult especially in Lycia and at Ortygia near Ephesus. In myth she is a Titan and another of Zeus' conquests. Hera was angry at her, and when she was pregnant by Zeus the places through which she wandered refused, out of fear of Hera, to allow her to sit down and give birth. At last the floating island of Delos put down roots and provided her with a haven; she gave birth under a palm tree. Her twin children were Apollo and Artemis. Delos was said to have been formerly called Ortygia, suggesting a connection with the quail as sacred bird (cf. Artemis). The palm-tree under which she sheltered is one of her symbols.

Leto then fled to Lycia. Being prevented from drinking at a well called Melite, she turned the local peasants into frogs.

Tityus tried to rape her and was shot by Apollo and Artemis.

**Leuce** The 'White Island' in the Black Sea to which Achilles, Helen and other heroes were translated after their death. See further *Elysium*. [Philostratus, *Heroicus*]

**Leucippides** Twin daughters of Leucippus, King of Messenia, named Phoebe (Light) and Hilaeira (Bright) who were engaged to the twins *Idas and Lynceus* but were carried off by the *Dioscuri*. In the subsequent battle between the rivals the Dioscuri died. See *Dioscuri*.

**Linus** The name of a dirge (the refrain *ai linon* means 'alas') which was sung to mourn the dying vegetation at harvest time. The name became personalized by analogy with other dying gods like *Adonis*, and became the name of a musician and poet, son of Apollo and (usually) one of the Muses. He taught the lyre to *Thamyris*, *Orpheus* and even Heracles.

**Lityerses** A Phrygian harvest song which became regarded as the name of its inventor (cf. *Linus*). Lityerses was the son of *Midas*, who forced passers-by to work in his fields and then beheaded them at the end of the day's work, binding the bodies into the stooks. The legend reflects the folk practice of binding the reaper of the last sheaf. Lityerses did this, according to a late development of the legend, to *Daphnis*, and Heracles then punished him with a dose of his own medicine.

**Lotus-Eaters** A people living on the Libyan coast, visited by *Odysseus*. Some of his men tasted the Lotus and promptly lost all desire to return home, becoming like the Lotus-Eaters themselves, who lived a life of perfect, empty-headed contentment. [Homer, *Odyssey* 9]

**Lycaon** An Arcadian king, founder of the city of Lycosura on Mt Lycaeum, who established a rite of child sacrifice. In some versions the child was his own son Arcas; the outrage marks the end of the community of men and gods, for Zeus would not accept the sacrifice by eating at Lycaon's table, and turned Lycaon into a wolf. At every subsequent sacrifice to Lycaean Zeus a man would turn into a wolf for a period of eight or nine years, but could be turned back if he abstained from human flesh during that period. The myth appears to reflect, if loosely, a rite of passage in which adolescents 'go wild' for a period before being accepted back into human society. It was also said that any creature which entered the santuary of Lycaean Zeus would lose its shadow: in a man's case, this was tantamount to becoming a *werewolf*, and offenders were stoned to death (Plutarch, *Greek Questions* 39). [Pausanias; Burkert; Buxton in Bremmer]

**Lycurgus** The best-known character of this name is the Thracian

king who drove Dionysus and his *maenads* out with an oxgoad (cf.
*Pentheus*). Like Pentheus, Dionysus drove him mad and, while he
was chopping down vines in the belief that wine was a poison (cf.
*Icarius*), he mistook his leg for a vine and chopped that off too. He
also killed his son Dryasa (Oak Tree) under the same delusion, and
for this crime his people, the Edonians, fed him to man-eating horses
on Mt Pangaeum. (Alternatively, Dionysus threw him to his panthers;
or he killed himself.) The moral is that those who oppose the rites
of Dionysus come to a bad end.

**Lycus 1.** King of Thebes who inherited the kingdom from his brother
Nycteus; or won it in battle. He then made war on Sicyon and brought
back Nycteus' daughter *Antiope*, who was thereafter persecuted by
Dirce. See *Dirce, Antiope*.
**2.** A descendant of (1) who usurped the kingdom after the death
of *Creon* (1). He was murdered by *Heracles* in revenge for his treatment of Heracles' family while Heracles was absent at Thespiae.

**Lynceus** See *Idas and Lynceus*.

# M

The dying Memnon and his mother Eos

**Machaereus** 'Knife Man'. The murderer of *Neoptolemus*. He was the ancestor of Branchus, who founded the oracle of Apollo at Didyma.

**Machaon** Son of *Asclepius* and brother of Podalirius: the two were healing heroes (naturally enough, considering their parentage). Healers are often paired: cf. the *Dioscuri*; SS Cosmas and Damian; Machaon's own sons Nicomachus and Gorgasus. Machaon and Podalirius were both suitors of *Helen* and both led a fleet to Troy. One of them healed *Philoctetes'* wound. Machaon was killed at Troy, by Eurypylus or *Penthesilea*, and was buried in Messenia.

**Maenads** Female votaries of Dionysus, who dressed in the skins of wild animals and carried thyrsoi, vine branches twined with ivy and tipped with pine cones. They assembled in the mountains and rampaged in Bacchic frenzy, catching small wild animals and eating them raw. The rites persisted in historic times. Some legends seem to reflect historical resistance to the introduction of maenadism to Greece; see *Dionysus*, *Lycurgus*, *Bassarids*. The most famous treatment is Euripedes' *Bacchae*, and the most famous legendary maenad is *Agave*. They are often portrayed on Attic vases, either in the retinue of Dionysus or as recipients of the unwelcome attentions of satyrs.

**Maia** One of the *Pleiades*, daughter of *Atlas* and the Oceanid Pleione. She bore Zeus a son, Hermes, on Mt Cyllene in Arcadia. Later she brought up *Callisto*'s son, *Arcas*, after his mother was killed by Hera (or turned into a bear).

**Marsyas** A Phrygian *satyr*, who picked up the double-reed pipe or aulos which Athena had discarded because of the grimaces it forced the player to make. The facial distortion suited the grinning cheeks of the satyr much better. A contest of musicianship between himself and Apollo, judged by Mt Tmolus (with contributions by King *Midas*) was won by Apollo, who suspended Marsyas in a pine-tree and flayed him alive. His blood became the River Marsyas. The scene was common in Hellenistic art and was also the subject of a late painting by Titian. [Ovid, *Met*. 6]

**Medea** The witch, and priestess of *Hecate*, Medea was the daughter of Aeëtes, King of Colchis, and thus granddaughter of *Helius*; her sister was *Circe*.

She entered Greek saga with her assistance to *Jason* in the quest for the Golden Fleece, betraying her father for love of the stranger (compare *Scylla*, *Ariadne*). (For a fuller rendering of their adventure, see *Argonauts*.) Her help and advice enabled Jason to yoke the fire-breathing bulls, sow the dragon's teeth and put to sleep the serpent which guarded the fleece. She then fled Colchis with Jason, murdering her brother Apsyrtus to deflect her father from the pursuit. She and Jason were then purified by Circe. Medea devised a way to dispose of the menacing bronze giant, Talus, the guardian of Crete. [Apollonius Rhodius]

On reaching Iolcus, Jason asked Medea to rejuvenate his father Aeson. This she did by draining his body of blood and filling the veins with a magical infusion of herbs. She then proposed to rejuvenate *Pelias*, who had sent Jason on his journey, demonstrating a second method to his dubious daughters by cutting an old sheep into bits, putting them in a cauldron, and drawing out of the brew a new-born lamb. Pelias' daughters then trustingly chopped up their father, but this time the magic did not work. The Argonauts were then able to take control of the city. [Ovid, *Met*. 7]

None the less, Jason did not stay in Iolcus but left with Medea for Corinth, where Aeëtes had perhaps once been king. The couple lived there happily for some years until Jason fell in love with the daughter of King *Creon*, Glauce. Realizing that her position as a resident alien was now precarious, the barbarian Medea devised a dreadful solution. She sent a poisoned robe to Glauce: when she put it on, it burnt her flesh and she died in agony. Medea then killed her children by Jason and left Corinth in a flying chariot sent by her grandfather Helius. [Euripides, *Medea*]

Medea fled to Athens and married *Aegeus*, though he already had a son, *Theseus*, by *Aethra*. Medea tried to get rid of her stepson by sending him to despatch the Bull of Marathon; but Theseus on his safe return showed Aegeus the tokens he had from his mother, and Aegeus banished Medea and their son, Medus.

They fled back to Colchis, stopping at Absoros to control a plague of snakes by confining them in Apsyrtus' tomb. She proposed to cure a failure of crops in Colchis by a human sacrifice, and King Perses suggested as victim her own son Medus. She then killed Perses. After this we hear no more of her.

She had cult in Thessaly and Corinth, and her children were also revered at Corinth. She is the central figure in Euripides' *Medea*, where her sinister and outlandish character is the vehicle for the tragedian's reflections on the problematic position of women in Athenian society.

**Medusa** One of the three *Gorgons* whose head, which had the power to turn creatures to stone, was removed by *Perseus*. Pindar refers to her in his telling of this episode as 'fair-cheeked', and though representations of the Gorgons as a group are uniformly hideous, vase-paintings of Medea's head protruding from Perseus' bag often show classical fine features. Her beauty led to her seduction by Poseidon; her hair was turned to snakes by Athena out of envy or spite. When beheaded, the severed neck gave birth to *Chrysaor* and *Pegasus* (the latter as horsey as his father). Though Perseus used the head for his own purposes, it was subsequently placed by Athena in the centre of her shield and the snake locks formed the fringe of her aegis. From the strange keening of her sisters over the corpse Athena invented the modes of music of the double-reed pipe (aulos).

**Melampus** A seer who acquired his gift as a result of rescuing the offspring of a dead snake while staying with the King of Messenia. When the snakes licked his ears as he slept, he acquired knowledge of the languages of birds and animals. (His name means Black Foot, because his mother left his feet in the sun when she laid him in the shade as a baby.)

He helped his brother Bias steal the cattle of King Phylacus, which Bias gave Neleus as the price of marrying his daughter. Melampus was caught and imprisoned, but when he overheard two woodworms discussing the imminent collapse of his prison roof, he asked to be moved to another prison. When the subsequent collapse of his first prison proved his foresight, the king realized his great powers and asked him to cure his son of impotence. Melampus discovered that this was the result of the boy having seen his father brandishing a bloody gelding-knife in his infancy. The knife was traced and an infusion of its rust was used to cure the lad. (Compare *Telephus*' wound, cured by Achilles.)

Melampus' best-known task was that of curing the daughters of

*Proetus* of Argos of madness; they thought themselves cows and roamed the countryside killing people. Melampus demanded shares in the kingdom for himself and Bias and then cured the women. The herbs he used were afterwards thrown into a river, which had a foul smell for evermore. Melampus and Bias married two of Proetus' daughters, Lysippe and Iphianassa; but once Melampus became king, his career as a seer ceased. His descendants formed the next Argive dynasty.

**Melanion** The name, the Black One, is consonant with the figure of the 'Black Hunter' who figures in the mythological complex concerning adolescent rites of passage (Détienne). It belongs to a chaste hermit, resembling *Hippolytus*, who lived in the mountains, far from men, and spent his time in hunting. [Aristophanes, *Lysistrata*] His nature represents an unduly prolonged antisocial adolescence. Paradoxically, this *Atalanta*-like figure also appears as the eventual bridegroom of Atalanta (though he also has another name, Hippomenes).

**Melanippe** The daughter of *Aeolus*, son of *Hellen*, and Hippe, daughter of *Chiron*. Her name means Black Horse. While Aeolus was in exile for a murder, Melanippe had twin sons by Poseidon, Aeolus and Boeotus. She hid them in an ox-stall and they were suckled by the beasts. When her father returned he decreed that these monstrous children should be burnt; he also blinded and imprisoned Melanippe. However, the children continued to be reared by the herdsmen.

Then Theano, wife of King Metapontus of Icaria, under pressure from her husband to produce children, adopted Melanippe's. When in due course she had two of her own, the two pairs fought and Aeolus and Boeotus killed their half-brothers. Theano committed suicide, but the two boys, like *Amphion* and *Zethus*, went to rescue their mother, who now recovered her sight.

Euripides wrote two plays, *Melanippe the Wise* and *Melanippe in Chains*, about these legends: they are preserved only in fragments. Her blindness seems to have given her a penchant for speculation on cosmology and divine justice. Some late unreliable sources say that in Euripides Melanippe was herself the daughter of Chiron, and that she was changed by the gods into a constellation in the form of a horse.

**Meleager** Son of Oeneus and *Althaea* of Calydon. The Fates appeared at his birth and, pointing to a stick burning in the fireplace, announced that he would die as soon as it was consumed. Althaea immediately put the brand out and hid it away.

Meleager sailed with the *Argonauts*, and afterwards returned to Calydon and married Cleopatra, daughter of Idas and Marpessa.

Artemis sent a boar to terrorize Calydon by way of punishing

Oeneus for forgetting to include her in the sacrifice of first-fruits. Numerous heroes took part in the hunt for the *Calydonian Boar*. Meleager succeeded in killing the boar. He then gave the skin to *Atalanta*, thus enraging his uncles the sons of Thestius, who took it from her. According to Ovid [*Met*. 8], Meleager then killed his uncles. In the *Iliad* he is said to have killed them rather in a war against the Curetes. Althaea in her anger at his murder of her brothers took out the magic brand from its place of concealment and set it alight, so that Meleager died of a wasting sickness.

Meleager's sisters mourned him bitterly, until at last Artemis turned them into guinea-fowl (meleagrides).

**Meliae** or **Meliadae** Nymphs of the manna ash-tree, born from the blood of the severed genitals of *Uranus*. The warlike race of bronze was born of these nymphs, and spears were commonly made from ash wood.

**Melicertes** Son of *Athamas* and *Ino*. When Ino leapt into the sea in her madness, carrying Melicertes in her arms, both were transformed into sea-deities. The boy's body was carried ashore by a dolphin and given funeral rites by his uncle *Sisyphus*, King of Corinth. These were the origin of the Isthmian Games. Melicertes was given the name Palaemon, and that hero's tomb is the oldest sacred spot in the Isthmian sanctuary. (For the change of name compare *Opheltes/Archemorus*.)

Melicertes may be a Greek form of the Phoenician god Melqart, who is often identified with *Heracles*.

**Melpomene** One of the *Muses*, mother of the *Sirens*. In Hellenistic times her role was specified as patroness of tragic poetry, and she is shown in art with a tragic mask and Heracles' club.

**Memnon** Son of *Eos* (Dawn) and *Tithonus*. He was regarded as a ruler of eastern peoples, Persians or Ethiopians, and shown in oriental costume in vase-paintings. He fought on the Trojan side at Troy and was killed by *Achilles*. The smoke from his pyre turned into birds known as memnonides, which sprinkled water (the tears of Eos) each year on his grave near Troy. [*Aethiopis*; Pindar, *Nem*. 3; Ovid, *Met*. 13]

The Colossus of Memnon was the name given by the Greeks to a statue of the Pharoah Amenophis near Egyptian Thebes. It 'sang' at dawn, because of expansion in the cracked stones. It was repaired by Queen Zenobia when she invaded Egypt in AD 270, after which it sang no more.

**Menelaus** King of Sparta and brother of *Agamemnon*: the two together were known as the Atridae (sons of Atreus). He married

*Helen* and as a result of her rape by *Paris* summoned the Greeks to the war against Troy; the Greek troops were commanded by Agamemnon.

At the end of the war Menelaus was ready to kill Helen for her adultery, but was overcome by her beauty and forgave her instead. For their further story see *Helen*.

**Mentor** Odysseus' right-hand man, who managed affairs in Ithaca while he was away at the Trojan War. Athena disguised herself as Mentor in order to give advice to the young *Telemachus*. The name means Adviser, and is commonly used in that sense in modern English.

**Mermaids** Mermaids appear in ancient Greek mythology under the name of *Nereids*, who have many of the characteristics associated with other European mermaids: they attract men and will marry them, but will disappear at once if the man attempts to engage them in conversation. Ancient Greek mermaids are, however, fully human in form, without fishes' tails; but they can, like other sea-deities, change their shape at will.

Mermaids in modern Greek folklore have two tails and are known as Gorgones. They are regarded as the daughters (or sisters) of *Alexander the Great*. If a ship is assailed by storms, mermaids will appear and ask the sailors 'Where is King Alexander?' If the sailors give the correct reply — 'Alexander the Great lives and rules and keeps the world at peace' — the mermaids will vanish and the storm will subside. [P. Leigh Fermor; Myrivilis]

**Merope** One of the *Pleiades* (the dimmest, because she married a mere mortal, unlike her sisters who married gods). She was the wife of *Sisyphus* and mother of *Glaucus*.

**Mestra** Daughter of *Erysichthon*.

**Metaneira** The wife of Celeus, King of Eleusis, who employed Demeter as her servant while the latter was searching for her daughter. One of her sons was *Demophoon*, whom Demeter placed on the fire to render him immortal. When discovered by Metaneira she abandoned the project. Another son was *Triptolemus*, through whom Demeter introduced the growing of grain to the human race.

**Midas** A king of Phrygia who once rescued *Silenus* from some peasants who had chained him up. Silenus (or his master, Dionysus) offered him a reward, and Midas asked that everything he touched should turn to gold. When his food and wine, his servants and family, all turned to gold as well as his furniture, Midas realized

his mistake and begged Dionysus to relieve him of the gift. Dionysus sent him to wash in the River Pactolus. The curse was removed
from Midas, but the river ever since has run with gold.

Midas was also involved in the musical competition of Apollo and
*Marsyas*. Asked for his opinion by the judge, Tmolus, Midas voted
for Marsyas, and Apollo in anger made his head sprout asses' ears.
Midas thereafter wore a tall Phrygian cap to conceal his shame, but
could not keep the secret from his barber. The latter, unable to keep
silent about it, whispered the secret to the reeds in the river, which
then began to whisper, eternally 'King Midas has asses' ears.'

Midas was also a historical name of kings of Phrygia; one of them
sent offerings to Delphi. [Ovid, *Met*. 11]

**Minos** King of Crete, son of Zeus and *Europa* and brother of
*Rhadamanthys* and *Sarpedon*. Like Sarpedon's his life appears to have
extended over several generations. To prove his claim to sole rule of
Crete he asked Poseidon to send a bull from the sea, which he would
then sacrifice to the god. The bull duly appeared and Minos won
his kingdom; but he failed to sacrifice it, wanting to breed from it
instead. To punish him the god made his wife, *Pasiphae*, fall in love
with the bull. *Daedalus* was employed to construct a wooden cow
in which Pasiphae could lie to copulate with the bull, and the result
of this union was the *Minotaur*.

His children by Pasiphae included *Ariadne* and *Phaedra*. He pursued *Britomartis* but she threw herself into the sea to escape him
and became the goddess Dictynna. In anger at his philandering
Pasiphae cast a spell on him, which caused his body to produce snakes
and scorpions which then devoured his mistresses. This curse was
lifted from him by *Procris* (see *Cephalus*) in exchange for his infallible spear and unbeatable hound Laelaps.

Minos was regarded by the Greeks as having been ruler of a sea
empire that included all of Greece, and thus when the Palace at
Knossos was excavated by Arthur Evans, its excavator immediately
dubbed it the palace of Minos. He made war on Athens, in the course
of which he defeated Megara through the treachery of *Scylla*. He
then imposed on Athens an annual tribute of seven youths and seven
maidens as food for the Minotaur. *Theseus* travelled on the last of
these shipments and destroyed the Minotaur.

When Daedalus escaped from Crete shortly afterwards Minos pursued him as far as Sicily but was killed by the daughters of King Cocalus who was harbouring Daedalus. The soldiers who had come with
him founded the city of Heraclea Minoa, and this contained a tomb
of Minos which was demolished by Theron when he founded the
new city of Acragas.

The laws of Minos were regarded as exemplary in their justice. In
the *Underworld* Minos functioned as a judge of the dead, with *Aeacus*
and his own brother *Rhadamanthys*.

**Minotaur** The offspring of the union of *Pasiphae*, wife of Minos, with the Cretan Bull. Minos was so horrified by the monstrous appearance of the creature, commonly represented as a man from the shoulders up, and the rest a bull, that he employed *Daedalus* to build a *Labyrinth* to contain it. The creature was fed an annual tribute of seven Athenian youths and maidens (a memory of Cretan empire in the Aegean?), until one year *Theseus* was of the Athenian party and, with the help of *Ariadne*, penetrated the labyrinth and killed it. The creature seems to perpetuate in distorted form a memory of the importance of the bull in Minoan religion, where numerous frescoes and statuettes attest to a bizarre ceremonial of bull-leaping.

**Minyas** King of Orchomenus, eponym of the Minyans (after whom a particular kind of grey Helladic pottery is named). His daughters Leucippe, Arsippe and Alcathoe resisted the introduction of the cult of Dionysus and even mocked it, preferring to sit at home weaving while their fellow women were out on the mountains with the god. Their stools were suddenly surrounded by a growth of ivy and mysterious music was heard; they went mad, tore apart Leucippe's son and set off for the mountains. The story recalls those of *Pentheus*, *Lycurgus* and the daughters of *Proetus*.

**Mnemosyne** Daughter of Uranus and Gaea, and Mother of the *Muses*. Her name means Memory.

**Moirae** The Fates, Clotho (The Spinner), Lachesis (The Allotter) and Atropos (The Inflexible), daughters of Zeus and Themis, who, like the Germanic Norns, spun the thread of each mortal's life and cut it when its end was due. In Homer there is a single Moira to whom even Zeus must yield, and Moira as Fate is commonly thought of as a single abstract power. In Plato's *Republic* the Three Fates are pictured seated around the Spindle of Necessity to do their spinning, accompanied by nine *Sirens*, one on each of the celestial spheres.

**Molionidae** Twin sons of Actor or Poseidon and Molione, later conceived of as Siamese twins (perhaps a misinterpretation of the archaic convention for drawing two warriors side by side?) They feature prominently in the *Iliad*. They were killed by *Heracles* in his war with *Augeas*, and their tomb at Cleonae was visited by Pausanias.

**Moly** A magical plant given by Hermes to *Odysseus* as protection against *Circe*'s enchantments. Dioscorides gives the name to a plant something like garlic with milky white flowers something like a violet, and grassy leaves. [Homer, *Odyssey* 10]

**Momus** Sarcasm, Mockery, daughter of Night. It was Momus who suggested to Zeus a plan to relieve Earth of the constantly increasing weight of the mortal race: he should marry *Thetis* to a mortal, and the resultant war would certainly reduce the numbers of the human race. The marriage of Thetis did, in fact, lead in due course to the *Trojan War*.

**Mopsus** The name of two seers, one of whom sailed with the Argonauts and was killed by a snake in Libya. The better known one was from Colophon and was son of *Tiresias'* daughter Manto. He made himself master of Caria, and defeated *Calchas* in a divination contest. Mopsus was revered as founder of the oracle of Apollo at Claros, and of many cities of Cilicia, including Mallus (with Amphilochus?), Aspendus, Phaselis and Mopsuestia. His name appears also in Hittite texts in the form Mukhshush.

**Mormo** A female demon or bogey, somewhat like *Lamia* or *Gello*. Nurses would chasten children with the threat, 'Mormo will get you!'

**Morpheus** One of the sons of sleep, winged and able to take the forms of other persons and appear in dreams. Often a synonym for sleep.

**Muses** The goddesses of poetry and song, daughters of Zeus and Mnemosyne (Memory). There was a grove of the Muses on Mt Helicon with which they are peculiarly associated — Hesiod invokes them as Heliconian Muses — but they figure most prominently as literary deities, regularly called upon by poets to supply the matter of their song (while the Graces supply the artistic polish).

Their names were Clio, Euterpe, Thalia, Melpomene, Terpsichore, Erato, Polyhymnia, Urania and Calliope. Later writers often associated individual names with a particular art (for example, Clio for history, Terpischore for choral poetry, Melpomene for lyric) but no two ever agree on the attributions. Few myths related to the Muses. They blinded the Thracian bard *Thamyris* who boasted of his song; they also blinded Homer's Demodocus but gave him minstrelsy as compensation. In practice many itinerant singers were blind (as they still are, where found), their handicap sharpening their powers of memory.

The *Sirens* once challenged the Muses to a singing contest. The Muses won and plucked out the Sirens' feathers. The Muses taught the riddle to the *Sphinx* and sang at the marriage of certain favoured mortals (*Cadmus* and *Harmonia*, *Peleus* and *Thetis*).

**Myrrha** See *Adonis*.

**Myrtilus** The charioteer of *Oenomaus* who was bribed by *Pelops* to remove the linchpins from Oenomaus' chariot-axle, so that it crashed;

Oenomaus died and Pelops won the king's daughter. Pelops then killed Myrtilus to keep the secret safe, and Myrtilus' curse was to be visited on Pelops' descendants for generations.

**Mystery** Mysteries were religious rites reserved for initiates, in contrast to the ceremonies of public religion which were open to all. Typical of such mystery cults were the Mysteries of Demeter at Eleusis and of the Cabiri on Samothrace. The precise nature of these cults was kept a mystery (in the modern sense) so that we know little of their content except that they involved a promise for the initiate of a richer reward in the after-life — pleasant days in the *Elysian Fields* rather than a bat-like flitting in the gloom of Hades. In the Hellenistic and Roman periods it became a mark of social standing to be an initiate, and many upper class Romans, including Nero, became initiates at Eleusis. In this period too there was an increase in the popularity of oriental mysteries such as those of Isis and Mithras.

In origin the rites had a strong element of fertility ritual, symbolizing the constant return of new life out of death.

With the rise of Christianity, the mystery religions were seen as a particular threat to the popularity of the new religion of resurrection and renewal. Christian writers therefore devoted a lot of ink to denouncing the mysteries, and a great deal of what we know of them is to be learnt from their bitterest enemies. [Burkert, *Ancient Mystery Cults*]

# N

A Nereid on a cuttlefish

**Naiads** See *Nymphs*.

**Narcissus** A son of the River Cephisus. *Tiresias* prophesied that he would have a long life if he 'never knew himself'. When he grew up he was loved by *Echo*, whom he spurned; but then he saw his reflection in a pool and fell in love himself, with himself. Thus he wasted away, unfulfilling the prophecy, and was transformed into the flower that bears his name.

**Nausicaa** Daughter of *Alcinous*, King of Phaeacia. She was the first to meet the shipwrecked *Odysseus* as he emerged naked from the sea. She kept her maidenly calm, helped him and introduced him to her parents, who set him safely on his way home. Her character is one of the most charming portraits in the *Odyssey* (books 6, 8). She was a popular subject of Victorian painters; especially Lord Leighton.

**Nectanebo** The last Pharaoh of Egypt; in the *Alexander Romance*, he is a wizard who escapes Egypt before the Persian conquest and takes refuge at the Macedonian court. Here he fell in love with Olympias the wife of King Philip, and contrived to sleep with her by disguising himself as the god *Ammon*. When Olympias bore a son, Alexander, the boy took himself to be a son of the god. Nectanebo was murdered by Alexander during an astronomy lesson.

**Neleus** King of Pylus, brother of *Pelias*. They were sons of Poseidon by Tyro, who exposed them to die; they were reared by horse-herders. Pelias drove Neleus out of Iolcus and Neleus came to Pylus. His daughter was Pero, who married Bias the brother of *Melampus*, and his 12 sons included *Nestor*, the oldest and wisest of the Greeks at Troy. Neleus was killed by *Heracles* (not in Homer) and Nestor survived to become king.

**Nemesis** Goddess of retribution, and daughter of Night. She represents the resentment felt by men both at evil deeds and at undeserved good fortune, and the hoped-for downfall of the victim. The name derives from *nemo*, to apportion.

**Neoptolemus** Son of *Achilles* and Deidameia, one of the girls he met while disguised as a woman on Scyros. He was also named Pyrrhus from Achilles' female name, Pyrrha. Neoptolemus was brought to Troy after Achilles' death and, according to Sophocles, helped bring *Philoctetes* there also.

His military prowess enabled the Greeks to win the war; he invented the war dance, pyrrhiche, which bears his name. He murdered *Astyanax* and sacrificed *Polyxena* at the tomb of Achilles.

In Homer, Neoptolemus then married Menelaus' daughter *Hermione*. In other writers, he travelled home via Thrace with *Helenus*, taking *Andromache* as his concubine, and settled in Epirus. He visited Delphi to inquire why his wife did not produce children. Here he was murdered, either by Orestes because he had stolen his own betrothed Hermione, or by a priest, Machaereus, because Neoptolemus objected to the custom of the priests taking all the sacrificial meat. Neoptolemus was buried in the Temple of Apollo at Delphi, where he received divine honours. [*Little Iliad*; see M. Davies; Pindar, *Paean* 6, *Nemean* 7]

**Nereids** Fifty sea-nymphs, daughters of *Nereus* and Doris, of whom the chief is *Thetis*, the mother of *Achilles*. The others are also named (variously) in Homer and Hesiod.

In modern Greece the name, in the form Neraïda, has become attached to the *Nymphs* of upland country and woodland, who can catch a man unawares at noonday and make him mad or dumb (nympholepsy). [R. and E. Blum; J.C. Lawson]

**Nereus** A sea-deity, father of the *Nereids*, sometimes confused with *Proteus* (the Old Man of the Sea).

**Nessus** A *Centaur* who attempted to rape *Heracles'* bride *Deianeira* while ferrying her on his back across the River Evenus. Heracles shot him with an arrow poisoned with Hydra-venom. The dying Nessus persuaded Deianeira to keep some of his blood, supposedly for use as a love-charm if Heracles' affections should wander. When Heracles betrayed Deianeira with *Iole*, Deianeira sent him a cloak soaked in the liquid; the poison burnt Heracles' flesh and caused him to die in agony. [Sophocles, *Trachiniae*]

**Nestor** King of Pylus in Messenia, one of the 12 sons of *Neleus*. In his youth he was involved in several battles with the men of Elis. He remained King of Pylus for three generations and was already old when the Trojan War began. He led 90 ships to Troy, and was esteemed as a wise, if somewhat loquacious, counsellor. He returned safe home to Pylus at the end of the war, where he entertained *Telemachus* during the latter's search for his father *Odysseus*.

The Mycenaean palace excavated by Blegen at Pylus is generally known as the Palace of Nestor. It was destroyed *c.* 1250 BC.

**Night** According to Hesiod, the daughter of Chaos, and sister of Darkness (Erebus), Earth (*Gaea*), *Tartarus* and *Eros*. By Erebus she bore Aether and Day. Alone she produced *Momus*, Thanatos (Death), Hypnos (Sleep), the *Moirae* and *Nemesis*. [Hesiod, *Theogony*]

**Nike** Goddess of victory, often depicted as winged, and accompanying Zeus, or Athena. She had a temple of her own (Athena Nike) on the Acropolis at Athens.

**Ninus** King of Babylon, and subject of a now fragmentary early Hellenistic Romance about his love for *Semiramis* — one of the earliest known Greek novels, in which the great conqueror is treated as a lovesick youth. [Reardon]

**Niobe** A daughter of *Tantalus*, King of Lydia, who boasted that her seven (or six) sons and daughters were fairer than the offspring of Leto (Apollo and Artemis). In revenge the two gods killed all the children, and Niobe was turned to a stone, weeping constantly, on Mt Sipylus. The scene is portrayed on a large krater in the Louvre, and was the subject of a famous sculptural group of the fourth century. The 'weeping rock' near Manisa is identified in George Bean's guide to *Turkey beyond the Maeander* (with photograph).

**Nisus** King of Megara whose daughter *Scylla (2)* betrayed him to King *Minos* when he attacked the city, by removing the purple lock of hair which preserved his life. After death Nisus was transformed into an osprey.

**Nymphs** *Daemones*, minor female deities, associated with particular habitats, such as mountains (oreads), trees (dryads and meliae), springs, rivers and lakes (naiads) or the sea (nereids). There are many legends of their amours with men (*Echo* and *Narcissus*; *Hylas and the Nymphs*; *Salmacis*) and their seductive charm is to be feared. Like Pan, these spirits of the wild have the power to drive a man mad or dumb (nympholepsy) especially at noonday. In modern Greek lore their functions persist but they have taken the name of the *Nereids*.

# O

Oedipus and the Sphinx

**Oceanus** Son of *Gaea* and *Uranus*, for Homer he is the progenitor, by his sister Titan Tethys, of all the gods as well as all rivers and three thousand Oceanids. His name is that of the River of Ocean which surrounds the Earth, thought of as a flat circular dish. The way to the *Underworld* lay across it, as did the Garden of the *Hesperides* and the home of the *Gorgons*.

**Odysseus** Perhaps the best-known of all the Greek heroes, son of Laertes and Anticleia the daughter of *Autolycus*, from whom he inherited his wily (and even sometimes dishonest) ways. Famed for his rhetoric and persuasive power — when the words began to fall 'like snowflakes' his hearers forgot his short stature — he was regarded by writers in the Dorian tradition as the epitome of the superficial cleverness of Athenian democracy, which they opposed to the simple nobility of the Doric system of values. Pindar is the clearest exponent of this attitude: see also Sophocles, *Philoctetes*.

In youth Odysseus was a great hunter. He once received a severe thigh wound from a boar while hunting with the sons of Autolycus. (The scar is important later in his story.)

Odysseus married *Penelope*, daughter of Icarius. Soon after the birth of his son, *Telemachus*, the heroes were summoned to the *Trojan*

*War*. Odysseus feigned madness to avoid call-up, sowing his land with salt and ploughing with an ox and ass to pull the plough; but he was unmasked by *Palamedes*, who placed the infant Telemachus in the furrow before him, at which point Odysseus acted like the sanest of fathers. Having joined the expedition, he in turn unmasked *Achilles* where he was in hiding on Scyros.

His part in the Trojan War is inconspicuous until after the death of Achilles, when he disputed with *Ajax* the right to the arms of Achilles: the Greek adjudicators, overhearing some captive Trojan girls praising Odysseus above Ajax, awarded them to Odysseus, and Ajax went mad with rage and killed himself. Later Odysseus captured *Helenus*, and fulfilled several of the conditions predicted by the seer for the capture of Troy: he fetched *Neoptolemus* from Greece and *Philoctetes* from Lemnos; with *Diomedes*, he stole the *Palladium*; most important of all, he devised the stratagem of the *Wooden Horse* by which Troy was finally taken.

His ten-year journey home is the subject of Homer's *Odyssey*, in which the first nine years' wanderings are recounted by the hero to his hosts in Phaeacia. (Each of his adventures is described in more detail under the relevant entry in this book.) His ship was blown off-course soon after leaving Troy and he and his crew were carried first to the land of the *Lotus-Eaters*, then to the land of the fierce *Laestrygonians*. His next adventure was the episode in the cave of the fierce *Cyclops Polyphemus*, whom he escaped by telling the giant that his name was 'Nobody', and then blinding him and getting his men to cling to the underside of his sheep when he let them out of the cave. They next came to the island of *Aeolus*, god of the winds, who gave him a bag of winds; thinking it was treasure, his men opened it and let the winds out, causing further storms. They were washed next to the island of Aeaea, where the sorceress *Circe* turned his men into swine. After persuading her to reverse the magic, Odysseus became Circe's lover for one year. He then sailed, on her advice, to the River *Oceanus*, where he summoned up the shades of the dead, first of all the prophet *Tiresias*, to advise him how to get safely home; Tiresias told him he and his men would arrive safely only if he left unharmed the cattle of the Sun on the island of Thrinacia. Odysseus then saw several of the other dead heroes in Hades, as well as his mother, and the great sinners *Tityus*, *Tantalus* and *Sisyphus*. From here he sailed past the islands of the *Sirens* and the dangers of *Scylla* and *Charybdis*. Being marooned on Thrinacia by adverse winds, his crew slaughtered and ate some of the cattle of the Sun, and were duly wrecked when they set sail again. Odysseus alone escaped and was washed up on *Calypso*'s island of Ogygia. Here Calypso made him her lover and wanted to make him immortal so that he would remain for ever; but after nine years Zeus sent Hermes to recall him to his duty, and Odysseus built a ship and sailed on. Close to Phaeacia he was wrecked again by Poseidon, who was still angry at him for

blinding his son Polyphemus; he was saved from drowning by Ino-
Leucothea who appeared in the form of a sea-mew and gave him
her scarf to keep him afloat. He was washed up on the beach of
Phaeacia where *Nausicaa* met him and introduced him to her father
King *Alcinous*. After hearing of Odysseus' travels Alcinous arranged
for his transport back to Ithaca — in an enchanted sleep — by a Phaeacian ship. He was deposited close to the Cave of the Nymphs on
Ithaca. Poseidon's last act of vengeance was to turn the ship to stone
on its return journey to Phaeacia.

On Ithaca, Odysseus' faithful wife Penelope was being besieged
by suitors living it up in the palace and waiting for her to decide
which of them she would marry. Odysseus was disguised by Athena
as an old man and visited the hut of the swineherd *Eumaeus* where
he was reunited with Telemachus. Together they hid the suitors'
weapons and prepared for a showdown. Odysseus' old nurse
Eurycleia, bathing him, recognized him by the scar on his thigh;
his aged dog Argus also recognized him with delight, these 20 years
on, and then died. But Odysseus kept his identity secret from
Penelope.

On Telemachus' advice Penelope devised a test for the suitors: she
would marry whichever of the suitors could bend Odysseus' great
bow and shoot an arrow through a line of 10 axe-heads. Odysseus
took part in the competition despite the suitors' derision, and was
the only one able to string the bow: he then fired a winning shot.
At this point Telemachus and other supporters rushed the suitors
and packed them off to Hades; Odysseus was reunited with his wife.

So ends the *Odyssey*. The later epic, the *Telegony*, by the sixth-
century poet Eugammon of Cyrene, told of his further wanderings
— a theme echoed in Tennyson's *Ulysses* — and his return home.
Here he was killed in battle by *Telegonus*, his son by Circe, who had
come to Ithaca to discover his father but did not know that it was
Ithaca on which he now stood. Telegonus then married Penelope.

Dedications to the hero Odysseus have been found in the Cave
of the Nymphs on Ithaca.

Nikos Kazantzakis wrote a lengthy symbolic continuation of Odysseus' adventures under the title *Odyssey*.

**Oedipus** The son of *Laius*, King of Thebes, and *Jocasta*. An oracle
had warned Laius that it would be dangerous to rear any son he had
by Jocasta. Accordingly, when the child was born, Laius had its feet
stapled together and the child was exposed on Mt Cithaeron. But
the child was rescued by shepherds and given to King Polybus of
Corinth and his wife. They named him Oedipus (Swollen Foot) and
brought him up as their own son.

When he was accused by his companions of not being a son of
Polybus, Oedipus consulted the Delphic *oracle*, which foretold that
he would kill his father and marry his mother. To prevent this horrific

prophecy coming true, Oedipus vowed never to return to Corinth.

On his way back from Delphi, at a place where three roads meet, he met a man in a chariot who refused to pull over and let him pass. In anger Oedipus killed the whole party, except one retainer, who escaped. He then went on to Thebes which was being subjected to the depredations of the *Sphinx*, who was challenging all the young men of Thebes to solve a riddle, and destroying them when they failed. The riddle was 'What goes on four legs in the morning, on two at noonday and on three in the evening?' Oedipus set off and gave the correct answer, 'Man' (who crawls in infancy, walks in adulthood, and uses a stick in old age). He then killed the Sphinx, or else she flung herself from the walls of Thebes to her death.

Oedipus was made King of Thebes and given the wife of the previous king, who had recently been murdered in mysterious circumstances. He and Jocasta had two sons, *Eteocles* and *Polynices*, and two daughters, *Antigone* and Ismene. But Thebes was then visited by a plague, which was revealed by the Delphic oracle to be the result of pollution because the murderer of King Laius was living in the city unpunished. Oedipus swore to find the murderer and punish him. The thriller-like course of his investigation provides the plot of one of the greatest of all Greek tragedies, Sophocles' *Oedipus the King*. In the end Oedipus realized that the man he had killed was Laius his father, and Jocasta realized that her husband was the infant they had exposed. Jocasta hanged herself, and Oedipus blinded himself with the brooches torn from her dress.

Oedipus was then exiled from Thebes by Creon, who assumed the kingship. His daughter Antigone accompanied the old blind man as guide. Oedipus cursed his sons because they acquiesced in his banishment, and the curse was fulfilled in the fratricidal war of the *Seven Against Thebes*.

According to Sophocles' *Oedipus at Colonus*, Oedipus came at last to Colonus near Athens and was given refuge by King Theseus. In a mysterious final scene the hero is taken silently from the earth by the gods; his tomb at Colonus became a sacred site.

Oedipus' name was used by Sigmund Freud to entitle his most famous 'discovery', the desire of the son to do away with his father and sleep with his mother. It is worth noting, however, that Oedipus was far from actually wanting to do either! [L. Edmunds; Bremmer in Bremmer]

**Oeneus** See *Althaea*, *Meleager*.

**Oenomaus** King of Pisa in Elis. His daughter was *Hippodamia*, and he used to challenge all her suitors to a chariot race from Pisa to the Isthmus of Corinth. As Oenomaus' horses had been given him by the God Ares, the suitors always lost and Oenomaus then killed them. Eventually *Pelops* beat him by driving a chariot team given to him by Poseidon and, in addition, bribing Oenomaus' charioteer *Myrtilus* to take out the axle pins of his chariot. It crashed and Oenomaus was killed.

**Oenone** A nymph of Mt Ida who married *Paris* but was abandoned by him when he ran off with *Helen*. Later, when Paris was wounded by *Philoctetes*, he begged her to save his life: she refused and then hanged herself in remorse when Paris died. The plight of the abandoned nymph is the subject of one of Ovid's *Letters of Heroines*.

**Old Man of the Sea** See *Proteus*.

**Olympia** A sanctuary of Zeus in Elis, the site of the Olympic Games which were traditionally founded by Heracles after his defeat of King *Augeas*. Historical records of the Games stretched back to 776 BC and their four-yearly cycle (Olympiads) was used as the basic dating system of the Greeks. It was the richest in dedications of all Greek sanctuaries, and Pausanias devoted books 5 and 6 of his *Guide to Greece* to its description.

**Olympus** The highest mountain in Greece, situated in Thessaly close to the Thermaic Gulf; usually cloud-capped, it was regarded by the ancients as the home of the gods. A distinctive spur of the mountain is still known as the Throne of Zeus. The name also belonged to other mountains of the Greek world, including one near Prusa (modern Ulu Dağ above Bursa).

**Omphale** A queen of Lydia who bought *Heracles* when he sold himself into slavery. She bore him a son, Lamus.

**Onocentaur** A *Centaur* with asses' legs and tail instead of horses'.

**Opheltes** The son of Lycurgus, King of Nemea, who was warned by an *oracle* not to let Opheltes touch the ground until he could walk. But when the *Seven against Thebes* came to Nemea his nurse *Hypsipyle* put him down to show them a spring; he was bitten by a snake and died. The Nemean games were founded in his honour under the new name of Archemorus (beginning of doom — because their expedition was fated to fail). His shrine is probably the large irregularly pentagonal archaic heroön at the south-west corner of the sanctuary at Nemea.

**Oracle** (Greek *manteion*, Latin *oraculum*). A holy place where inquirers could obtain responses to their questions about the future: usually, about what they should or should not do (for example, marry a certain person, go on a journey, dedicate an altar in one place rather than another). Major Greek oracles were situated at Delphi, Didyma,

Claros (all Apollo), Dodona (Zeus), and Ephyre (the dead); at each the responses were given in a different form. At Dodona the shaking of the leaves in Zeus' sacred oak, signified the god's answer; at Delphi the ravings in ecstatic trance of the *Pythia*. These responses were interpreted to the inquirer by the priests, who in some cases put them into hexameter verse. These responses are also called in English 'oracles' (Greek *chresmos*, *—moi*, Latin *oraculum*, *—la*).

Many fictitious oracles were composed, often *ex post facto*, by wandering prophets (*manteis*) and were recited in public, or found a home in historical writings like that of Herodotus. The famous riddling oracles which led men to make the wrong decision and proceed to their doom are almost certainly literary inventions.

By the Christian era the oracles no longer gave replies in verse, and they entered a decline. When the Emperor Julian sent to the Oracle of Delphi, he was told it had ceased to operate. That at Didyma was closed by the Christian Emperor Theodosius in 395 when he abolished all pagan observances. [H. W. Parke *Greek Oracles*; Oracles of Apollo in Asia Minor; Parke and Wormell, *The Delphic Oracle*; J. Fontenrose, *The Delphic Oracle*]

**Oread** A mountain *nymph*.

**Orestes** The son of *Agamemnon* and *Clytemnestra*, who escaped after Agamemnon's murder to the court of King Strophius of Phocis, brother-in-law of Agamemnon. Here he became the inseparable companion of Strophius' son Pylades. When he reached manhood, Orestes returned to Argos with Pylades to avenge his father by murdering his mother and her lover *Aegisthus*. The Delphic oracle enjoined the act, but none the less the *Furies* of his mother pursued him and drove him mad. He returned to Delphi for advice; Apollo sent him on to Athens, where he was acquitted by a special court on the Areopagus over which Athena presided. Thus the ancestral curse was finally absolved. This at any rate is the version of Orestes' cure given by Aeschylus in *Eumenides*. Other traditions had it that he drove away the Furies by biting off one of his fingers at Megalopolis; or that the madness left him at Gythion.

Euripides did not let Orestes off so easily. In *Orestes* he has the young man condemned to death by the Argives, following which Orestes and Pylades try to murder Helen because of Menelaus' refusal to help them, and then hold Hermione hostage until Apollo appears and orders Orestes to be banished. This weird story seems to be Euripides' own invention. In *Iphigeneia in Tauris* Orestes' madness continues after the trial in Athens, and Apollo sends him to Tauris to bring home the statue of Artemis which will cure him. Here he encounters his sister *Iphigeneia*, transported there by Artemis to be her priestess. They narrowly escape the murderous Taurians and flee to Athens. The statue was then set up in Attica, or in the temple of Artemis Orthia at Sparta, and Iphigeneia became priestess at Brauron. Orestes became King of Mycenae and Sparta.

Hermione recurs in Orestes' next adventure. Orestes had been betrothed to her in childhood, but Menelaus then gave her to Neoptolemus, so that Orestes arranged to have Neoptolemus murdered at Delphi.

Orestes died an old man and was succeeded as king by Tisamenus. Herodotus (1,167) tells how the Spartans were told that they could conquer Tegea if they brought Orestes' bones to Sparta. They eventually found them in a forge at Tegea and brought them triumphantly home.

**Orion** A giant hunter who was given to King Hyrieus in answer to his prayer for a child. Zeus, Poseidon and Hermes took an ox-hide, urinated on it and buried it. After nine months it produced the baby Urion; his name later became Orion.

He made love to Merope the daughter of King Oenopion of Cos, and Oenopion blinded him. Orion as a son of Poseidon was able to walk on the water, and made his way to Lemnos, where he took Hephaestus' servant, the boy Cedalion, to be his guide; the boy sat on his shoulders and gave him directions towards the sunrise (this unusual detail is the subject of a painting by Poussin). The sun's rays healed him and *Eos* fell in love with him, and carried him to Delos.

Here he shared the pleasures of the hunt with Artemis, but she was also responsible for his death, though its manner was variously reported. Either he boasted of his hunting prowess to Artemis, or he tried to rape one of her attendants, Opis, and Ge sent a scorpion to kill him; or Artemis killed him by accident with a discus; or Apollo challenged her to some target practice while Orion was swimming, and she hit the unfortunate giant's head, not realizing what it was.

Orion was placed among the stars where, accompanied by his dog, he pursues perpetually the seven daughters of *Atlas*, the *Pleiades*, one of whom was also called Merope, and whom he is said also to have pursued in his lifetime.

**Orpheus** A legendary Thracian singer and poet, son of Oeagrus and one of the Muses, credited with the composition of a number of theogonic poems, of which only fragments survive. They were influential on the theology and practice of the Pythagoreans (from sixth century BC) as well as later cults. 'Orphic' doctrine is one of the most intractable puzzles in the history of Greek religion. The most plausible explanation of the human Orpheus is that he was a 'shaman', a type of medicine-man or ecstatic prophet familiar from Central Asia and the regions to the north-east of Greece (including Thrace).

He entered the legendary accounts of early Greece as a musician the power of whose song could move animals, rocks and trees to follow him. He took part in the expedition of the *Argonauts* and introduced them to the mysteries of Samothrace, as well as carrying out the crucial task of putting to sleep with his music the dragon which guarded the *Golden Fleece*.

His wife was *Eurydice*, who was killed by a snakebite while being pursued by *Aristaeus*. Orpheus descended to Hades and tried by his playing to charm the gods of the *Underworld* into returning her. They agreed to let her follow him back to the Upper World on condition that he did not look back until he emerged. He failed to restrain his anxiety, and lost her for ever. He then wandered the plains of Thrace until he was torn apart by maenads. They buried his body, but his head floated down the River Hebrus, continuing to sing, and was washed to Lesbos where it finally found a grave. The reward of the Lesbians was their skill in music. [Apollonius; Ovid *Met.*; Vergil, *Georgius IV*; West, *Orphic Poems*]

**Orthros** The dog of *Geryon* and father, by his own mother Echidna, of the *Sphinx*.

**Otus and Ephialtes** Twin giants, sons of Poseidon and Iphimedeia. They planned to make an assault on the home of the gods, and to do so piled Mt Pelion on Mt Ossa, and both on Mt Olympus. They captured Ares and imprisoned him in a jar; when they tried to rape Artemis and Hera, Apollo shot them down; or, Artemis took the form of a deer which ran between them and, in their attempt to shoot it, they killed each other. They were punished in Hades, bound back to back against a pillar, with snakes as bonds. They were regarded as founders of Hesiod's home, Ascra, at the foot of Mt Helicon.

**Owl** The sacred bird of Athena, one of whose epithets is *glaukopis*, generally interpreted as 'owl-faced' (rather than 'grey-eyed'), indicating a prehistoric identification of goddess and bird.

# P

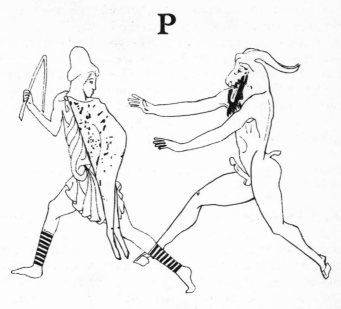

Pan and a boy

**Paeon** Or Paean. A healing god, identified with Apollo. The name is often simply a title of Apollo.

**Palaemon** See *Melicertes*. When the latter drowned he became a sea-god, and was honoured under this name as the presiding hero of the Isthmian games.

**Palamedes** A hero of Nauplia, the inventor of the alphabet (but see also *Cadmus*), dice, chess, weights and measures, fire signals, etc. (Palamai means hands, with the implication of dexterity or cleverness.) He tricked *Odysseus* into joining the expedition against Troy. Odysseus had feigned madness by yoking his plough to an ox and an ass and sowing the ground with salt; but Palamedes unmasked him by placing his infant son in the furrow before him, at which point Odysseus revealed his sanity by leaping to rescue the child, Cypria.

At Troy Odysseus took revenge on Palamedes by planting a quantity of gold in his tent and arranging for the interception of a forged letter from Priam to Palamedes. Palamedes was convicted of treachery and stoned to death. In another version Odysseus and Diomedes murdered him while fishing.

**Palladium** A wooden image of Athena preserved in the citadel at Troy. It had been made by Athena as a monument to her friend *Pallas* whom she killed. Zeus threw it out of heaven when *Electra* the daughter of Atlas tried to take refuge at it to avoid his lust; it fell in Troy. Odysseus and Diomedes stole it as one of the conditions for victory in the *Trojan War*, and it was then claimed by both Argos and Athens.

**Pallas** A title of Athena for which the Greeks gave various explanations. It was the name of one of the *Giants*, and in the war of the Gods and Giants Athena killed him and used his flayed skin as a shield. Or the title (which seems to mean 'girl') was derived from Athena's accidental killing of a girlfriend named Pallas — perhaps a symbol of Athena's usurpation of the place of a pre-Olympian goddess. See also *Palladium*.

Pallas is also the name of a Titan, who married Styx and was father of Victory, Strength, Violence and Emulation. A hero of this name was half-brother of *Aegeus* and helped him to regain the throne of Athens, but then with two other brothers rebelled; he and his 50 sons were eventually killed by *Theseus*.

**Pan** The god of Arcadia *par excellence*, half-goat and half-man in form, beautifully described in the Homeric Hymn to Pan:

> the chief of Hermes' love-got joys,
> Goat-footed, two-horned, amorous of noise,
> That through the fair greens, all adorn'd with trees
> Together goes with nymphs. . .

He is son of Hermes by one or another *nymph*; his mother was so scared by his appearance that she abandoned him at birth and Hermes introduced him to Olympus.

His name is probably related to the same root as Latin *pasco*, and thus means 'shepherd' (though a link with the Vedic Puśan, the nourisher, has also been proposed). His home is the wild landscape beyond the borders of cities: when he receives cult within the city limits it is not in a temple but in a grotto or niche which represents the wild country (examples at Athens, on the Acropolis, and on Thasos).

He is associated with the Great Mother (Pindar calls him 'hound of the Mountain Mother') and represents the unbridled instinctual drive of the he-goat and, perhaps, of the goatherd too: his loves are typically unfulfilled or sterile (boys) and he is credited with the invention of masturbation. He did, however, once seduce the Moon by spreading out a beautiful white fleece, and also the insubstantial *Echo* who bore him a daughter, *Iynx*. He is connected none the less with fertility, as in the Arcadian rite of beating an image of Pan with squills to ensure fertility of the land. A common term for rape was Panic Marriage.

Best-known of his loves is the nymph *Syrinx*; when he pursued her, she begged the nymphs of the River Ladon for help, and was transformed into a clump of reeds. From these Pan invented the pan pipes, a set of tuned reeds bound together with wax. His musical competition with Apollo on the lyre led to his defeat.

Pan, unlike other gods, is not approached in silence. He is thus most dangerous at the tranquil noontide hour of siesta time, when 'the choler sits in his nostril' [Theocritus], and a man may be seized by Pan (or the nymphs) and made mad, or dumb: there is little difference between nympholepsy and panolepsy. Laughter also belongs to Pan.

He also represents the terror of the noonday or the night, especially the panic fear that affects armies in camp. He seems to have used this gift to help the Athenians at Marathon in 479 BC: when Pheidippides ran from Marathon to Athens to warn of the Persian invasion, Pan met him on Mt Parnes and promised his help. After the Athenian victory the cult of Pan was introduced to Athens for the first time. His popularity with the Athenians is indicated by his centrality to the plot of Menander's *Dyscolus*.

In Orphic theology Pan acquired a quite different significance: because of the resemblance of his name to the word *pan*, 'all', he became a universal high god, but this is simply the aberration of theologians at play. Like satyrs and silens, Pan may also be multiplied, and Plato in the *Laws* refers to the inclusion of 'panes' in carnival-like processions in the Greek city. [*Homeric Hymn to Pan*; *Orphic Hymn to Pan*; P. Bourgeaud]

**Pandareus** A Cretan king who was killed, along with his wife, by the gods, for stealing from a shrine of Zeus. Aphrodite rescued their daughters, Hera gave them beauty and Athena taught them weaving; but when Aphrodite went to arrange marriages for them,

> The ravishing Harpie snatched the maids away
> And gave them up, for all their loving eyes,
> To serve the Furies who hate constantly.
> [Homer, *Odyssey* 20]

**Pandarus** A Lycian leader on the Trojan side, a skilled archer. He was killed by *Diomedes*. His role as Pandar in the story of *Cressida* belongs to that medieval legend only.

**Pandora** The first woman, created by the gods to punish man for *Prometheus*' theft of fire; she was made from clay by Hephaestus, given life by Athena, decked with jewellery by the Graces and Peitho, with flowers by the Horae, with beauty by Aphrodite, and with treachery by Hermes. Hermes gave her to *Epimetheus* as bride; her dowry was a jar full of evils. When the jar was opened, all these were released among men — except Hope, which remained in her keeping. This ambiguous parable seems to mean that despite all his woes, man can still cling to Hope, [Hesiod. *Works and Days*]

**Paris** The second son of *Priam* and *Hecuba* of Troy, exposed by them on Mt Ida because of a warning dream Hecuba had, in which she gave birth to a firebrand which destroyed their city. The baby, however, was suckled by a bear and then brought up by a shepherd, who gave him the name Alexander, Protector, because of his skill in protecting the flocks. When he reached adolescence Paris returned to the city to take part in the funeral games which had been arranged to commemorate his own death; he won all the events and was recognized by his sister *Cassandra*; or revealed his identity by showing the clothes in which he had been exposed.

Despite being recognized and welcomed by his family, Paris continued his shepherd's life and became the lover of a *nymph* called Denone. His life took a marked change of course when he was invited to judge between three goddesses — Hera, Athena and Aphrodite — which of them had the best claim to the golden apple, inscribed 'for the fairest' which Eris (Discord) had thrown among the guests at the wedding of Peleus and Thetis. Zeus sent the three to Mt Ida to the handsomest man in the world, Paris. Hera offered him rule over Asia, Athena wisdom and military supremacy, but Aphrodite offered the love of the most beautiful woman in the world. So Paris gave the prize to Aphrodite, thus earning the undying hatred of Athena and Hera for Troy.

The most beautiful of women was *Helen*, and Paris at once abandoned Denone and set off for Sparta to wrest her away from her husband Menelaus. The eloping couple spent their first night on the island of Cranae off the southern tip of Mani, and then made straight for Troy. Menelaus summoned the Greek heroes to keep their oath to defend the rights of Helen's husband, and thus began the Trojan War.

In the 10 years' fighting Paris excelled in the art of archery. He killed *Achilles* by hitting him on his one vulnerable spot, his heel, but was presently wounded by an arrow from the bow of *Philoctetes*. He repaired to Ida to be healed by the magic powers of his erstwhile lover Oenone, but she refused to help him and he died. She then hanged herself in remorse. [*Cypria*; *Aethiopis*; *Iliad*]

**Parnassus** A mountain in central Greece, on whose southern slope Delphi is situated. It is the home of Apollo, where he holds court with the Muses when they come over from neighbouring Helicon, their home. Many poets localized the Muses too on Parnassus.

**Pasiphae** The daughter of Helius and Perseis and wife of *Minos*, king of Crete. She fell in love with a bull which Poseidon had given to her husband. *Daedalus* constructed for her an artificial cow in which she could lie to copulate with the bull. In due course she gave birth to the *Minotaur*.

Her name means 'all-brightest' and she was worshipped as a moon-goddess in Laconia. Of her several offspring, *Ariadne* ('all-holy') and *Phaedra* ('shining') also seem to be faded gods of the Cretan religion.

**Patroclus** Son of Menoetius and uncertain mother, from Opus. Patroclus killed a friend in a quarrel, and he and his father fled to the court of *Peleus*. Patroclus became the inseparable friend of Peleus' son *Achilles*, and his lover; when Achilles went to Troy, Patroclus accompanied him as his squire. When Achilles withdrew from the fighting at Troy, Patroclus tried to save the situation by going into battle wearing Achilles' armour; but he was wounded by Euphorbus and then killed by *Hector*. The fight to recover his body was a lengthy one. Patroclus' death incited Achilles to return to battle for revenge, after a period of extravagant mourning, and he then killed Hector in a duel. Patroclus was translated, like Achilles after his death, to the White Island in the Black Sea. [Homer, *Iliad*]

**Pegasus** The winged horse born from the severed neck of *Medusa* (brother of *Chrysaor*). He created the spring Hippocrene (Horse's Spring) on Mt Helicon by a stamp of his hoof. He was tamed by *Bellerophon*, with the gods' help, and carried the latter on his adventures until Bellerophon dared to try to fly to heaven itself. Then Zeus sent a gadfly to sting Pegasus and the hero plunged to his death. The horse then made his home on Olympus. [Hesiod, *Theogony*, Pindar, *Ol.* 13]

**Peitho** Goddess of the rhetorical or amatory power of Persuasion — a personified abstraction.

**Pelasgus** The eponym of the Pelasgians, the name of the autochthonous inhabitants of Greece. The Athenians, Argives and Thessalians claimed descent from Pelasgus, but he is usually made King of Arcadia, either the son of Zeus and *Niobe* or born directly from the Arcadian soil. For its people he invented huts and sheepskin coats, and he introduced them to the superior diet of acorns. He was father of *Lycaon*.

**Peleus** Son of *Aeacus*, brother of *Telamon*, father of *Achilles*. In his youth he and Telamon murdered their half-brother *Phocus* and were banished. Peleus came to Phthia and married *Antigone* the daughter of King Eurytion: but he accidentally killed the latter and fled to Iolcus. Here he was purified by King Acastus. Unfortunately Acastus' wife Astydamia fell in love with Peleus and, being spurned, accused him of attempted rape. She also told Antigone that he was about to marry Acastus' daughter, and Antigone killed herself.

As revenge, Acastus took Peleus hunting on Mt Pelion and hid Peleus' sword, leaving him asleep and at the mercy of Centaurs. However, he was saved by *Chiron* and enlisted the help of *Jason* and the *Argonauts* to take vengeance on the Iolcan couple by killing Astydamia, cutting her body in half and marching his army between the pieces.

Peleus then became King of Phthia. Now Zeus, who had fallen love with *Thetis*, had been warned that she would bear a son greater than his father. This dissuaded him from taking her for his own and he arranged for her to marry a mortal. The choice fell on Peleus. Chiron explained to Peleus how to capture the sea-nymph: he surprised her while sleeping on the beach at Sepias, and though she transformed herself into fire, then water, then a lion, a snake and a tree, and perhaps other forms as well, he clung on and made her his wife.

The wedding of Peleus and Thetis was attended by all the gods, who brought gifts, while the Muses sang the wedding hymn. (There is a long description in Catullus' 64th poem.) However, *Eris* was left off the guest list and in pique flung among the guests the Golden Apple inscribed 'For the fairest', the dispute over which led to the *Trojan War*. (See also *Paris*.)

When Thetis bore a child, Achilles, she tried to make him immortal, either by dipping him in the Styx (but his ankle, which she held him by, was not dipped and remained vulnerable) or by placing him on the fire (compare *Demophoon*). Peleus caught her in the act and cried out, thus violating the taboo that mortals should not speak to their mermaid wives; Thetis at once disappeared and returned to the sea, her home. Peleus then gave Achilles to Chiron to bring up.

Peleus was driven from Phthia in old age by the sons of Acastus, and at last joined Thetis in the depths of the sea and became immortal.

**Pelias** King of Iolcus, son of Poseidon and Tyro: his twin brother was *Neleus*. Their mother exposed them at birth but they were reared by horse-herders. Tyro then married Cretheus, King of Iolcus, and her son was Aeson. However, Pelias managed to make himself King of Iolcus rather than Aeson, and banished Neleus to Messenia, where he became king.

Pelias' children were *Alcestis* and Acastus.

An oracle warned Pelias to beware the man who would arrive wearing one sandal. In due course Aeson's son *Jason* arrived at Iolcus to claim his inheritance; he had lost one sandal in a river while helping an old woman to cross it. Pelias decided to get rid of him by sending him to fetch the *Golden Fleece* (see *Argonauts*).

On his safe return with *Medea*, Jason claimed the kingdom and Medea persuaded Pelias' daughters to chop him up under the pretence that by boiling the pieces she could rejuvenate him. Though she had demonstrated this trick on an old sheep, she made sure it did not work for Pelias. However, this did not make Jason and his wife popular, and they left for Corinth, so that Pelias' son Acastus became king. He celebrated funeral games for Pelias which became legendary for their magnificence and for the number of *heroes* who took part.

**Pelops** The son of *Tantalus*, who served him up to the gods in a stew to test their omniscience (compare *Lycaon*). Demeter ate a piece of the shoulder before the ruse was discovered; the gods pieced him together again and gave him a new shoulder of ivory. The boy was now so beautiful that Poseidon fell in love with him and took him off to Olympus.

However, Tantalus tried to steal the nectar and ambrosia of the gods, and as punishment they sent the boy back to earth. Here Pelops fell in love with *Hippodamia*, daughter of *Oenomaus* of Pisa, and determined to win her as his bride. To do this he had to beat Oenomaus in a chariot race. Poseidon helped him by giving him a chariot with horses of divine swiftness, in which he won the race and the girl. So the story is told by Pindar (*Ol.* 1) who omits any reference to the commoner tale that Pelops won by bribing the charioteer *Myrtilus* to remove the axle-pins from Oenomaus' chariot so that it crashed. Pelops killed Myrtilus to conceal the secret, and the dying Myrtilus cursed Pelops.

His sons include *Atreus*, *Thyestes*, Plisthenes and *Sciron* as well as the eponyms of many Peloponnesian cities. His illegitimate son *Chrysippus* was loved by *Laius*, who thus instituted pederasty on earth and brought a curse on his descendants.

Pelops' tomb was one of the central objects of devotion at Olympia, where the games were established by his great-grandson *Heracles*. The bringing of his bones to Troy was one of the conditions for the Greeks winning the *Trojan War*.

**Penelope** The daughter of *Icarius* of Sparta and therefore cousin of *Helen*, Penelope married *Odysseus*, King of Ithaca, to whom she bore a son *Telemachus*. When her husband failed to return from the *Trojan War* (he was away for 20 years), the palace filled up with local princelings hoping to marry her, and eating her out of house and home meanwhile. To delay her decision as to which of them she would agree to marry, she announced that she would make her choice when the tapestry she was making (or it may have been a shroud for her still living father-in-law, *Laertes*) was finished; but every night she unravelled the work she had done in the day, and so it was never finished. When it was scarcely possible to put off the choice any longer, Odysseus returned at last and killed the suitors.

When Odysseus was killed by *Telegonus*, his son by *Circe*, Telegonus married Penelope while Telemachus married Circe. Penelope and Telegonus had a son, Italus, eponym of Italy.

A local legend of Arcadia said that Penelope was divorced by Odysseus for infidelity, and returned home to Sparta, and thence to Mantinea where she bore to Hermes the god Pan. [Homer, *Odyssey*; Telegony.]

**Penthesilea** An Amazon who led an army of *Amazons* to Troy. She was killed by *Achilles*, who fell in love with her at the moment his spear penetrated her. *Thersites* mocked his passion, and Achilles killed him with a blow. [*Aethiopis*]

**Pentheus** King of Thebes, grandson of *Cadmus* and son of *Agave*. His story is famous from Euripides' *Bacchae*. He attempted to outlaw the ecstatic orgiastic rites of Dionysus, which were exclusively pursued by women (*maenads*), of whom his mother was one of the most prominent. Overcome none the less by a prurient desire — induced by the temptations of the wheedling stranger who is Dionysus himself — to spy on the women at their rites, which involved catching, rending and eating raw small animals and deer, he disguised himself as a Bacchant (maenad). He was discovered as an intruder. In their bacchic frenzy the women mistook him for a wild beast and tore him limb from limb. Agave bore his head in triumph back to the palace. Brought back to her senses by Cadmus, she went into exile.

The story pattern resembles that of other *heroes* who resisted the rites of Dionysus: see *Dionysus*.

**Persephone** The daughter of Zeus and Demeter, Persephone was carried off by Hades while gathering flowers in the fields of Enna, in Sicily — 'that fair field / Of Enna, where Proserpine, gathering flowers, / Herself a fairer flower, by gloomy Dis / Was gathered, which cost Ceres all that pain / To seek her through the world. . .' [Milton, *Paradise Lost*] Demeter's search for her missing daughter ended at Eleusis, after she had brought famine on the earth for a year (see *Demeter*). Zeus sent Hermes to the *Underworld* to bring back Persephone. Unfortunately while there she had swallowed some pomegranate seeds; for every seed she had swallowed she was bound to spend a month of each year in the Underworld, and so she could spend only part of each year above the earth. Her presence on the earth represented the seasons of growth and fruitfulness, her redescent the lean days of winter.

As Queen of the Underworld she wielded considerable power and was responsible, for example, for restoring *Alcestis* to her husband.

Under the name of *Kore* (the Maiden) she was worshipped jointly with Demeter in the Mysteries of Eleusis, at the Thesmophoria in Athens, and elsewhere. The two were often known simply as The Two Goddesses. [*Homeric Hymn to Demeter*]

**Perseus** The son of *Danae*, who was made pregnant by Zeus in the form of a shower of gold. Her father *Acrisius* set mother and son adrift in a chest, which floated to Seriphos where it was rescued by one Dictys (Net) who took them into his home. Dictys' brother Polydectes was King of Seriphos; he fell in love with Danae but she refused him. Polydectes then announced that he would marry *Hippodamia*, and charged all his subjects to provide him with horses as bridal gifts. Perseus, having no horses, offered to bring the head of the *Gorgon*, *Medusa*.

In this apparently fatal enterprise Perseus had the help of three gods: Athena, who gave him her shining shield; Hermes, who lent him his winged sandals and a sickle; and Hades, who lent him his cap of invisibility. He also carried a special bag, called a kibisis. With these, Perseus travelled to the home of the *Graeae*, whose single eye and tooth he stole while invisible through the aid of Hades' cap. They then revealed to him the home of the Gorgons, which was either beyond the Western Ocean, or in Scythia (Aeschylus), or beyond the Hyperboreans in the far north (Pindar).

When he arrived, Perseus protected himself from the Gorgons' gaze, which had the power to turn men to stone, by looking at them only in the reflective surface of Athena's shield. He struck off Medusa's head with the sickle, placed it in the bag and flew off. From the severed neck were born *Pegasus* and *Chrysaor*. The two other Gorgons pursued Perseus but could not catch him. The drops of blood which fell from the head turned into the serpents which infest the Libyan desert.

Pausing to rest in the land of the Hesperides, Perseus was rudely treated by the giant Atlas who had been warned to expect a son of Zeus, who would come and try to steal his golden apples. (In fact the prophecy was fulfilled much later by *Heracles*.) In anger Perseus showed Atlas the head and turned him into stone: he became Mt Atlas.

Perseus then flew to the sea-kingdom of the Ethiopian king Cepheus, often located at Joppa, where he rescued *Andromeda*, the king's daughter, from the rock to which she had been chained as prey for the sea-monster. He killed the sea-monster. A party was held to celebrate. Perseus was hoping to marry Andromeda but learned that she was already bethrothed to Cepheus' brother Phineus. To remove his rival he turned Phineus and his retinue into stone. The two then married, and their son Perses inherited the kingdom, becoming the ancestor of the Persians.

Returning to Seriphos, Perseus found Polydectes still harassing his mother. He entered the king's banqueting hall with his gift, and held it up for all to see. More statues! Perseus then returned his accoutrements to the gods who had lent them to him, and gave the Gorgon's head to Athena who placed it in the centre of her shield, using its snake-locks to make a fringe for her aegis.

Perseus then sailed home to Argos with his mother and tried to make peace with Acrisius, but accidentally killed him in a discus-throwing competition in Larisa. Perseus then swapped kingdoms with the King of Tiryns, because he was ashamed to sit on Acrisius' throne. He founded a new city, Mycenae. Andromeda bore him a daughter, Gorgophone, and five sons; his grandson was *Eurystheus*.

**Phaeacia** The mythical kingdom of *Alcinous* on which *Odysseus* was washed up after the shipwreck which he suffered after leaving the island of the *nymph Calypso*. It was situated on the island of Scherie, often identified in classical times and since with Corfu, because of the lush fruitfulness Homer attributes to it.

Its king Alcinous and his daughter *Nausicaa* gave Odysseus a hospitable welcome and provided the audience for the narrative of his adventures which makes up much of the *Odyssey*.

Their friendliness to seafarers was well-known and made Poseidon, who liked a shipwreck, their enemy. When they conveyed Odysseus in a magic sleep back to his own island of Ithaca, Poseidon revenged himself by turning the returning ship into stone — identified with the islet of Pondikonisi.

**Phaedra** Daughter of *Minos*, King of Crete, and *Pasiphae*. (Her name, like her mother's, means 'shining' and suggests we have here a faded goddess, perhaps of the moon.) She married *Theseus* and then fell in love with her stepson *Hippolytus*: when he in his chastity rejected her, she accused him to Theseus of attempted rape. Theseus cursed his son, who was then killed by a bull sent from the sea by Poseidon; Phaedra then hanged herself. [Euripides, *Hippolytus*; Seneca, *Phaedra*]

**Phaëthon** The son of *Helius*, the Sun, and Clymene a daughter of Ocean. Anxious to confirm his paternity to his schoolmates who doubted it, he visited his father in his palace, and Helius promised him any boon he cared to ask for as proof. Phaëthon asked to be allowed to drive the chariot of the Sun for a day. Unable to dissuade him, the god had reluctantly to grant his promise.

Phaëthon proved unequal to the task. The horses would not obey the unfamiliar hand. In their headlong career with the blazing chariot they first etched the Milky Way on the sky, then plunged down and scorched the tropics, turning their inhabitants black. These regions were turned to desert.

To prevent further disasters, Zeus hurled a thunderbolt at Phaëthon, who was hurled from the chariot and fell into the River Eridanus (Po). His sisters the *Heliades* gathered on the riverbank and wept unceasingly for their brother, until they were turned into poplar trees. Their tears became amber which dripped into the waters of that river.

According to Hyginus, Phaëthon took the chariot without permission, and Zeus let loose the Flood to quench the heat of the scorched earth. [Ovid, *Met.* 1]

**Phaon** See *Sappho*.

**Philemon and Baucis** An elderly Bithynian peasant couple who one day unwittingly entertained Zeus and Hermes as they wandered the earth in disguise (clearly a common event as Paul and Barnabas were once mistaken for the same two gods). Giving unstintingly to their guests of what little they had, they found the food and wine were magically replenished. They then recognized that their guests were gods; the latter transformed their hut into a temple and made them its keepers, also granting their request that they should both die at the same moment. When that time came they were changed into an oak and a linden tree that continued to grow and flourish side by side, next to the temple. [Ovid, *Met.* 8]

**Philoctetes** The Malian hero Philoctetes, son of Poeas, received *Heracles'* bow and arrows as a parting gift when he lit the great hero's pyre on Mt Oeta. He joined the Trojan expedition with seven ships, but was bitten by a snake while sacrificing to Athena on Tenedos. The bite became septic and stank so badly that the Greeks refused to have him on board ship with them; on the advice of *Odysseus* they sent him off to Lemnos to get him out of the way. Here for most of the duration of the war the lame hero supported himself by shooting down gulls with his bow and arrow and gathering what other food he could.

In the last year *Helenus*, the Trojan seer captured by the Greeks, revealed that Troy could only be taken if Philoctetes were brought from Lemnos. Odysseus was sent with Diomedes (or, according to Sophocles, *Neoptolemus*) to fetch him back, but Philoctetes was unwilling to help as he felt so bitter towards the Greeks, especially Odysseus.

In Sophocles' *Philoctetes* Odysseus tried to trick Philoctetes: he persuaded Neoptolemus to tell the hero that he was to be taken back home. Once on board, they would then sail instead for Troy. But Neoptolemus, an honest young man, gave the plot away and determined to keep his promise. At this point Heracles appeared from heaven and ordered Philoctetes to go to Troy, prophesying that one of his arrows would kill *Paris*. (Usually, however, Paris is dead by the time of the embassy to Philoctetes.)

At Troy Philoctetes' wound was healed by *Asclepius* or one of his sons. After the war was over, Philoctetes was said to have travelled to southern Italy and founded there several towns, including Croton, and a sanctuary of Apollo where he dedicated his arrows.

**Philomela** See *Tereus*.

**Philyra** A daughter of Oceanus and Tethys, with whom Zeus coupled in the form of a stallion. She bore the Centaur *Chiron*, horse from the waist down, and a wise teacher. To cover her own shame she received from Zeus the boon of being turned into a linden tree.

**Phineus** King of Salmydessus, brother of *Cadmus* and *Europa*, a seer who had been blinded by Zeus for revealing too much of the gods' plan for the human race. A further punishment was his continued harassment by *harpies*, who snatched all his food and befouled the table. When the *Argonauts* put in at Salmydesseus, they found Phineus half-starved. The sons of Boreas finally chased away the harpies, driving them to the Echinades islands. Phineus in gratitude explained to the Argonauts how to pass safely through the Clashing Rocks. [Apollonius Rhodius].

Another, incompatible story gave Phineus two wives, Cleopatra daughter of Boreas and Idaea daughter of a Scythian king. The latter lady accused his sons of raping her. In anger he blinded them; then Boreas and the Argonauts blinded him and rescued his sons. Idaea was sent home to her father, who killed her. [Diodorus Siculus]

**Phocus** A son of *Aeacus* of Aegina by the *Nereid* Psamathe, and half-brother of *Peleus* and *Telamon*, who killed him by accident in a discus match — or deliberately, on the instructions of their own mother Endeis.

A person of this name — which means Seal, a suitable name for a sea-nymph's child — became the eponymous founder of the region of Phocis, but this latter was son of Poseidon. However, the sons of the Aeginetan Phocus settled in Phocis after their father's death. [Pindar, *Nem.* 5; Hesiod, *Theogony*]

**Phoenix 1.** One of the sons of Agenor of Tyre, brother of *Cadmus* and *Europa*. Phoenicia was named after him.
**2.** Son of Amyntor, King of Ormenium on Mt Pelion. He was persuaded by his mother to seduce his father's concubine. Amyntor then cursed or blinded him. Phoenix' sight was restored by *Chiron* after he had been befriended by *Peleus*, who made him King of the Dolopes and also tutor to his own son *Achilles*. He accompanied Achilles to Troy and took part in the embassy to Achilles when he had withdrawn from the fighting. He died on the way home to Greece.

**Pholus** A Centaur who entertained Heracles on Mt Pholus in Elis. The other *Centaurs* tried to steal their wine. In the ensuing battle Pholus was struck by one of *Heracles*' poisoned arrows and died.

**Phorcys** A sea-god, son of *Gaea*, married to Ceto and father of the *Gorgons*, the *Graeae*, *Echidna* and the serpent Ladon. He had cult on Ithaca. [Hesiod, *Theogony*]

**Phrixus** Son of *Athamas* and Nephele of Orchomenus, rescued, on the point of being sacrificed by his father, by a Golden Ram which flew down from the sky and bore him and his sister away. Though his sister, *Helle*, fell off in their flight, Phrixus reached Colchis, sacrificed the ram and hung its fleece in a grove sacred to Ares. Phrixus married the daughter of King Aeëtes of Colchis and had four sons, who left Colchis when the *Argonauts* came to fetch the *Golden Fleece*.

**Pirene** A nymph of Corinth whose sons by Poseidon, Leches and Cenchrias, gave their names to the two gates of Corinth. Leches was accidentally killed by Artemis, and Pirene's tears were so copious that she became a spring. There were in fact two springs of this name at Corinth, one in the elegant Roman fountain house in the lower town, and one on Acrocorinth.

**Pirithous** Successor to *Ixion* as King of the Lapiths, he led the war against the *Centaurs* for control of his kingdom of Thessaly. Pirithous became a close friend of *Theseus* and helped him carry off *Antiope*. He married Hippodamia (not the same as the wife of *Pelops*) and the Centaurs were invited to the wedding. A great brawl ensued: the west pediment of the Temple of Zeus at Olympia shows Apollo stilling the fracas.

Pirithous and Thesus then decided to marry daughters of Zeus. First Pirithous helped Theseus to kidnap *Helen*, and then Theseus accompanied Pirithous to the *Underworld* to seize *Persephone*. Hades invited them to sit down, but when they did their flesh stuck fast to the chairs. *Heracles* released Theseus when he came down to Hades to collect *Cerberus*, but an earthquake dissuaded him from releasing Pirithous, who remained there forever: 'And Theseus leaves Pirithous in the chain / The love of comrades cannot take away.' (A. E. Housman's translation of Horace, *Odes* 4.7) [Ovid, *Met.* 12]

**Pleiades** Seven daughters of Atlas and Pleione. Their names are Electra (who coupled with Zeus and bore Dardanus and Iasion), Taygete (who coupled with Zeus and bore Lacedaemon), Maia (who coupled with Zeus and bore Hermes), Celaeno (who coupled with Poseidon and bore Lycus and Nycteus), Alcyone (who coupled with Poseidon), Asterope (who coupled with Ares and bore Oenomaus), and Merope (who married Sisyphus and bore Glaucus). Because Merope only managed to wed a mortal, she was ashamed and tried to hide her light; thus she is the dimmest star in the constellation that bears their name.

Zeus placed them in the stars either because they died of grief for their sisters the *Hyades*, who died of grief weeping for Hyas, or to save them from the pursuit of *Orion* — who still pursues them nightly across the sky.

**Pluton** An epithet of Hades; his name means 'the Wealthy One'.

**Plutus** The god of wealth (the meaning of his name), son of Demeter and *Iasion*. He became a largely symbolic figure in fifth-century Athens, as in Aristophanes' play where he is represented as a blind god with no discrimination in who he attaches himself to; or the statue by Cephisodotus in the Athenian agora where the baby god is nursed by Peace.

**Podalirius** Son of *Asclepius*, brother of Machaon. Like his father he was a healer, and cured *Philoctetes'* festering wound.

**Polydeuces** See *Dioscuri*.

**Polyhymnia** One of the *Muses*. Her name is cognate with *hymos*, hymn, and she is associated especially with the lyre, with pantomime and with geometry.

**Polyidus** An Argive seer, a descendant of *Melampus*. He helped *Bellerophon* to tame *Pegasus*. He also revived *Glaucus* (4) after solving the Curetes' riddle — to find the aptest analogy for Minos' cow which changed colour from white to red to black every day. He suggested the blackberry and revived Glaucus with a magic herb revealed to him by a snake which had used it to revive its dead mate.

**Polynices** One of the sons of *Oedipus*. He and his brother *Eteocles* were cursed by Oedipus because they refused him sanctuary after his disgrace — and so they were doomed to quarrel over the kingship they were supposed to share. Eteocles banished Polynices, refusing to take shares in the kingship, so Polynices raised an army at Argos which was known as the *Seven against Thebes*. Polynices was killed in battle by Eteocles, and was refused burial by the new King of Thebes, *Creon*. For the sequel see *Antigone*.

**Polyphemus** One of the *Cyclopes*, but a son of Poseidon unlike the rest of the tribe. He fell in love with Galatea but she spurned him for his ugliness and was in love with *Acis*: so Polyphemus killed Acis: the rocks he hurled at him became the Isole Ciclopee off Acireale in Sicily.

   This same Cyclops appears in the story of *Odysseus* as a cannibal giant. When Odysseus and his men took refuge in his cave, he ate the men two by two (though his usual diet was the pastoralist's milk and cheese). When he asked Odysseus his name, Odysseus told him that it was 'Nobody'. Odysseus eventually contrived an escape for the remainder by first blinding Polyphemus' single eye and then getting each man to cling to the underside of a sheep as the giant let them out to pasture in the morning. After a while Polyphemus realized what had happened. He called the other Cyclopes to his aid, explaining 'Nobody is doing me harm.' So of course no help came. The furious giant hurled rocks blindly into the sea towards Odysseus' ship, but fortunately missed. However, his prayers to his father Poseidon delayed Odysseus' return home for many years. [Homer, *Odyssey* 9; Euripides, *Cyclops*; Theocritus, *Idyll* 11]

**Polyxena** A daughter of *Priam* and *Hecuba* of Troy. After the fall of Troy she was sacrificed by the Greeks on *Achilles*' grave as his ghost demanded. The deed was done by Achilles' son *Neoptolemus*.

**Poseidon** Though known as god of the sea (= Neptune) and of sweet waters, driver of his watery chariot drawn by hippocamps, Poseidon is also the Earthshaker, Ennosigaios, the god of earthquakes. In this role he is especially associated with horses (which he created) and their thundering hooves; he may also be conceived as equine in form. Sacrifice of horses, as well as bulls, in his honour was common.

In classical times his role as sea-god was predominant. He had major temples in the Peloponnese and Arcadia as well as one of the most famous of all, at Sunium. The Isthmian Games were dedicated to Poseidon, and he was invoked both before horse-races and before sea-voyages.

An Arcadian legend told that to save him from *Cronus*, *Rhea* gave the latter a foal to swallow in his stead, and a Rhodian one said that he was reared by the Telchines on Rhodes. Otherwise he is assumed to have been released from Cronus' bowels along with the other gods, by Zeus.

Poseidon's name is found in the Linear B tablets and may mean 'spouse of the earth' — a role especially alluded to in his title *Phytalmios*, fruitful.

The three brothers Zeus, Hades and Poseidon divided up the universe between them and Poseidon's portion was the land and sea, Zeus' the sky and Hades' the *Underworld*. As sea-god he made himself master of the older sea-deities such as Nereus, Proteus and Phocus.

He struggled with other gods for the areas of Greece that were peculiarly his own: he disputed Corinth with Helius, and lost, but was awarded the Isthmus instead by *Briareus*. When the river-gods of Argos awarded that region to Hera he dried up the rivers in anger and only restored them after his liaison with *Amymone*. He was allotted by Zeus equal shares with Athena in Trozen, but was forced to cede Athens to the goddess by the judgement of *Cecrops*, who valued her olive-tree above his spring of water.

His home in Homer is Aegae, probably the place of that name on the north coast of the Peloponnese. His wife was *Amphitrite*, who bore him *Triton*. His loves include Amymone for whom he created the springs of Argos with a blow of his trident. Numerous other springs were also created by him. He mated with *Medusa*, from whose severed neck sprang *Chrysaor* and *Pegasus*, and with Demeter who bore the horse *Arion*, and with Caenis whom he turned into *Caeneus*. His wedding gift to *Peleus* was the horses *Xanthus and Balius*.

He used his power of metamorphosis in these amours, and also gave the gift to *Mestra* and Periclymenus (see *Neleus, Heracles*).

His offspring include the giants *Antaeus*, by *Gaea*, and *Polyphemus*, *Otus and Ephialtes*, and perhaps the water-walker *Orion*; savages *Busiris, Sciron* and *Cycnus (3)*; also *Phineus, Euphemus, Eumolpus*. His most famous son was *Theseus*, by *Aethra*; for him he sent the Bull from the sea which killed his son *Hippolytus*.

He was lover also of *Pelops*, and gave him the divine chariot in which he won his race with *Oenomaus*.

He supported the Greeks at Troy, but was enemy to *Odysseus* because the latter blinded his son Polyphemus.

**Potnia Theron** 'Mistress of the Animals'. A title sometimes used for Artemis in her capacity as goddess of wildlife: it is now commonly used to refer to the goddess figure represented in Minoan art flanked by lions, panthers, or other animals — a presentation of the deity that derives from Near Eastern iconography of the Mother Goddess, for example *Cybele*.

**Priam** Son of *Laomedon* and King of Troy. His second wife was *Hecuba*, who bore him *Hector, Paris, Helenus, Cassandra, Polyxena*, Deiphobus, *Troilus* and many others, a total of 14 of Priam's full complement of 50 sons and 50 daughters. Priam features in the *Iliad* when, as an old man, he visits *Achilles* by night to reclaim the body of Hector. On the fall of Troy he was murdered by *Neoptolemus* at the altar of Zeus Herkeios.

**Priapus** A god generally represented in the form of a pillar with a human torso and head, and an enormous phallus. His origin is in Asia Minor — he was the chief god of Lampsacus — and in Greece and Rome functioned as a territory marker, a guardian of gardens and orchards. (Male monkeys protect their tribe's territory against interlopers by sitting at its corners displaying their erections as talismans of power, and a threat to invaders.) A collection of bawdy Latin verse celebrates the god. [*Priapea*]

**Procne** See *Tereus*.

**Procris** Daughter of *Erechtheus* and wife of *Cephalus*. Only Apollodorus tells the story of her seduction by one Pteleon, her flight to Crete and her liaison with *Minos* whom she cured of a fearsome disease. Minos gave her a hunting spear and a dog, Laelaps. She then returned to Athens and appeased Cephalus' anger by giving him these gifts.

*Eos* fell in love with Cephalus and Procris became jealous: she hid in a bush to spy on him when he went hunting on Mt Hymettus, and Cephalus, seeing the movement in the bushes, flung at her the infallible spear, and killed her.

**Procrustes** Procrustes dwelt by the road from Eleusis to Athens and would invite travellers to spend the night in his house. But if they did not fit his bed exactly, he would stretch or lop them as necessary. *Theseus* finished his career by fitting him to his own bed.

**Proetus** A king of Argos, son of Abas, who quarrelled with his brother *Acrisius* and thus split the kingdom. Proetus seduced Acrisius' daughter *Danae* and was exiled to Lycia, where he married the daughter of King Iobates, *Stheneboea*. From here he made war on Argos and became ruler of Tiryns. He built its walls with the aid of the *Cyclopes*.

Stheneboea fell in love with *Bellerophon* and, when he rejected her, accused him to Proetus of attempted rape. Proetus sent Bellerophon off to Iobates with the letter that was supposed to cause his death.

An unrelated tradition concerns the daughters of Proetus, who were inflicted with madness either by Hera or by Dionysus for neglecting the god's rites; they thought themselves cows and were finally cured by *Melampus*.

**Prometheus** 'Forethought', a Titan, son of Iapetus and Themis or an Oceanid. Prometheus was a champion of the race of men, whom he had created from clay. He stole fire from the gods, hiding it in a fennel stalk, to bring its warmth to mankind. He also established the custom that only the poorer parts of sacrificed animals should be given to the gods. He hid the lean meat in a paunch and covered the bones and entrails with rich fat, and then offered Zeus the choice: Zeus chose the latter and thus left the best parts to men.

When he realized how he had been tricked, Zeus had Prometheus chained to a rock in the Caucasus and sent a vulture to peck out his liver daily: it grew again each night. He also made life awkward for men by getting Hephaestus to create the first woman, *Pandora*, and presenting her as bride to Prometheus' more dim-witted brother *Epimetheus*.

Prometheus was finally released by *Heracles* who shot the vulture that was tormenting him, and broke his chains. In gratitude Prometheus advised Heracles to get *Atlas* to stand in for him in fetching the Apples of the *Hesperides*. According to Aeschylus, his release was prompted by Zeus' anxiety to know his secret — that Thetis would bear a son who would be stronger than his father. However, this fact is more often said to have been revealed to Zeus by Themis. [Hesiod, *Works and Days*; Aeschylus, *Prometheus Bound*]

**Protesilaus** Protesilaus led a Greek force from Phylace against Troy. An oracle foretold that the first Greek to go ashore would be killed: when others hesitated, Protesilaus defied fate and leapt ashore (his name means First Leaper) and after killing several Trojans was himself cut down. He was buried on the European side of the Hellespont and had a temple near Sestus. According to Philostratus, his ghost could still be seen haunting the region of the Troad, with those of other *heroes*, in his own day (third century AD). [Philostratus, *Heroicus*]

**Proteus** The Old Man of the Sea (compare *Nereus*) who looked after Poseidon's seals. Menelaus consulted him to find out how to reach Sparta again from Troy. By the advice of the nymph Eidothea, he and his companions disguised themselves as seals. When Proteus lay down for his siesta, they seized him and held on as he turned himself into a lion, snake, leopard, boar, water and a tree. Then he resumed his own form and told Menelaus what he wanted to know. [Homer, *Odyssey* 4]

The name also belongs to a human king of Egypt, husband of Psamathea, who looked after *Helen* (in the Stesichorean version of the legend) during the *Trojan War*. He was succeeded, while Helen was still there, by his son Theoclymenus. [Euripides, *Helen*]

**Protogonus** In the Orphic theogonies, Protogonus (First Born) is a god born from the world-egg created by Unaging Time. The myth is closely related to others known from Phoenicia, Iran and India, and direct Near Eastern influence is quite likely. Protogonus had golden wings, bull's heads on his flanks and a serpent on his head, and combined in himself the two sexes. (A parody of this kind of theology is given a choral ode in Aristophanes' *Birds*.) He is also known as the bright Phanes, 'he who makes manifest'. By copulating with himself he performed the functions of Demiurge or Creator, which are not carried out by the supreme god Time. (This division of labour resembles later Neoplatonic doctrine.) Thus were born monsters, the heavenly bodies and the Golden Race of men. This theogony is incompatible with that given by Hesiod which was regarded as canonical, but later Zeus came to be identified with Protogonus. Other gods were also identified with him in various sources. [West, *Orphic Poems*]

**Psyche** The fairy-tale of Cupid (Eros) and Psyche comes to us from Apuleius' *Golden Ass* but probably has Hellenistic roots. It repays reading in full, as one of the most enchanting stories of antiquity.

Psyche's beauty aroused Aphrodite's jealousy, and the oracle of Apollo commanded her to be brought to a castle in the mountains to marry a demon. At night a secret presence came to her in her room and made love to her, but without allowing her to light the lamp. On the fourth night she disobeyed, and lit the lamp as her lover lay sleeping to see what kind of demon was giving her such pleasure. It turned out to be the beautiful boy Cupid himself. Just then a drop of oil from the lamp fell on his shoulder, and he flew away.

Aphrodite was furious when she discovered what had been happening, and set Psyche a series of impossible tasks. 1. She had to separate a pile of millet, wheat, barley and other grains into separate heaps. But the ants came to her aid and did the job for her. 2. She had to bring some wool from a flock of man-eating sheep. This she did by waiting until they were asleep and gathering the tufts of wool on the thorn bushes. 3. She had to bring a jar of water from the River Styx. But Zeus' eagle saw her plight and fetched it for her. 4. She had to bring a box of Persephone's ointment from Hades. Psyche prepared to throw herself from a tower (always a quick way of reaching the land of the dead); but the tower spoke to her and told her how to enter the *Underworld* at Taenarum, carrying two obols for the ferryman and two honey cakes for *Cerberus*. Psyche made the journey successfully and Persephone gave her the ointment. But when Psyche got back to the upper world she opened it in curiosity, and a sleep of death wafted up from the pot and enveloped her. Just in time, Cupid arrived to fan away the noxious gas, and while she delivered the box to Aphrodite he begged Zeus to let him marry Psyche. And so they lived happily ever after. [Apuleius, *The Golden Ass*]

**Pygmalion** A king of Cyprus and a sculptor. Only Ovid tells the famous story of Pygmalion's loneliness for lack of a wife. He carved a statue of the most beautiful woman he could imagine, and then fell in love with it. He prayed to Aphrodite, who caused the image to come to life. Pygmalion then made her his wife. Their daughter was Paphos. [Ovid, *Met.* 10]

**Pylades** The son of King Strophius of Phocis and companion to the exiled *Orestes*. He accompanied Orestes when he returned to Argos to murder his mother. In Aeschylus *Choephori* he takes a silent part, uttering just one sentence to remind Orestes of Apollo's orders at the crucial moment — his utterance thus has the force of the word of the god himself. He appears also in the *Electras* of Sophocles and Euripides, and the latter's *Orestes*.

**Pyriphlegethon** 'Flaming with Fire', one of the four rivers of the *Underworld*.

**Pythia** The priestess and mouthpiece of Apollo in his oracle at Delphi. She was an old woman of no education who, in order to convey the oracular responses of the god, sat on the tripod and delivered inspired utterances, apparently in a trance perhaps induced by some kind of drug or mediumistic techniques (though two popular theories, the chewing of laurel leaves or the inhaling of 'mephitic vapours' from a chasm below the temple, have been shown to have no basis in fact). Her 'ravings' were then interpreted and put into hexameter verse by the priests.

**Python** The serpent at the oracle of Mother Earth at Delphi, killed by Apollo. Its name is explained in the *Homeric Hymn to Apollo* by a pun: Apollo leaves the dead creature in the hot sun to rot (*pythein* = rot). [Fontenrose, *Python*]

# R

Rhea, mother of the gods

**Rhadamanthys** The son of *Zeus* and *Europa*, brother of *Minos* and *Sarpedon*. He was either banished by Minos or made part ruler of Crete, and law-giver of the kingdom. Both he and Minos became judges of the dead in Hades.

**Rhea** A Titaness, wife and sister of *Cronus* and mother of the Olympian gods. As Cronus was eating each of her children as they were born, Rhea concealed Zeus and gave Cronus a stone in swaddling clothes instead. When Zeus grew up and overthrew the Titans, Rhea retained her status as Mother of the Gods, in which capacity she was often identified with *Cybele*.

**Rhesus** A Thracian king, borne by one of the *Muses* after wading in the River Strymon (though in Homer his father is Eïoneus); the child was brought up by *nymphs*. He brought troops to assist the Trojans in the tenth year of the war. His arrival was revealed to the Greeks by Dolon, who killed Rhesus and captured his horses. Rhesus was worshipped as an oracular spirit in Thrace. [Euripides *Rhesus*]

# S

Odysseus and the Sirens

**Sacrifice** Sacrifice is the means by which man the hunter seeks reconciliation with the animal he has hunted for food. In historical times this takes the form of offering the meal to a god. Commonly the hunter uses the skin and especially the feet and head to reconstitute the animal in effigy after slaughter: this practice is reflected in myths like those of *Lycaon*, *Tantalus* and *Thyestes*, where the murderer leaves out of the child-stew the head, hands and feet, so that the unlucky diner then recognizes what he has eaten. Some Greek rituals involve the sacrificers dressing in the skins of the slaughtered beast, thus identifying with the victim, rather as *Actaeon* was turned from hunter into hunted beast. [Burkert, *Homo Necans*]

Gods were honoured with sacrifice of many animals from hare to bull. The beast was sprinkled with water, which caused it to shake its head indicating assent to its butchery. The animal was then slaughtered on the altar and burnt.

In legend, *Prometheus* devised the system of sacrifice by which the best parts were reserved for men (at Delphi, the priests alone) and the fat and bones were given to the gods. Commonly some of the meat was roasted and some boiled, the processes being carried out in that order. A puzzling reversal of the processes occurs in the Orphic myth of Dionysus/Zagreus.

Heroes received a different form of sacrifice called *enagismos*, on a lower altar; the offerings were generally not burnt but poured into a hole in the ground or in the hero's tomb. The latter form of sacrifice was also used for Chthonic deities such as Demeter. [Farnell, *Greek Hero-cults*]

**Sappho and Phaon** Sappho, the poetess of Lesbos, was a historical figure of the sixth century BC, famous for her poems declaring love for young girls of her society. In later antiquity she was thought to have entertained a hopeless love for a young man called Phaon, a ferryman. In despair she threw herself off a rock on Leukas (about as far from Lesbos as it is possible to go in Greece) which was and is known as Sappho's leap. [Ovid, *Letters of Heroines*]

**Sarpedon** The leader of the Lycian forces in the *Trojan War*, but also the brother of *Minos*, exiled by him to Lycia: his son married *Bellerophon*'s daughter. Apollodorus explained his apparent extraordinary longevity by a special dispensation, as was essential in a rational compilation like his.

He was a son of Zeus, who tried to save him from death in the battle at Troy, but was overruled by the other gods. When he was killed by *Patroclus*, Zeus sent Apollo to rescue the body, and Sleep and Death carried it safely home to Lycia.

**Satyrs** Wild men of the woods, imagined as human in form with ugly snub-nosed features and horses' tails (goats' tails, and sometimes legs, in later periods). They are devoted to drink and sex and are generally shown in art with uncontrollable erections, or actually masturbating, or raping *nymphs*. They form part of the retinue of Dionysus and are represented in the satyr-plays which form part of the festivals of Dionysus, under the leadership of *Silenus*.

They belong to the world of anomie and the instincts and unbridled fertility which characterizes devotion to Dionysus. They may be derived from, or related to, festivals in which animal mummery was prominent: such festivals developed into drama, and in a more carnivalesque form have been common in modern times in Greece and the Balkans (not to mention the hobby-horses of Cornwall). Such processions are referred to by Plato in the *Laws*, and the inhabitants of Ephesus dressed as satyrs and pans to welcome Mark Antony when he visited their city. In this aspect the satyrs have affinities with *Centaurs* and their descendants the *Kallikantzaroi*. [J. C. Lawson; Brommer; R. A. S. Seaford, *Euripides Cyclops*]

**Scamander** A river running across the Trojan plain, and father of *Teucer* the first king of the Troad. In the fighting at Troy, *Achilles* blocked his course with corpses. In rage, Scamander flooded the plain and Achilles fought the river with his weapons single-handed, until Hephaestus sent a blaze of fire to dry up his waters. [Homer, *Iliad* 20-21]

**Sciapodes** Legendary men of India or Ethiopia who when sleeping used their huge single foot as a parasol.

**Sciron** A bandit who dwelt near the Isthmus of Corinth on the Megarian side — modern Kaki Skala. He forced travellers to stop and wash his feet, then kicked them down the cliffs into the sea, where they were eaten by a turtle. *Theseus* despatched him by his own preferred mode of death.

**Scylla** 1. A nymph whom *Glaucus* loved. But *Circe* loved Glaucus and in jealousy turned Scylla into a horrible sea-monster with six dog's heads around her waist. She lived in a cliff face in the straits of Messina, opposite *Charybdis*, and devoured sailors unlucky enough to be caught by her; *Odysseus* lost the last of his men between these two terrors.
2. Daughter of *Nisus*, King of Megara. When *Minos* attacked Megara, Scylla fell in love with him and betrayed her father by cutting the single purple lock in his hair which preserved his life. Minos was so disgusted at her treachery that he drowned her. Scylla became a small seabird called a ciris and Nisus became an osprey. [Vergil, *Ciris*; Ovid, *Met.* 8]

**Selene** The moon-goddess, daughter of *Hyperion* and *Theia*. Mother of Pandion, by Zeus. She was seduced by *Pan*, but the love of her life was *Endymion*.

**Semele** The daughter of *Cadmus* and *Harmonia*, loved by Zeus. Hera in jealousy disguised herself as Semele's nurse and urged her to ask Zeus to reveal himself to her in his true form. He did — as a thunderbolt — and Semele was incinerated. From her ashes Zeus took the infant Dionysus whom he hid in his thigh until he was ready for birth. He was then brought up by *nymphs* on Nysa.

When Dionysus grew to manhood he descended to Hades to bring back his mother, and she ascended with him to Olympus where she had the name Thyone.

**Semiramis** A legendary queen of Babylon (her name means 'Shammu is exalted'), daughter of the fish-goddess Derceto of Ashkelon, who married Ninus king of Assyria and conquered large parts of the Middle East. A Hellenistic novel treats the love of the youthful couple. When he died she built him a mausoleum at Nineveh, and a huge palace for herself near the Euphrates. She consulted the oracle of Ammon as to when she would die, and was told that it would be when her son conspired against her. Before that happened she conquered large parts of India; when she died she was turned into a dove and ascended to heaven where she became a goddess.

Alexander is said to have pursued some of his conquests in emulation of her. [Diodorus Siculus; Reardon, *Collected Greek Novels*; G. Pettinato, *Semiramide*]

**Seven against Thebes** Seven Argive champions who made war on Thebes to support the claim of the banished *Polynices* to the throne of Thebes, which he was supposed to share in alternation with his brother *Eteocles*.

Polynices, exiled from Thebes, married the daughter of *Adrastus* (the other daughter married *Tydeus*), and Adrastus raised an army. Its commanders were Capanaeus, *Amphiaraus*, Hippomedon and Eteoclus. (Thus Aeschylus, but Euripides *Phoenissae* and Hyginus omit Eteoclus.) Tydeus joined the expedition on condition that, when it was over, Adrastus would help him in his claim to Calydon. Polynices and Tydeus are not always counted as among the seven, and in these sources two other warriors are added; Mecisteus and Parthenopaeus.

Amphiaraus, a seer, foresaw the failure of the expedition and the death of all its leaders except Adrastus, and was disinclined to go. Polynices therefore sought the support of Amphiaraus' wife *Eriphyle*, by bribing her with the necklace of Harmonia. She talked Amphiaraus into going.

The expedition set out and made a halt at Nemea to seek water. Here *Hypsipyle* showed them a well; in doing so she put down the baby *Opheltes* whom she was nursing: he was bitten by a snake and died. The Seven buried him and celebrated funeral games, which became the origin of the Nemean Games. Opheltes was renamed Archemorus (beginning of doom). (For the pattern see also *Melicertes*.)

Reaching Thebes, each of the champions led the assault against one of its seven gates: Aeschylus' *Seven against Thebes* is devoted to a series of messenger speeches describing the champions and their opponents at each gate, and their defeat. Capaneus scaled the walls but was struck down by Zeus. Tydeus, mortally wounded, killed Melanippus: Athena was about to make him immortal, but then saw that he was preparing to eat the brains of the dead Melanippus, and in disgust revoked her gift. Amphiaraus was pursued by Periclymenus; to save him, Zeus opened the earth and Amphiaraus disappeared, chariot and all, re-emerging at Oropus, where he became a healing hero.

Polynices and Eteocles killed each other in single combat. Polynices was refused burial as a traitor by *Creon*, who now assumed the rule of Thebes; for the consequences of this see *Antigone*.

The Seven were avenged by their descendants the *Epigoni*, who mounted a successful expedition against Thebes just before the *Trojan War*.

**Sibyl** The name of a prophetess, located perhaps in Libya and the daughter of *Lamia* (Euripides), but more commonly associated with Ionia. The sixth-century philosopher Heraclitus described her thus: 'Sibylla with raving mouth uttering things without laughter and without charm of sight or scent, reaches a thousand years by her voice on account of the god.' By the late fourth century the name had become generic, and Varro in the first century BC lists 10: the Persian, Libyan, Delphic, Cimmerian (of Italy), Erythraean, Samian, Cumaean, Hellespontic, Phrygian and Tiburtine Sibyls. Sibyls are also referred to at Delos, Claros, Colophon, Sardis and Dodona. The rock from which the Delphic Sibyl, whose name was Herophile, made her prophecies, was described by Pausanias and can still be seen there.

Sibylline prophecies were made in ecstatic trance and written down by her attendants (at Cumae, on palm leaves).

The Cumaean Sibyl offered the nine books of Sibylline prophecies to King Tarquin of Rome. When he refused to buy them, she burnt three and offered him six for the same price. He still refused, and she burnt three more before offering him the last three still for the same price as before. Tarquin then realized what he was missing and paid the price for the three.

Nine books of Sibylline prophecies were none the less preserved at Rome until they were destroyed in the fire on the Capitol in 63 BC.

In the Christian period 14 books of Sibylline prophecies in hexameter verse were composed, many of which tell the history of Rome in prophetic form (a style of narrative previously practised by the riddling poet Lycophron of Alexandria) among much other material. [H. W. Parke, *Sibyls and Sibylline Prophecy*; J. H. Charlesworth (ed.), *The Old Testament Pseudepigrapha* vol. I]

**Silenus** Silenus is the leader of the *satyrs* in the satyr plays dedicated to Dionysus. But the name is a generic one and there are many Sileni. They are scarcely to be distinguished from satyrs though Sileni seem to be Attic-Ionic in origin and satyrs Peloponnesian. Sileni are often older, fatter and more drunken than the lusty satyrs; they also, surprisingly, can purvey wisdom. Midas once captured one who taught him a great deal, and in Vergil's sixth *Eclogue* two young shepherds corner one and force him to give an account of the creation of the world.

Silenus as an individual was given various parentages, including Pan or Hermes, and was father of the Centaur *Pholus*.

**Sinis** A bandit of the Isthmus, who tied his victims by the arms to two down-bent pine-trees, and then released the trees so that the unfortunates were torn apart. *Theseus* meted out the same treatment to him.

**Siren** A bird with a woman's head. The creature resembles the *harpy*, but in addition she has the gift of enchantingly sweet song. When *Odysseus* and his men sailed past the islands of the Sirens, Odysseus had himself bound to the mast and his men's ears stopped with wax so that none of them should give way to their lures and be wrecked on that shore of whitening bones. For the sirens are birds of death, and reappear in this guise in the mermaids that tempted the blacksmith in *Moby Dick* as well as in the angelic inhabitants of a mysterious island described in a Pomeranian legend (Benwell and Waugh). In some of the comic poets they offer Odysseus the more prosaic attraction of excellent cooking!

The Sirens of legend are regarded as daughters of a sea-god (e.g. Phorcys) and one of the *Muses*. In Homer there are two; later three. Later legend made them take part in a musical contest with the Muses, which they lost.

Plato makes quite different use of the Sirens in his cosmology in the *Republic*, where each of the nine circles of the heavens has one Siren sitting on it: each sings a different note which together make up a celestial concord, while the circles revolve on the spindle of necessity controlled by the three *Fates*. These celestial Sirens bear a remarkable resemblance to the heavenly musical bird-women, the Ginnari, of Buddhist mythology.

Plato too associates the Sirens with death: they are 'ensnared by love of Hades'. Because of this association sirens were a common adornment to funereal monuments, including that of Sophocles, where it was doubly appropriate because of the sweet music of his poetry. They were also used as acroteria on temples. A remarkable South Italian terracotta group in the Getty Museum shows Orpheus accompanied by a pair of 'baffled-looking Sirens' — again perhaps with an association with the afterlife. [E. Baer, *Sphinxes and Harpies in Medieval Islamic Art*; E. Buschor, *Die Musen des Jenseits*; J. T. Pollard, *Seers, Shrines and Sirens*]

**Sisyphus** King of Ephyra (Corinth) and a noted trickster. He outwitted *Autolycus*, who was stealing his cattle, by marking the undersides of their hooves; when Autolycus transformed the appearance of the cattle to conceal the theft, the marks were left and the theft discovered.

Sisyphus was known as one of the great sinners in Hades, because he had told Asopus that Zeus had carried off his daughter Aegina, or because he had seduced his brother Salmoneus' daughter Tyro. Zeus condemned him eternally to push a rock up a hill: just as he reached the top, the stone would roll down again.

Albert Camus' book, *The Myth of Sisyphus* treats this myth as an allegory of the human condition.

**Sleep** The son of Night and brother of Death. He appers in anthropomorphic form in the *Iliad*, where he puts Zeus to sleep at Hera's

162

request; and helps his brother, at Apollo's command, to carry
Sarpedon's body to Lycia for burial.

**Snake** The snake in Greek lore is commonly regarded as the embodiment of a dead hero or chthonic god. As a matter of observation
snakes are often found around graves and a connection was made
between the two. Reliefs from Sparta and elsewhere show worship-
pers approaching seated *heroes* over whose throne towers a huge
snake. Snakes were also regarded as protectors of the household (also
at Rome). The god Asclepius also took the form of a snake, in which
guise he travelled when his cult was introduced to Athens.

Snakes seem also to have been important in Cretan religion, as witness the ivory statues of snake-handling goddesses from Knossos.
In Asia under the Roman Empire snake-handling cults became popular and even influenced some branches of Christianity.

**Solomon** In the Greek Middle Ages King Solomon had acquired the
reputation of a wizard, through a work probably of the first to third
century AD known as the *Testament of Solomon*. This records
Solomon's interviews with a great variety of demons, which are summoned for him by a special demon, Ornias, and by Beelzebul. All
these Solomon controls with his magic ring, which was given to him
by the archangel Michael. [J. H. Charlesworth, *Old Testament Pseudepigrapha* Vol. I]

**Spartoi** See *Cadmus*. The leading families of Thebes claimed descent from these Sown Men, sprung from the earth of Thebes. This
claim of autochthony may be compared with that of the Athenians
to be sprung from the soil of Attica, or that of the Arcadians who
said that they were in Arcadia before the creation of Sun and Moon.

A group of Sown Men was also created by *Jason* from the remaining *dragon*'s teeth in Colchis: they were destroyed like the earlier
ones, by throwing a stone in their midst which led them to quarrel
until they were all dead.

**Sphinx** A creature with a lion's body, a woman's head and wings.
In the ancient Near East this and similar composite creatures, such
as winged man-bulls and eagle-headed men, were used as heraldic
beasts on royal gateways, thrones and corridors. The Egyptian sphinx
at Giza, already 14 centuries old when the Pharaoh Thothmes excavated around it in 1420 BC, was a symbol of royal power and probably also a guardian of the underworld, lord of the setting sun.

In Greece the sphinx was adopted as an artistic motif, but its mixed
nature represented to the Greek mind not royalty but anxiety. Its
unsettling composite nature and savage ways emblematized the non-
human forces man must fight against.

In legend, the Sphinx, daughter of Echidna by Orthros or Typhon, dwelt on a mountain near Thebes and devoured a regular tribute of Theban youths, who failed to answer the riddle she set them: 'What is it that goes on four legs in the morning, on two legs at midday, and on three legs at evening?' In some versions of the story the last to suffer this fate was *Haemon* the son of *Creon*. At last *Oedipus*, arriving as a stranger in Thebes, solved the riddle (the answer is 'Man') and was made King of Thebes. The Sphinx threw herself to her death, or was killed by Oedipus.

Later writers, include Palaephatus and Pausanias, rationalized the Sphinx as a female bandit whose refuge was on Mt Phix outside Thebes. [J. M. Moret, *Oedipe, la Sphinx et les Thébains*, 1984]

In Baroque Europe the Sphinx again became a heraldic emblem (Vienna Belvedere) until Romantic painters (Gustave Moreau, Elihu Vedder) turned her into a nightmare figure once more.

**Stentor** The herald of the Greek at Troy, noted for his strong voice; hence 'stentorian'.

**Stheneboea** See *Bellerophon*.

**Strigla** A woman with the ability to transform herself into a beast or a bird of prey. Ovid [*Fast*. 6. 131 ff], John of Damascus [*Peri strygon*] in the eighth century and Michael Psellus in the eleventh, all allude to Strigles' propensity for creeping through keyholes and throttling children, or devouring their internal organs. Leo Allatius assimilates them to medieval witches, old women who have made a pact with the devil. Sometimes (J. C. Lawson 182 f) their activities differ little from those of *Lamia*. The word is a diminutive of the classical word *strix*, a kind of bird.

**Striglos** A demon of modern Greek lore — a male version of *Strigla* — who takes many forms. He may be snake-like in form, or appear as a tormented ghost. In half-human form he dances or utters a death-bearing screech. He has the ability to change his shape, and he couples with sheep so that they die, or suckles goats to dry up their udders. In general his activity is related to the misfortunes of animals. [Richard and Eva Blum, *The Dangerous Hour*]

**Styx** A river in Arcadia and also one of the four rivers of the *Underworld*. Dead souls were ferried across it by Charon into Hades. Oaths sworn by its waters could not be broken, even by the gods. Its water was said to be so poisonous that it corroded clay and metal containers and could only be carried in a horse's hoof. In some versions of the *Alexander Romance* this water was used to poison the hero, being sent by Antipater in Macedon to Alexander's cupbearer in Babylon.

**Symplegades** The Clashing Rocks at the northern end of the Bospho-

rus, which clashed together each time a vessel passed through, and
crushed it. The *Argonauts* outwitted them by sending a dove on
ahead: the rocks clashed, just clipping its tail feathers, and as they
drew apart again the oarsmen pulled on their oars and hastened
through. Even so they needed a helping push from Athena. After
being tricked this once, the Rocks never clashed again. [Apollonius
Rhodius]

**Syrinx** An Arcadian *nymph*. Pan fell in love with her and pursued
her to the River Ladon; here she prayed to the gods and was turned
into a clump of reeds. From these, Pan fashioned the first Pan-pipes,
a row of tuned reeds fastened with wax.

There is an exotic poem by Elizabeth Barrett Browning about the
legend. [Ovid, *Met.* 1]

# T

Theseus and Triton

**Talos** A bronze giant, guardian of Crete. When he menaced the *Argonauts* on their return from Colchis, *Medea* identified his one weak spot, where his single vein of ichor came close to the surface at the ankle. She withdrew the nail that plugged the ankle, or caused him to graze it; alternatively, she instructed the archer Poeas to shoot him in the ankle, and he collapsed. [Apollonius Rhodius 4]

**Tantalus** A Lydian king, son of Zeus. He proved himself unworthy of the favour the gods showed him, either by telling their secrets to mortals and stealing their nectar and ambrosia after being invited to dinner on Olympus, or by tricking the gods in the following way. To test their omniscience, he cut up his own son *Pelops* and served him to the gods in a stew. They all realized what was in it except Demeter, who ate a piece of the shoulder. The gods restored Pelops to life and gave him an ivory shoulder. Tantalus, however, was condemned to a tantalizing torture in Hades: standing up to his neck in a pool of water, he found the water receded from him every time he stooped to drink. A bunch of grapes dangled above his head just out of reach, mocking his hunger. Alternatively, a huge stone was permanently balanced just above him on the point of falling. [Pindar, *Ol.* 1]

**Tartarus** A dark region as far below Hades as Hades is below the earth, and prison of the *Giants* and *Titans*, who were guarded there by the *Hundred-Handers*. According to Homer, an anvil dropped from heaven would fall nine days before reaching Tartarus. The King of Tartarus was also called Tartarus, and was a son of Chaos, and father by his sister Earth of *Typhoeus* and *Echidna*. [Hesiod, *Theogony*]

**Telamon** Son of *Aeacus* and Endeis, and brother of *Peleus*, with whom he killed their half-brother *Phocus* in a discus accident, or deliberately. The brothers were banished from Aegina: Peleus went to Phthia while Telamon became King of Salamis after marrying King Cychreus' daughter. He took part in the expedition of the Argo and the *Calydonian Boar Hunt*, and accompanied *Heracles* in his assault on Troy to punish *Laomedon*. He then married Laomedon's daughter *Hesione*, who bore *Teucer*; by yet another wife, Eëriboea, he was father of *Ajax*. He plays no part in the legends of his children's generation.

**Telchines** Web-footed or fish-tailed *daemones*, the first inhabitants of Rhodes who nursed the infant Poseidon to protect him from *Cronus*. They were noted artificers and originators of the art of sculpture (for which Hellenistic Rhodes was famous). They were also able to control the weather by sorcery. Callimachus used the name to denigrate his literary opponents.

**Telegonus** The son of *Odysseus* and *Circe*, born to the latter during the year Odysseus spent on her isle of Aeaea. (His name means 'born afar'). When he grew up he went to seek his father. In the course of his journey he led a raiding party against Ithaca, not realizing what island it was. In the fighting he killed his father with a spear tipped with the sting of a stingray, thus fulfilling the prophecy that Odysseus would meet 'a death from the sea'. The story is in the *Telegony*, a lost poem by Eugammon of Cyrene, *c.* 560 BC [M. Davies, *The Epic Cycle*]

**Telemachus** The son of *Odysseus* and *Penelope*. Too young to drive out the suitors who pestered his mother in Odysseus' absence, he received assistance from Athena in the guise of Odysseus' deputy *Mentor*, who advised him to visit *Menelaus* at Sparta for news of Odysseus. By the time Telemachus returned to Ithaca, Odysseus had arrived, and together they drove out the suitors. When Odysseus was killed by *Telegonus*, Telegonus married Penelope, while *Circe* married Telemachus and made him immortal. [Homer, *Odyssey*]

**Telephus** A son of *Heracles* by Auge, he was exposed on a mountain by Auge's father, but found and reared by shepherds. Following an oracle he travelled to Mysia, where he was rewarded with the kingdom for helping Teuthras of Teuthrania against invaders. He married one of the 50 daughters of *Priam* of Troy.

Telephus and his army repelled an attack by *Achilles* on his way to the *Trojan War*. Telephus was wounded by Achilles and the wound refused to heal. The oracle of Apollo told him that only the inflictor of the wound could cure it. Dressed in rags as a suppliant (as portrayed in Euripides' lost play, much parodied by the comic poets), Telephus went to visit Achilles at Argos. He seized *Agamemnon*'s son *Orestes* and threatened to kill him if Achilles did not help him. Achilles was at a loss until *Odysseus* explained that it was the spear itself that must heal the wound. Some rust scraped from it into the wound was found to have the desired effect.

The Greeks knew that they could not take Troy without Telephus' guidance. He accordingly led them to Troy but refused to fight against his father-in-law's city, and returned home to Teuthrania.

**Tereus** A king of Daulis who married Procne, the daughter of Pandion king of Athens. Their son was Itys. But Tereus then fell in love with Procne's sistern Philomela: he raped her and cut out her tongue to prevent her revealing the act. But Philomela wove an embroidery which portrayed the events and sent it to her sister. In revenge, Procne killed Itys and made him into a stew. When Tereus discovered and tried to kill Procne and Philomela, they were changed into, respectively, a swallow and a nightingale, and Tereus into a hoopoe. [Ovid, *Met*. 6]

**Terpsichore** *Muse* of choral poetry, often represented in the long robe of a citharode and bearing a lyre or other instrument. She was the mother of *Linus*, Hymenaeus and the *Sirens*.

**Tethys** A Titaness, daughter of *Gaea* and *Uranus*, wife of *Oceanus* and mother therefore of the Oceanids. As foster-mother of Hera, she refused to allow *Callisto*, who had been Zeus' concubine and then turned into a constellation (the Great Bear), ever to set in her realm, the sea. [Hesiod, *Theogony*; Homer, *Iliad* 14; Ovid, *Met*. 11]

**Teucer 1.** The first king of the Troad, succeeded by his son Dardanus. **2.** The son of *Telamon* and *Hesione*, a skilled archer who fought alongside his brother *Ajax* in the *Trojan War*. When Ajax committed suicide, Teucer defended his cause and upheld his right to burial. [Sophocles, *Ajax*] But Telamon exiled him from Salamis on suspicion of complicity in Ajax' death; Teucer founded a new Salamis in Cyprus, on Delphi's instructions, and married a daughter of *Cinyras*.

**Thalia** *Muse* of comedy and pastoral poetry; her attributes are mask and crook. She is the mother of the *Corybantes*.

**Thamyris** A mythical Thracian bard. He fell in love with *Hyacin-*

*thus* and was said to have been the first man to love one of his own sex. After winning a singing contest at Delphi he became vain and challenged the *Muses* to a contest. They won, and deprived him of his sight. (Many bards are in practice blind — like Homer — a handicap which improved their powers of memory.)

**Thanatos** Death, the brother of *Sleep*, son of Night. In Euripides' *Alcestis*, *Heracles* wrestles with Thanatos to win back the dead Alcestis — a foreshadowing of such episodes of modern Greek lore as *Digenis Akritas'* wrestling with *Charon*, the modern equivalent of Thanatos.

**Theagenes** A Thasian athlete who won the boxing at Olympia in 480 BC, and many other victories. When he died a bronze statue of him was erected in Thasos: an enemy came to flog it every night, but one night it fell on him and killed him. The man's son prosecuted the statue for murder and it was drowned in the sea.

The soil of Thasos became barren and the Delphic oracle commanded the Thasians to 'take back the exiles'. They restored a number of men, to no effect. A second consultation elicited the response, 'You leave great Theagenes unremembered.' Then, by chance, some fishermen's nets became entangled with the statue; they brought it to land and re-dedicated it in its former place, and offered it divine sacrifices. The barrenness of the land was cured. [Pausanias, 6. 11]

**Theia** 'Goddess of Many Names, and Mother of the Sun', as Pindar calls her [*Isth* 5], she is the daughter of *Gaea* and *Uranus*, a Titaness. She is mother of the Sun by *Hyperion* and of the *Cercopes* by *Oceanus*.

**Themis** A Titaness, daughter of *Uranus* and *Gaea*. Her name implies communal order and right dealing. As second wife of Zeus she gave birth to the Seasons (Horae), Eunomia (Order), Dike (Justice), Eirene (Peace) and the Fates (Moirae). She held the oracle at Delphi until ousted by Apollo. Her prophecies included the warning to Zeus that a son born to *Thetis* would prove greater than his father — which deterred Zeus from attempting to make her his mistress.

**Theogony** A narrative (in verse) of the origins of the gods. The only surviving one is that by Hesiod, giving the canonical succession of *Uranus — Cronus — Zeus*, and in many respects resembling similar accounts from the Near East. Numerous other theogonies existed in antiquity, ascribed to *Orpheus* and others. Their accounts, which essentially treat cosmology in mythical terms, are often conflicting. The Orphic theogonies were pressed into the service of mystery cults and the theology of such groups such as the Pythagoreans. [M. L. West, Hesiod: *Theogony*]

**Thersites** A Greek soldier in the *Trojan War*, mocked by the Greeks and reviled by Homer himself for his attempts to criticize his betters. He was a common man, ugly and misshapen. His beating by *Odysseus* after he complained at *Agamemnon*'s seizing *Briseis* gave the rest of the Greeks a good laugh. When he mocked *Achilles* for falling in love with *Penthesilea*, Achilles killed him. [Homer, *Iliad* 2]

**Theseus** The son of King *Aegeus* of Athens by *Aethra* of Trozen, who though not his wife relieved his childlessness. Poseidon lay with her in the same night so that Theseus claimed him too as father; through his mother he was great grandson of *Pelops*. When he left Trozen, Aegeus hid a sword and sandals beneath a rock, and told Aethra to send her son, when he grew up, to fetch the tokens, if he could lift the rock, and bring them to him in Athens. Of course the young man succeeded in the task, and set off for Athens via the Isthmus of Corinth. Bacchylides in his seventeenth ode described his progress as he slays the various ruffians who infested the route: Periphetes at Epidaurus who cracked travellers' heads with his club, *Sinis* of the Isthmus who stretched his victims between bent pines and then released the trees; the wild sow of Crommyon; *Sciron* who made passers-by wash his feet and then kicked them off the cliff (at modern Kaki Skala); Cercyon of Eleusis who wrestled with all comers; *Procrustes* who fitted all travellers to his bed, lopping or stretching them as necessary. All these were despatched by the means of death they themselves practised (except the sow, which was simply speared).

After purification of all these killings by some men he met at a shrine of Zeus Meilichius, Theseus continued to Athens, where he was given a hero's welcome. *Medea*, however, who had become Aegeus' consort and borne him a son, Medus, recognized who Theseus was and decided to get rid of him; she persuaded Aegeus to send Theseus off to capture the *Cretan Bull*, which was now terrorizing Marathon. To her chagrin he was successful. At the celebration banquet, Medea laced a cup with poison and got Aegeus to offer it to Theseus — but just in time Aegeus saw Theseus' sword and recognized it as the token he had left under the stone.

Now Theseus was acknowledged as Aegeus' son. But the due time was approaching when Athens must send to Crete the nine-yearly tribute of seven youths and seven maidens imposed by King *Minos*, to be food for the *Minotaur*. Theseus volunteered to be one of the 14, intending to finish off the Minotaur. He rigged the ship with black sails and promised to change them to white if he should return victorious.

On the voyage Theseus and Minos quarrelled and cast doubt on each other's paternity. Minos called Zeus to send thunder and lightning to prove his son's status; after this had been duly sent, Minos flung his ring into the sea and challenged Theseus to fetch it back from the realm of his alleged father Poseidon. Theseus dived in, was

welcomed by *Nereids* and led to the underwater palace of *Amphitrite*: *Thetis* gave him not only the ring but a crown she had received
from Aphrodite as a wedding gift. Theseus then returned to the ship
and gave the ring to Minos [Bacchylides, *Ode* 16]

On arrival in Crete, Theseus was seen by Minos' daughter *Ariadne*,
who fell in love with him and determined to help him. She got *Daedalus* to reveal how he could safely penetrate the *Labyrinth* where the
Minotaur was imprisoned, and gave him a clew of thread to enable
him to find his way out again. The Minotaur was vulnerable only
to its own horns, so Theseus tore one off in a wrestling hold and
stabbed the creature to death.

Theseus and his companions then made their escape with all speed,
accompanied by Ariadne. However, on the island of Dia, Theseus
abandoned her and sailed off while she slept. [Ovid, *Letters of
Heroines*] In her distress she was found by Dionysus, who made her
his bride.

Theseus stopped next at Delos and instituted the festival of the
Crane Dance around an altar of twisted horns, a dance which imi-
tated in its intricacies the windings of the Labyrinth.

Unfortunately Theseus forgot to change the sails as he had promised. When Aegeus, at his lookout on the Acropolis, saw the ship
with black sails approaching, he jumped to conclusions, and to his
death.

Theseus, now king, made himself master of all Attica and was
regarded by fifth-century Athenians as the original founder of their
democracy. (He is thus celebrated in a number of plays, including
Euripides' *Heracles* and Sophocles' *Oedipus at Colonus*. He
refounded the Isthmian games and dedicated them to Poseidon. His
other adventures include accompanying *Heracles* against the
*Amazons*, where he carried off their queen *Antiope* or *Hippolyta*,
who bore him a son *Hippolytus*, but later died; and going with the
Lapith *Pirithous* to kidnap first *Helen* for himself and then Persephone for his friend. The two descended to Hades together and were
invited to sit down. The chairs were magic and they were bound fast.
Theseus was at last rescued when Heracles came to fetch *Cerberus*,
but Pirithous remained for ever.

Theseus married (surprisingly) another daughter of Minos, *Phaedra*.
When exiled for one year from Athens for killing the sons of Pallas
who tried to usurp his throne, he and Phaedra went to Trozen. Here
Phaedra fell in love with her stepson Hippolytus and, being rejected
by the chaste youth, accused him of attempted rape. Theseus believed
her and in hasty rage cursed his son. As Hippolytus fled away in
his chariot along the shore, Poseidon sent a bull from the sea which
killed the lad. Phaedra hanged herself. [Euripides, *Hippolytus*]

Theseus returned to Athens but found the hearts of the people were
now with Menestheus, whom the *Dioscuri* had placed on the throne
while rescuing *Helen*. Theseus left Athens for Scyros, where he died

after falling off a cliff (or was he pushed by King Lycomedes, who was apparently jealous of Theseus' fame).

Theseus was thought to have led the Athenians to victory at Marathon, and in the fifth century a cycle of legends was developed about him to rival those of the Dorian *Heracles*: this is enshrined in Bacchylides as well as in the sculptural adornment of temples such as that of Hephaestus in Athens. Despite the uncertainties of his chronology, he was regarded as essentially a historical figure and Plutarch wrote a life of him.

**Thetis** Chief of the *Nereids*. Zeus and Poseidon both loved her, but on being told by *Themis* (or *Prometheus*) that any son of Thetis would be greater than his father, they decided to marry her to a mortal. That mortal was *Peleus*: he captured her on the coast at Sepias (cuttlefish-place) despite her transformations into many shapes, and made her his wife. The wedding was attended by all the immortals, who brought gifts — except *Eris*, whose anger at not being invited caused her to throw among the guests the apple inscribed 'for the fairest', which ultimately caused the *Trojan War*.

Sophocles calls the marriage of Peleus and Thetis 'speechless'. Commonly men who marry mermaids are forbidden to speak to their wives on pain of losing them. Thetis tried to make their son *Achilles* immortal by dipping him in the *Styx* or (like Demeter with *Demophoon*) placing him on the fire. Peleus caught her in the act and cried out, and Thetis vanished back to the sea.

She continued, however, to care for Achilles through his short life, concealing him on Scyros in the hope of avoiding his doom of death at Troy, bringing him the armour made for him by Hephaestus, and comforting him when he wandered in gloomy rage by the thundering sea. [Homer, *Iliad*; Pindar, *Isth*. 8; Catullus poem 64]

A modern folktale about the capture and flight of a Nereid, taking precisely the form of that of Peleus and Thetis, was recorded in Iraklion by a folklorist in 1825: the only difference is that the hero was a peasant not a king, and after her return to the sea the Nereid is shunned by her companions because she has borne a human child. [Megas, *Modern Greek Folktales*]

**Thyestes** See *Atreus*.

**Tiresias** A Theban seer who lived for seven generations. In his youth he saw two *snakes* copulating: on killing the female, he was transformed into a woman. Seven or eight years later, in a similar situation, he killed the male and was transformed back into a man. This unique experience made him useful as an arbiter when Zeus and Hera were disputing whether man or woman gained more pleasure from sexual intercourse. Tiresias assured them that the woman gained nine times as much. Hera was so angry (though it is hard to say why) that she blinded him; but Zeus gave him long life and the gift of prophecy.

Callimachus said that he was blinded for seeing Athena bathing, and that Athena's nymph Chariclo gave him second sight. According to Apollodorus, Apollo gave him the power to understand the language of birds. [Ovid, *Met.* 3]

A coeval of Cadmus, with whom he celebrated the rites of Dionysus [Euripides *Bacchae*], Tiresias' fame came when he revealed to *Oedipus* that he was the murderer of his father and cause of the pollution of Thebes. [Sophocles *Oedipus Tyrannus*] He later predicted the fall of the city to the *Epigoni*. He fled with the rest of the population, and died while drinking from the spring Telphusa; his daughter Manto was taken prisoner by the Argives and dedicated at Delphi.

He continued his prophetic powers after death, advising *Odysseus*, who consulted him in the *Underworld*, how to reach home in safety. [Homer, *Odyssey* 11]

**Tisamenus** The son of *Orestes*, who inherited the kingdoms of Argos and Sparta. Overthrown by the *Heraclidae*, he fled to the Northern Peloponnese. His bones were later returned to Sparta on the orders of Delphi (Pausanias 7,1).

**Tisiphone** The daughter of *Alcmaeon* and Manto; also one of the *Erinyes*. See also *Creon 2*.

**Titans** The children of *Uranus* and *Gaea*: they are *Oceanus* and *Tethys*, *Hyperion*, *Themis*, *Rhea*, *Mnemosyne*, Coeus, Crius, *Theia*, *Cronus* and Phoebe. This ancient set of nature divinities came to power when Cronus overthrew his father. Their reign ended when Cronus' own son Zeus overthrew him. After a war lasting 10 years he imprisoned the Titans in Tartarus under the guard of the *Hundred-Handers*. The myth resembles in form the Hittite myth of the overthrow of his father by the weather-god Kumarbi. [Hesiod, *Theogony*, with M. L. West's commentary] See further *Cronus*.

The Titans have a specific role in the Orphic theodicy of Zagreus, identified with Dionysus, whom they tore apart. Zeus swallowed his heart and gave birth to Dionysus a second time by *Semele*. It seems that the Titans in this myth are not in fact the pre-Olympian gods but a race of primeval men: the name is perhaps connected with titanon, quick-lime, because the murderous Titans smeared themselves with gypsum. See further *Dionysus*.

**Tithonus** See *Eos*.

**Tityus** A giant, son of Zeus and the nymph Elara. He tried to rape Leto at Delphi: Apollo and Artemis shot him down, and he was then chained down in Hades where his body covered two acres. Here two eagles constantly devoured his liver, which grew again according to the phases of the moon. Alternatively, it was Zeus who felled him with a thunderbolt.

**Tlepolemus** A son of *Heracles*, he killed his uncle Licymnius and was forced to leave Argos for Rhodes where he became king and founded the cities of Lindus, Ialysus and Camirus. He also led nine ships to Troy.

**Triptolemus** The son of *Metaneira* and Celeus, King of Eleusis. After Demeter was entertained by his parents, she taught him how to sow grain and sent him through the world to do so everywhere, riding on a chariot drawn by dragons. The goddess is represented instructing him on the Eleusinian relief in Athens Museum. He was said to have introduced the festival of the Thesmophoria to Athens. After his death he became a fourth judge in the *Underworld*. [*Homeric Hymn to Demeter*; Ovid, *Met.* 5]

**Triton** A sea-god, son of Poseidon and *Amphitrite*. He directed the *Argonauts* to the sea from Lake Tritonis. Attic black-figure vases show *Heracles* in battle with the fish-tailed Triton, who is labelled with this name, though the scene seems to be simply an iconographic development of his better-attested fight with *Nereus*.

Pausanias has a long disquisition on Tritons (9, 20, 4-21, 1), with mention of their attacks on the people of Tanagra, and bodies of Tritons which he had seen at Rome — an early precursor of mariners' tales of mermen.

**Troilus** A son of *Hecuba* by *Priam* or Apollo, killed by *Achilles* in the Trojan War. The story of his love for *Cressida* (the Greek *Chryseis*) is not classical but medieval, well known from Chaucer's *Troilus and Criseyde* and Shakespeare's *Troilus and Cressida*.

**Trojan War** The war waged by the Greeks (Achaeans) against Troy, a city which stood at modern Hisarlik in Asia Minor. The Greeks fought to reclaim *Helen* who had been stolen from her husband *Menelaus* by the Trojan prince *Paris*, because Aphrodite had promised to reward him for awarding her the Golden Apple by giving him as wife the most beautiful woman in the world.

Helen's suitors had sworn to defend her and all joined the expedition which was summoned by Menelaus and commanded by his brother *Agamemnon*. Many of the most famous heroes of Greece joined the expedition, including *Odysseus*, *Diomedes*, *Nestor*, *Ajax* and *Achilles*.

The fleet assembled at Aulis where Agamemnon had to sacrifice his daughter *Iphigeneia* to secure a fair wind. When they finally were able to sail, the Greeks came first to Mysia where they were driven off by *Telephus*. They returned home, but when Telephus came to Achilles to have his wound healed he agreed to show them how to reach Troy. On their second attempt they arrived safely, except *Philoctetes*, whom they abandoned on Lemnos because a snake bite in his foot had festered and produced a terrible stench.

At Troy the first ashore was doomed to die: this man was *Protesilaus*.

The war went on for nine years with little progress being made. The god-built walls of Troy were invulnerable. Homer's *Iliad* covers a brief period in the last year of the war when Achilles retired from the fighting. His friend *Patroclus* went into battle in Achilles' armour and was killed by *Hector*: Achilles then returned to battle and killed Hector.

Subsequent events were told in the lost epics *Aethiopis*, *Little Iliad* and *Sack of Troy*, as well as the late epic of Quintus of Smyrna. On the Trojan side fought the *Amazon Penthesilea* and the Ethiopian prince *Memnon*, both killed by Achilles. Achilles was at last shot by Paris. *Helenus* was captured by the Greeks and revealed that Troy could only be taken if Achilles' son *Neoptolemus* joined the troops, if the bones of *Pelops* were brought to Troy, if the *Palladium* was removed from Troy, and if Philoctetes were to come with Heracles' bow and arrow.

When all these conditions had been fulfilled, Odysseus devised the scheme of the *Wooden Horse* to enter Troy. Through this, the army was admitted at night and put the city to fire and the sword. King *Priam* was murdered at the altar of Zeus, *Cassandra* raped at a shrine of Athena. Neoptolemus sacrificed *Polyxena* on Achilles' grave and threw Hector's son *Astyanax* from the walls. Menelaus was about to kill his wife for her infidelity, but just in time she opened her bodice, and he was so overcome by her beauty that he relented and took her home with him.

The stories of the *heroes*' returns were full of event, and were told in the lost *Returns*; Odysseus' in particular took a further 10 years and is the subject of the *Odyssey*.

**Trophonius** The son of King Erginus of Orchomenus in Boeotia: his brother was Agamedes. The brothers are credited with the building of many early temples and other edifices, including Alcmene's bridal chamber at Thebes and the first Temple of Apollo at Delphi: but its beauty was so great that pilgrims pined away on seeing it and never returned home: so the gods destroyed it. [Pindar, *Paean* 8].

Trophonius and Agamedes also built a treasury for King Hyrieus of nearby Hyria. They made in it a secret entrance which Agamedes used in order to rob the treasure. Hyrieus caught Agamedes in a trap; Trophonius, afraid that their secret would be revealed, cut off his head and removed it so that the king would not recognize the thief when he found him in the trap. But the earth opened up at Lebadeia and swallowed Trophonius.

The gulf where he vanished became the site of an *oracle*, which was first discovered by one Saon, led by a swarm of bees. Trophonius instructed him in the procedures of the oracles. These are described in great detail by Pausanias who consulted the oracle himself. (Pausanias 8,9)

**Tyche** Goddess of Fortune, she became a popular object of cult in the fourth century BC and later. The presiding deity of a city in later times was regularly its Tyche — for example the Tyche of Antioch whose statue, portrayed on coins of that city, was one of the most famous works of antiquity.

**Tydeus** The son of King Oeneus of Claydon, banished for killing an uncle (or brother). He fled to Argos and married *Adrastus'* daughter Deipyle. Their son was *Diomedes*. Tydeus then joined the expedition of the *Seven against Thebes*. He killed *Melanippus* in single combat but was mortally wounded himself. In a berserk fury he ate Melanippus' brains. Athena, who was fond of him, was about to give him immortality but was so shocked at this act that she changed her mind. The scene is portrayed on some vases and an Etruscan relief — immortality taking the form of a maiden, Athanasia, or a little bottle. [Pindar, *Nem.* 10 with scholia; Bacchylides fr. 41; Krauskopf]

**Tyndareus** King of Sparta, possibly son of *Perseus'* daughter Gorgophone. His brothers or half-brothers were Aphareus (see *Idas and Lynceus*) and Leucippus (see *Leucippides*). Expelled from Sparta by his other brothers Hippocoon and Icarius, he was restored by *Heracles*, whose descendants later claimed Sparta as theirs.

He married *Leda* the daughter of Thestius of Aetolia. Their children include *Clytemnestra*, *Helen*, *Castor* and *Polydeuces*, though Helen and Polydeuces were generally regarded as children rather of Zeus. Because Tyndareus had once failed to sacrifice to Aphrodite, the goddess made his daughters unfaithful to their husbands.

**Typhoeus** or Typhon. A son of *Tartarus* and *Gaea*, a gigantic monster with a hundred snakes' heads for arms, wings on his back and eyes of flame, who tried to oust Zeus from power. He cut out the tendons of Zeus' legs and hid them in a bearskin; but Hermes and Pan stole the tendons and gave them back to Zeus. Typhoeus then fled to Mt Nysa to gain strength from the magic fruits that grew there. Zeus pursued him, and as they ran Typhoeus hurled mountains at Zeus; Zeus threw them back again. One of them became covered with Typhoeus' blood and was named Mt Haemus (from *haima*, blood). At last Zeus crushed him under the island of Sicily, where his breath is the source of Mt Etna's constant flame and smoke.

# U

Cerberus, guardian of the Underworld

**Underworld** The world of the dead, the realm of *Hades*; often called Hades itself, or the House of Hades. Through it ran the four rivers, *Styx*, Cocytus, Pyriphlegethon and *Lethe*. Souls were ferried across the first by *Charon*, and by drinking in the last they forgot their former lives and entered on the batlike existence of the shades. Blessed souls went to a special part of Hades known as the *Elysian Fields*. Hades and Persephone were the rulers of the dead, but there were also three judges, *Minos*, *Rhadamanthys* and *Aeacus*. Though the Underworld was not generally a place of punishment, it did contain the great sinners *Tantalus*, *Tityus*, *Ixion* and *Sisyphus* in their various torments.

**Urania** The *Muse* of astronomy and the sciences. Her name, which simply means 'heavenly', is also a title of Aphrodite (and of other goddesses).

**Uranus** The sky, son and husband of *Gaea*, Earth, who bore him the *Cyclopes*, the *Hundred-handers* and the *Titans*. He imprisoned the first two in *Tartarus*; to save the rest Gaea gave the Titan *Cronus* a sickle with which he castrated Uranus as he lay with her. The severed genitals fell into the sea and the foam gave birth to Aphrodite; the drops of blood which fell on the ground engendered the *Erinyes*, Giants and *Meliae*. The myth resembles that of the separating of Apsu and Tiamat, the sweet and bitter waters, in Babylonian myth. [Hesiod, *Theogony*, with M. L. West's commentary]

Sword and scimitar to exorcise a vampire

**Vampire** Modern Greek legend shares with that of Transylvania and other parts of Europe the figure of the man or woman who returns from the dead in bodily form and feeds on the blood of the living. The origins of the figure have been much disputed, and cross-influence on Greece from the north supposed: but there are enough instances of vampires in ancient Greek literature to make clear that the Greeks had no need of outside influence. The best-known is the story in Philostratus' *Life of Apollonius of Tyana*, of the young man of Lycia, Menippus, who held a wedding feast to celebrate his union with a lady. She provided the gold and silver and the elaborate food, but in the course of the feast both these and all the servants vanished under the gaze of the philosopher Apollonius. He questioned the woman, who then confessed that she was a 'siren' or *Lamia* (not the usual application of this term); as Apollonius explained to Menippus, her purpose was to ensnare a man and then to eat his body. The story is that of Goethe's *Bride of Corinth* and Keats' *Lamia*.

A similar story is given by Phlegon of Tralles concerning one Philinnion who acquired a lover Machates, before he discovered that she had been dead six months. Then he killed himself in despair. [Montague Summers, *The Vampire in Europe*]

The ancient vampire thus exhibits some of the characteristics of the *Sirens*, birds of death who by their enchantments lured men to their death on a shore white with bones.

In modern Greek the vampire is called Vrykolakas, a word of unknown origin. The vrykolakas was described by Leo Allatius in the seventeenth century as 'the body of a man of evil and immoral life'. It does not decompose after death but acquires a skin of drum-like toughness and emerges from its grave to make a nuisance of itself (or, occasionally, to be helpful, like the shoemaker of Santorini who came back by night to repair his children's shoes and chop wood for his family). The famous folksong of Constantine and Arete concerns another kindly revenant, the dead son Constantine who brings the living daughter to visit their mother before the latter dies — 'a spirit of the dead leading a lovely lady'.

Normally it was required to dispose of vrykolakes by exorcism and burning of the corpse. Such a ceremony is described in vivid detail by J. P. de Tournefort (see Summers): the devil could not leave the corpse because the swords with which they pierced it were in the shape of a cross, and it was necessary to use curved Ottoman scimitars before the vrykolakas could be disposed of. (Curiously, the spirit is inhibited rather than exorcized: contrast the ancient Lamia, which gave way before the philosopher Apollonius. Thus one sees how uneasily Orthodox doctrine is welded onto ancient beliefs.)

For more vampire stories, and on the special connection of vampires with the island of Santorini, see Richard Stoneman *A Literary Companion to Travel in Greece* 253. [Summers; J. C. Lawson]

**Vrykolakas** See *Vampire*.

# W

The Wooden Horse of Troy

**Wandering Rocks** Treacherous rocks in the sea off Sicily, avoided by *Odysseus* by going instead between *Scylla* and *Charybdis*. The *Argonauts* achieved a safe passage by the help of the *Nereids*. Some writers confused them with the Clashing Rocks or *Symplegades*.

**Water of Life** The legendary *Alexander the Great* travelled through the Land of Darkness in search of the Water of Life. In due course his expedition reached a place where there were a number of springs. His cook Andreas took some water from one to boil a dried fish, which immediately came to life again. But Andreas did not tell Alexander until they had left the place again. He then gave a share of it to Alexander's daughter, and in anger that she had won immortality and he had not, Alexander banished her to the mountains, where she was henceforth to live as a *Nereid* or mountain-nymph. As for the cook, he had a millstone tied around his neck and he was flung into the sea. [*Alexander Romance*]

**Werewolf** Men who are transformed into wolves are known to Greek mythology, and indeed to medical observers: see especially the story of *Lycaon*, whose name means wolf-man.

The myths associated with the sanctuary of Zeus Lycaeus tie the idea of the wolf-man to ephebic initiation rites. One example is the ritual of the Arcadian boy (described by Varro) who, once in every generation of a particular family, leaves his clothes, swims across a river, becomes a wolf for nine years, and on his return — if he has abstained from human flesh — reclaims his clothes and is transformed back into a man. The story reflects the activities of male secret societies 'wavering between demonic possession and horseplay'. [Burkert, *Homo Necans* 88]

At the feast of Zeus Lycaeus a cauldron of miscellaneous entrails of animals and a man was stirred: anyone of the participants who got one of the human bits was transformed into a wolf.

Such rites and tales seem to reflect primeval man's anxiety about hunting: man, in killing, becomes himself beast-like. The banishment of the werewolf re-establishes the distinction of beast and man. The practice can be viewed as part of a continuum with *sacrifice*, which also attempts to neutralize the same anxiety. [Burkert; Buxton in Bremmer]

**Witch** Witches were thought to be especially prevalent in Thessaly, which had been imbued with *Medea*'s magic herbs when she came there from Colchis with *Jason*. Witches were devotees of the underworld goddess *Hecate* (also associated with the moon), and had such powers as drawing down the moon and moving crops from one field to another. Binding magic was a speciality, and lovers would often resort to a witch to make their beloved responsive; the classic description is Theocritus' second *Idyll* where the witch uses an *iynx* to enchant the loved one. ('Turn, magic wheel, draw home the one I love...Bethink thee, mistress Moon, whence came my love.')

In Roman times witches were credited with increasingly gruesome practices: Horace envisages them haunting graveyards to gather bits of corpses for their spells (*Epode* 17), while Lucan's witch Erichtho yields nothing to those of Shakespeare's *Macbeth* in grisly extravagance.

**Wooden Horse** The stratagem by which the Greeks finally gained entry to Troy through its impregnable walls. *Odysseus* devised the plan, and a large Wooden Horse was built by Epeius, in which a number of Greek soldiers could lie concealed. It was inscribed 'To Athena from the Greeks for their safe return' and left outside the walls of Troy. The Greek fleet then sailed away and concealed itself behind a headland.

The Trojans, believing the Greeks to have gone, debated what to do with the horse. A captured Greek named Sinon, suborned by Odysseus, said that if they destroyed it Athena's anger would come on them, but if they brought it inside the walls they would conquer many Greek cities. It was too large to come through the gates so the Trojans broke down the walls, thus circumventing the destiny that the god-built walls could never fall through enemy action.

Some Trojans were suspicious. *Cassandra* revealed that troops were concealed inside but as usual was not believed. *Laocoön* hurled a spear at it to test its hollowness, but was then strangled with his sons by two enormous sea-serpents. Deiphobus led his wife *Helen* around it to speak to the Greeks in the voices of their own wives; but Odysseus forced them all to keep silent.

At last the Horse was left in peace and night fell. When all Troy was asleep the Greeks poured out, admitted their comrades, who had sailed back under cover of darkness, and put all Troy to fire and the sword.

# X

Achilles and his horses Xanthus and Balius

**Xanthus and Balius** The horses of *Achilles*, immortal offspring of Zephyrus, the west wind, and the *Harpy* Podarge. They were a wedding present to Achilles' father *Peleus*. They wept at the death of *Patroclus*; and Xanthus briefly was given speech by Hera to warn Achilles of his approaching death. [Homer, *Iliad* 19, 392-424]

**Xuthus** A king of Athens, brother of Dorus and Aeolus, the sons of Hellen, who divided Greece among them. Xuthus was allotted the Peloponnese, but came instead to Athens and married *Creusa* the daughter of *Erechtheus*. Their son was *Ion*. (In Euripides' *Ion* the boy is rather the son of Apollo.)

In Pausanias Xuthus was not king of Athens, but appointed *Cecrops* to that role, and was banished by Cecrops' brothers.

# Z

Zetes, son of the North Wind

**Zagreus** A name given to Dionysus in the Orphic myth of his dismemberment by the Titans: see *Dionysus*.

**Zalmoxis** A Thracian god resembling Dionysus, who provided his votaries with immortality after death. Petitions to the god were accompanied by the ritual of hurling a man on to the points of three spears. If he died, it was taken as a sign that the prayers were accepted; if not, they tried again. [Herodotus 4, 93-5]

**Zetes** See *Argonauts*.

**Zethus** See *Amphion and Zethus*.

**Zeus** Zeus, the king of the gods, is clearly the Indo-European sky-god corresponding to Sanskrit Dyaus, Latin *Dies-piter* (Jupiter): compare such Greek words as *eu-dia*, good weather. Zeus is god of sky, weather, thunder and lightning, gatherer of the clouds, especially associated with mountaintops (where his shrines have now mainly become chapels of Prophet Elias, who ascended into the sky), though his greatest temples (Dodona, Olympia, Nemea) lie in peaceful valleys.

Zeus is also revered as god of home and hearth, of hospitality to strangers, and of oaths, and identified with the snake-formed Meilichios (the placable) and Ktesios (the god of store-rooms).

In Crete, Zeus is a young god, consort of the dominant Mother Goddess: in historical times he is 'Father of Gods and Men', but his mythological character was too entrenched to allow him to become a universal god when monotheism was advancing. (Normally an anonymous 'god', or even Pan, took this role.) None the less, Homeric and Aeschylean theology gives him a strong moral role as arbiter of the justice of the gods. An unidentified character in a fragmentary play of Aeschylus made Zeus the one god who is identified with all things. He was identified in Hellenistic times with other gods, especially oriental ones, including the Egyptian Sarapis and *Ammon*, and the Anatolian Sabazios.

He had one oracle, at Dodona, where the oracular responses were given by the priests from their interpretation of the rustling of the leaves in the sacred oak. (The oak is especially Zeus' tree because it is more often struck by lightning than any other species.)

It is impossible to construct a narrative of Zeus' life beyond his childhood and conquest of heaven. He was the son of *Cronus* by *Rhea*. Cronus swallowed each of his children as they were born to prevent them growing up to overthrow him, as he had done his own father Uranus. But when Zeus was born Rhea gave Cronus a stone wrapped in swaddling clothes to swallow, and hid Zeus in a cave on Crete where he was nursed by the goat-nymph *Amalthea*. The *Curetes* danced and clashed their shields to drown the sound of the baby's cries; and so the baby grew up in safety.

When he was grown up, Zeus induced the Oceanid Metis to give Cronus an emetic: he vomited up Zeus' brothers and sisters as well as the stone, which fell at Delphi and became the navel-stone of Earth. Then Zeus released the *Hundred-handers* and *Cyclopes* from *Tartarus*: they helped him to depose Cronus, after which he shut them up in Tartarus again. Zeus and his brothers Poseidon and Hades now divided the world between them: Zeus won the sky and became king of all the gods.

He led the gods in the war against the *Giants*, who assailed him as the *Titans* had assailed Uranus. Zeus also defeated *Typhoeus* and buried him under Sicily.

Zeus' first wife was Metis, who conceived a child by him. For fear it should be a son who would overthrow him, Zeus swallowed her. He then gave birth himself to Athena through his forehead, after Hephaestus had split it open for him with an axe.

His other liaisons with goddesses include *Themis*, mother of Good Order, Justice, Peace and the Fates; Eurynome, mother of the *Graces*; Demeter, mother of Persephone; Leto, mother of Apollo and Artemis; and Maia, mother of Hermes.

His wife in all Greek mythology is Hera, notable for her jealousy

of and cruel behaviour towards the *nymphs* and mortal women whom
Zeus pursued in such numbers: see *Semele*, *Alcmena*, *Io*, *Europa*,
*Danae*, *Leda*. He and Poseidon both desired Thetis, but gave up their
claims on learning that any son she bore would be greater than his
father. He also seized the boy *Ganymede* to be his catamite and cupbearer. [Hesiod, *Theogony*; A. B. Cook, *Zeus*]

**Zodiac** The region of the sky parallel with the ecliptic and extend-
ing 12-14 degrees on either side. The name means 'band of animals'
and was so named after the supposed resemblance of the constellations to certain creatures. The origin of the zodiac is uncertain: similar
divisions of the sky are known from ancient Egypt and Mesopot-
amia, but the creatures of our zodiac are of Greek origin. Anaxi-
mander in the fifth century seems to have conceived a zodiac with
11 signs. The zodiac with 12 signs was probably invented in the third
century BC.

The twelve signs are Aries (Ram), Taurus (Bull), Gemini (Twins),
Cancer (Crab), Leo (Lion), Virgo (Virgin), Libra (Scales), Scorpio
(Scorpion), Sagittarius (Archer), Capricorn (fish-tailed Goat),
Aquarius (Water-carrier) and Pisces (Fishes). The sky was divided
into 12 regions each of 30 degrees, each ruled by one sign. With the
precession of the equinoxes over the centuries, the signs are all now
approximately 24 degrees out.

Besides its importance in navigation, the zodiac was fundamental
to the practice of astrology. Each sign had its corresponding month,
gemstone, planet and god. The position of the sun at sunrise determined which was the dominant sign for each twelfth of the year.

Different signs were thought to rule particular regions of the world
and to determine their climate, and to establish the seasons for
agricultural activities (e.g. sow seed in the Ram). It was also supposed that men's fates were influenced by the zodiacal conjunctions
at the time of the birth (an excellent example is the calculation made
by Nectanebo at the birth of *Alexander the Great* in the *Alexander
Romance*).

The creatures of the zodiac were identified with those occurring
in the stories of Greek myth. For example Aries is the Ram with the
*Golden Fleece*. However, this was only systematized at a late stage,
for example by Hyginus, and there are many rival candidates for most
of the signs.

# Bibliography

Pegasus

## List Ai: Texts in Translation

The Penguin editions of the Greek and Roman authors are the most accessible. Where there is no Penguin edition, I give details of the best available translation. The order in List Ai is chronological.

Hesiod, *Theogony*: tr. M. L. West (Oxford 1988)
Homer, *Iliad*
Homer, *Odyssey*
*Homeric Hymns*: tr. Thelma Sargent (New York 1973)
Pindar, *The Victory Odes*: tr. Frank Nisetich (Johns Hopkins University Press 1980)
Aeschylus, *Plays*
Sophocles, *Plays*
Euripides, *Plays*
Herodotus, *Histories*
Plato, *Republic*
Callimachus, *Hymns and Epigrams*: tr. A. W. and G. R. Mair; and *Iambi, Hecale and Fragments*: tr. C. A. Trypanis; (Loeb Classical Library 1968 and 1969)
Apollonius Rhodius, *The Voyage of Argo (Argonautica)*

Plautus, *Amphitruo*
Catullus, *Poems*
Ovid, *Metamorphoses*
*Priapea*, tr. W. H. Parker (Croom Helm 1988)
Seneca, *Plays*
Pausanias, *Guide to Greece*
Diodorus Siculus, *History*, tr. C. H. Oldfather *et al.* (Loeb Classical Library 1933–)
Lucian, *Works*, tr. H. W. and F. G. Fowler (Oxford UP 1905)
Plutarch, *On the Cessation of Oracles*, tr. F. C. Babbitt (Loeb Classical Library 1936)
Apuleius, *The Golden Ass*
Charlesworth, J. H., *The Old Testament Pseudepigrapha* (1983)
*The Greek Alexander Romance*, tr. Richard Stoneman (Penguin 1991)
Colluthus, *Rape of Helen*, and Tryphiodorus, *Capture of Troy*, tr. A. W. Mair (Loeb Classical Library 1928)
Nonnus, *Dionysiaca*, tr. W. H. D. Rouse (Loeb Classical Library 1962)
*Quintus of Smyrna, Posthomerica*, tr. A. S. Way (Loeb Classical Library 1913)
Reardon, B. P. (ed.), *Collected Ancient Greek Novels* (California UP 1989)

## List Aii: Untranslated texts

*Fragmenta Hesiodea*, ed. R. Merkelbach and M. L. West (Oxford UP 1968)
Artemidorus, *On The Interpretation of Dreams*
John of Damascus [Michael Psellus], *On the Operation of Demons*, ed. J. F. Boissonade (Nürnberg 1838)
Palaephatus, *On Incredible Things*, ed. N. Festa (Leipzig 1902)
Parthenius, *Erotic Tales*
Philostratus, *Heroicus*
Orphic *Argonautica*
Orphic *Hymns*, ed. D. P. Papaditsas and E. Ladia (Athens 1984)
Pseudo-Vergil, *Ciris*, ed. O. Lyne (Cambridge UP 1978)

## List B: Handbooks, Ancient and Modern

Apollodorus, *The Library*, tr. Sir J. G. Frazer (Loeb Classical Library 1963)
Graves, Robert, *The Greek Myths* (Penguin 1955)
Grimal, Pierre, *The Dictionary of Classical Mythology* (Blackwell 1986)
Henle, Jane, *Greek Myths: A Vase Painter's Notebook* (Indiana University Press 1973)
Hyginus, *Fabulae* (no translation)
—, *Poetica Astronomia* (no translation)

Morford, M. P. O., and Lenardon, R. J., *Classical Mythology* (Longman, 3rd edn 1985)

Otto, W. F., *The Homeric Gods: The Spiritual Significance of Greek Religion* (Thames & Hudson 1955)

Rose, H. J., *A Handbook of Greek Mythology* (Methuen, 6th edition 1958)

Tripp, Edward, *The Meridian Handbook of Classical Mythology* (New York 1970)

### List C: Secondary Works on Greek Mythology

Baer, Eva, *Sphinxes and Harpies* (Jerusalem 1965)

Baur, Paul, *Centaurs in Ancient Art* (1912)

Bolton, J. D. P., *Aristeas of Proconnesus* (Oxford 1962)

Borgeaud, Philippe, *The Cult of Pan in Ancient Greece* (Chicago UP 1989)

Brelich, Angelo, *Gli Eroi Greci* (repr. 1978)

Bremmer, Jan (ed.), *Interpretations of Greek Mythology* (Routledge 1987/1988)

Brommer, Frank, *Satyroi* (Wurzburg 1937)

Burkert, Walter, *Greek Religion* (Blackwell 1985)

—, *Ancient Mystery Cults* (Harvard UP 1987)

Buschor, Ernst, *Die Musen des Jenseits* (Munich 1944)

Cary, G. A., *The Medieval Alexander* (Cambridge UP 1956)

Cole, S. G., *Theoi Megaloi: The Cult of the Great Gods at Samothrace* (Leiden: E. J. Brill 1984)

Cook, A. B., *Zeus* (5 vols. 1914-25)

Croon, J. H., *The Herdsman of the Dead* (1952)

Davies, Malcolm, *The Epic Cycle* (Bristol Classical Press 1989)

Détienne, Marcel, *The Gardens of Adonis* (1977)

—, *Dionysos Slain* (Johns Hopkins UP 1979)

—, and J. P. Vernant, *Cunning Intelligence in Greek Culture and Society* (Harvester Press 1978)

—, and Giulia Sissa, *La vie quotidienne des dieux grecs* (1989)

Doob, Penelope Reed, *The Idea of the Labyrinth from Classical Antiquity through the Middle Ages* (Cornell UP 1990)

Du Bois, Page, *Centaurs and Amazons* (Michigan UP 1983)

Dumézil, Georges, *Le Problème des Centaures* (Paris 1929)

Edmunds, Lowell, *The Sphinx in the Oedipus Legend* (Koenigstein 1981)

—, *Oedipus: The Ancient Legend and its Later Analogues* (Johns Hopkins UP 1985)

—, *Explorations of Greek Mythology* (1989)

Farnell, L. R., *Cults of the Greek States* (5 vols: 1896-1909)

—, *Greek Hero-Cults and Ideas of Immortality* (1921)

Ferguson, John, *Among the Gods* (Routledge 1989)

Folliot, K. A., *Atlantis Revisited* (1984)

Fontenrose, Joseph, *Python* (California UP 1959)

—, *The Delphic Oracle* (California UP 1978)

Forsyth, Phyllis Young, *Atlantis: The Making of Myth* (Croom Helm 1980)

Friedrich, Paul, *The Meaning of Aphrodite* (Chicago UP 1978)

Frontisi-Ducroux, F., *Dédale* (1975)

Galinsky, Karl, *The Herakles Theme* (1972)

Grigson, Geoffrey, *The Goddess of Love* (Constable 1976)

Harris, J. Rendel, *The Heavenly Twins* (1906)

Harrison, Jane Ellen, *Prolegomena to the Study of Greek Religion* (1903)

Hooke, S. H. (ed.), *The Labyrinth* (1935)

Hoyle, Peter, *Delphi* (1967)

Kahn, Laurence, *Hermès Passé: ou les ambiguités de la communication* (Paris 1978)

Kirk, G. S., *Myth: its Meaning and Function in Ancient and Other Cultures* (Cambridge and California 1970)

—, *The Nature of Greek Myths* (Penguin 1974)

Krauskopf, Ingrid, *Der thebanische Sagenkreis und andere griechische Sagen in der etruskischen Kunst* (Mainz 1974)

Lessing, G. E., *Laokoon* (1766)

Lloyd-Jones, Hugh, *The Justice of Zeus* (California UP 1971)

Lovejoy A. O. and Boas, G., *Primitivism and Related Ideas in Antiquity* (Baltimore 1935)

Luce, J. V., *The End of Atlantis* (1969)

Matthews, W. H., *Mazes and Labyrinths* (1922)

Merivale, Patricia, *Pan the Goat-God: his Myth in Modern Times* (Harvard UP 1969)

Moret, J. M., *Oedipe, la Sphinx et les Thébains* (1984)

Mylonas, George, *Eleusis and the Eleusinian Mysteries* (Princeton 1961)

Nilsson, Martin, *The Mycenaean Origin of Greek Mythology* (California UP 1932)

Onians, R. B., *The Origins of European Thought* (Cambridge UP 1951)

Otto, W. F., *Die Musen* (1956)

Page, D. L., *Folktales in Homer's Odyssey* (Harvard UP 1973)

Parke, H. W., *Greek Oracles* (Hutchinson 1967)

—, *Festivals of the Athenians* (Thames and Hudson 1977)

—, *The Oracles of Apollo in Asia Minor* (Croom Helm 1985)

—, *Sibyls and Sibylline Prophecy in Classical Antiquity* (Routledge 1988)

—, and D. E. W. Wormell, *The Delphic Oracle* (1956)

Pettinato, Giovanni, *Semiramide* (1985)

Pollard, J. T., *Seers, Shrines and Sirens* (1965)

Renault, Mary, *The Bull from the Sea* (1962)

Rodd, J. Rennell, *Homer's Ithaca* (1927)

Ross, D. J. A., *Alexander Historiatus* (Warburg Historical surveys 1, 1963)

—, *Illustrated Medieval Alexander Books in Germany and the Netherlands* (Cambridge UP 1971)

Rothery, Guy Cadogan, *The Amazons in Antiquity and Modern Times* (1910)

Seaford, Richard, *Euripides: Cyclops* (Oxford UP 1984)

Sourvinou-Inwood, Christiane, *Studies in Girls' Transitions* (Athens 1988)

Svoboda, K., *La démonologie de Michael Psellos* (Brno 1927)

Tyrrell, W. B., *Amazons in Athenian Mythology* (Johns Hopkins UP 1984)

Veyne, Paul, *Did the Greeks Believe in their Myths?* (Chicago UP 1988)

Vidal-Naquet, P., 'The Black Hunter and the Origins of the Athenian Ephebeia', *Proceedings Camb. Philological Soc.* ns. 14 (1968)

Walcot, Peter, *Hesiod and the Near East* (Univ. of Wales Press 1964)

West, M. L., *The Orphic Poems* (Oxford UP 1983)

—, *The Hesiodic Catalogue of Women* (Oxford 1985)

Wilhelm, Kaiser, *Die Gorgonen* (1936)

Zuntz, G., *Persephone* (Oxford 1971)

## List D: Works on Modern Greek Folklore

Abbott, G. F., *Macedonian Folklore* (Cambridge UP 1903)

Allatius, Leo, *De Graecorum hodie quorundam opinationibus epistola* (1645)

Argenti, Philip, and H. J. Rose, *The Folklore of Chios I-II* (Cambridge UP 1949)

Benwell, Gwen and Sir Arthur Waugh, *Sea Enchantresses* (Hutchinson 1961)

Blum, Richard and Eva, *The Dangerous Hour: the Lore of Crisis and Mystery in Rural Greece* (Chatto 1970)

Buondelmonti, Cristoforo, *Description des Iles* (French tr. 1897 from Italian of 1414)

Davey, Richard, *The Sultan and His Subjects* (1879)

Dawkins, R. M., *Modern Greek Folktales* (Oxford UP 1953)

—, *More Greek Folktales* (Oxford UP 1955)

*Digenis Akritas*, tr. J. Mavrogordato (Oxford UP 1956)

Fermor, Patrick Leigh, *Mani* (John Murray 1958)

—, *Roumeli* (John Murray 1966)

Ioannou, Giorgos, *Paramythia tou Laou Mas* (Tales of our People: in Greek) (Athens 1979)

—, *Karagiozis* (Athens 1978)

Kornaros, Vinzenzos, *Erotokritos*, tr. Th. Stephanides, (Papazissis Publishers Athens 1984)

Lawson, J. C., *Modern Greek Folklore and Ancient Greek Religion* (1910 repr. 1964)

Mandeville, Sir John, *Travels* (c. 1375)

Megas, Georgios A., *Folktales of Greece* (Chicago UP 1970)

Miller, William, *The Latins in the Levant* (1908)

Myrivilis, Stratis, *The Mermaid Madonna* (Athens: Efstathiadis 1981)

Paton, J. M., *Medieval and Renaissance Visitors to Greek Lands* (Princeton 1951)

Politis, N. G., *Kleftika Demotika Tragoudia* (Athens n.d.)

Rodd, J. Rennell, *Customs and Lore of Modern Greece* (1929)

Stoneman, Richard, *A Literary Companion to Travel in Greece* (Penguin 1984)

—, *Across the Hellespont* (Hutchinson 1987)

Summers, Montague, *The Vampire in Europe* (1929)